SCANDINAVIAN EUROPE
phrasebook

Ingibjörg Árnadóttir   Peter A Crozier
Markus Lehtipuu   Doekes Lulofs
Pär Sörme

Scandinavian Europe phrasebook
2nd edition

Published by
Lonely Planet Publications
Head Office:PO Box 617, Hawthorn, Vic 3122, Australia
Branches:155 Filbert Street, Suite 251, Oakland CA 94607, USA
10 Barley Mow Passage, Chiswick. London W4 4PH, UK
71 bis rue de Cardinal Lemoine, 75005 Paris, France

Printed by
Colorcraft Ltd, Hong Kong

Cover Photograph
Window, Den Fynske Landsby open-air museum, Odense, Denmark.
Photograph by Glenda Bendure

Published
April 1997

National Library of Australia Cataloguing in Publication Data

Árnadóttir, Ingibjorg.
Scandinavian Europe phrasebook
2nd ed.
Includes index.
ISBN 0 86442 505 8.

1. Icelandic language - Conversation and phrase books - English. 2.
Danish language - Conversation and phrasebooks - English. 3. Finnish
language - Conversation and phrase books - English. 4 Norwegian
language - Conversation and phrase books - English. 5. Swedish language - Conversation and phrase books - English. I. Crozier, Peter A.
II. Lehtipuu, Marcus. III. Title. (Series: Lonely Planet language survival
kit)

439.5

Contents

Acknowledgements

The Danish section was written by Peter A Crozier. Markus Lehtipuu wrote the Finnish chapter and the Icelandic was written by Ingibjörg Árnadóttir. Doekes Lulofs wrote the Norwegian chapter. Swedish was updated by Anna Herbst, based on an original chapter by Pär Sörme.

The editor of this book is Sally Steward, and Tamsin Wilson was responsible for design and illustrations. Thanks to Dan Levin for computer assistance and David Kemp for the cover design.

From the Publisher

In this book Lonely Planet uses a simplified phonetic translation, based on the International Phonetic Alphabet. While this can only approximate the exact sounds of each language, it serves as the most useful guide for readers attempting to speak the various words and phrases. As you spend time in a country, listening to native speakers and following the rules offered here in the pronunciation sections, you should be able to read directly from the language itself.

All the languages in this book have masculine, feminine and sometimes neuter, forms of words. The different forms are separated in the text by slashes and/or the bracketed letters (m), (f) and (neut), when appropriate. Many words share the same form, so no indication of gender is required.

Several of the languages in this book have both formal and informal ways of speech, which means that for one word in English you may find two in the other language, one being the polite, formal, word and the other being more casual, informal. For the purposes of this book the formal way of speech has been adopted throughout, as this will ensure that at least you will not offend anyone by using the more intimate speech. In instances where the informal is commonly used, we have included it in brackets after the formal, or indicated with the letters (inf).

DANISH

Danish

Introduction

The Danish language belongs to the North Germanic language group, together with Swedish, Norwegian, Icelandic and Faroese. Consequently written Danish bears a strong resemblance to these languages. Spoken Danish, on the other hand, has evolved in a different direction, introducing sounds and pronunciation not found elsewhere. Grammatically it has the same general rules and syntax as the other Germanic languages of Scandinavia. Nouns have two genders: masculine *(en)* and neuter *(et)*. Definite articles ('the' in English) are added to the noun: *-en* and *-et* for singular nouns, and *-ne* (indefinite) and *-ene* (definite) for plural nouns regardless of gender.

Danish has a polite form of address, using the personal pronouns *De* and *Dem*. The words and phrases in this chapter are mostly in the familar form using *du* and *deg*, except where it is more appropriate to use the formal form. In general, use the formal form when speaking to senior citizens and officials, and the familiar form the rest of the time.

As Danish is a minor language and few visitors take the time or effort to learn it, most Danes speak English. However, an effort to at least learn the basics is well received. It's a good idea to memorise the words for 'thank you', 'goodbye', 'hello' and 'I'm sorry'. This minimum effort will be appreciated, and with an increased command of the language you'll be rewarded by gaining a greater insight into Denmark and the Danes. The pronunciation of each phrase and word in this chapter is transcribed using a simplified phonetic system, so with not too much effort it should be possible to grasp the basic sentence structure and begin creating your own sentences.

Pronunciation

Danish varies from island to island as well as from north to south, with each region having its distinct dialect. The translation and pronunciation presented here follows the form of Danish known as *Nudansk*, (literally 'Now Danish'). This is the form of Danish spoken in Copenhagen, and understood throughout the country.

In Danish the stress is usually placed on the first syllable, or on the first letter of the word. Stressed syllables in polysyllabic words are printed here in bold type, and some longer syllables have been split into more manageable lengths.

Danes do not necessarily pronounce what they write. The pronunciation of vowels in particular varies depending on the word, and unfortunately there are no hard and fast rules as to how a given letter is to be pronounced. Following is a list of Danish letters, how they sound using English words, and their equivalent in our pronunciation guide. Letters in parenthesis determine when the letter in bold type is to be pronounced as described. This should make it easier for the reader to pronounce words encountered which are not included in the text. In general though, the best advice for good pronunciation is to listen and learn. Good luck.

10 Danish

Danish	Pronunciation Guide	Sounds
a	aa	a long flat 'a' as in 'father'
a, æ	a	a long sharp 'a' as in 'act'
u(n), å, o	ã	a long rounded 'a' as in 'walk'
e(g)	ai	as in 'eye'
e, I	e	a short flat 'e', as in the Italian *che*
I	i	a long sharp 'e' as in 'see'
æ	eh	a long flat 'e' as in 'bet'
ø	er	as in 'fern' and 'earn'
i	i	a short flat 'i' as in 'pit' and 'in'
o, u	oo	a long 'o' as in 'zoo'
o	o	a short 'o' as in 'pot'
o(v)	ow	somewhat shorter sound than 'out' or 'vow'
o(v)	or	with less emphasis on the 'r', as in 'more'
u	u	as in 'pull'
y	ü	a long sharp 'u' as in the German *über*

Semiconsonants

w	w	similar to the 'wh' in 'what'
j	y	as in 'yet'
	'	the glottal stop, similar to the swallowed sound in 'bottle' as pronounced by a cockney: 'bo'l'. Usually occurs with words ending in 'er'.

Consonants

sj	sh	as in 'ship'
ch	tj	as the 'ch' in 'cheque'

j(o)	j	a short sharp 'j' as in 'jaw' or 'age'
(o)d	ð	a flat 'dth' sound as in 'these'
ng	ng	as in 'sing'
g	gh	when followed by a vowel, a hard 'g' as in 'get'
h	h	as the 'h' in 'horse', but silent before j and v
k	k	as the 'c' in 'cat'
b	b	as in 'box'
r	R	a rolling r abruptly cut short – there's no English equivalent
v	v	as in 'very'
c	c	as in 'cell'

All other consonants are pronounced as in English.

Greetings & Civilities
Top Useful Phrases

Hello./Goodbye.
   haa-lo/faar-vel   Hallo./Farvel.

Yes./No.
   ya/naay   Ja./Nej.

Excuse me.
   ān-sghül   Undskyld.

May I? Do you mind?
   mā yai? te-laÞ' dee?   Må jeg? Tillader De?

Sorry. (excuse me, forgive me)
   ān-sghül. be-klaa   Undskyld. Beklager.

Please.
   mā yai beðe. vehrs-gho   Må jeg bede. Værsgo.

Thank you.
   taagh   Tak.

Many thanks.
  maang-e taagh   Mange tak.
That's fine. You're welcome.
  de ehR ee oh-den   Det er i orden.
  sehl taagh   Selv tak.

Greetings
Good morning.
  gho mor-on   God morgen.
Good afternoon.
  gho efd'-meda   God eftermiddag.
Good evening/night.
  gho-aafden/gho-nad   Godaften/Godnat.
How are you?
  vo-dan haa dee de?   Hvordan har De det?
Well, thanks.
  gaad, taagh   Godt, tak.

Forms of Address
Madam/Mrs	*froo*	fru
Sir/Mr	*hehr*	herr
Miss	*frer-ghen*	frøken
companion, friend	*kaame-rad, ven*	kammerat, ven

Small Talk
Meeting People
What is your name?
  vað he-ð' du?   Hvad hedder du?
My name is ...
  mid naown ehR ...   Mit navn er ...

I'd like to introduce you to ...
  yai vel ad du sgha merðe ...   Jeg vil at du skal møde ...
I'm pleased to meet you.
  det ehR hüge-lid ad   Det er hyggeligt at træffe
  tref-feh dem   Dem.

Nationalities

Where are you from?
  *vor-**fraa** k'm-m' du?*   Hvorfra kommer du?

I am from ...
  jai ehR fra ...   Jeg er fra ...

Australia	*aaow-**sdraa**-lien*	Australien
Canada	***kan**-ada*	Canada
Denmark	***dan**-maagh*	Danmark
England	***ehng**-lan*	England
Ireland	*i**R**-lan*	Irland
New Zealand	*nü-se-lan*	New Zealand
Scotland	*sgh'd-lan*	Skotland
the USA	*dee f'-eneðe*	De Forenede
	sdaa-d'	Stater
Wales	*wa-**ehls***	Wales

Age

How old are you?
  *vor **gaa**-mel ehR du?*   Hvor gammel er du?
I am ... years old.
  *yai ehR ... ā **gaa**-mel*   Jeg er ... år gammel.

Occupations

What do you do?
  *vað f' ed **aa**-baay-de*   Hvad for et arbejde
  lav' du?   laver du?

I am (a/an) ... /I work as ...

yai ehR ...   Jeg er ...

yai aa-baay-d' sām ...   Jeg arbejder som ...

artist	*kāns-d'*	kunster
business person	*f'-radnengs-dree-vene*	forretningsdrivende
doctor	*leh-e*	læge
engineer	*enshe-nyerR*	ingeniør
farmer	*bāne*	bonde
journalist	*shuRna-lisd*	journalist
lawyer	*aðvo-kaa-d*	advokat
manual worker	*kr'bs-aa-baay-d'*	krobsarbeider
mechanic	*me-kaa-nigh'*	mekaniker
nurse	*süe-plaay'*	sygeplejer
office worker	*k'nto-risd*	kontorist
scientist	*for-sgh'*	forsker
student	*sdu-dehd*	student
teacher	*leh'*	lærer
waiter	*kehl-n'*	kelner
writer	*sghree-behnd*	skribent

Religion

What is your religion?

vað f' en reli-ghyoon haa du?   Hvad for en religion har du?

I am not religious.

yai ehR eghe relee-ghyers   Jeg er ikke religiøs.

I am ...
  yai ehR ...   Jeg er ...
Buddhist   *bu-**deesd***   buddist
Catholic   *kato-**leegh***   katolik
Christian   ***krehs**-den*   kristen
Hindu   *hen-du*   hindu
Jewish   ***yer**-ðe*   jøde
Muslim   *mus-**leem***   muslim

Family

Are you married?
  ehR du gheefd?   Er du gift?
I am single.
  *yai ehR u-**gheefd***   Jeg er ugift.
I am married.
  *yai ehR **gheefd***   Jeg er gift.
How many children do you
have?
  *vor **maang**-e berRn haa du?*   Hvor mange børn har du?
I don't have any children.
  yai haa eng-en berRn   Jeg har ingen børn.
I have a daughter/a son.
  *yai haa en **da**-d'/en sern*   Jeg har en datter/en søn.
How many brothers/sisters do
you have?
  *vor **maang**-e brer-ðr'/*   Hvor mange brødre/søstre
  ser-ðr' haa du?   har du?
Is your husband/wife here?
  ehR deen man/koone hehR?   Er din mand/kone her?

Do you have a boyfriend/
girlfriend?

haa du en kehR's-de?   Har du en kæreste?

brother	*broR*	bror
children	*bern*	børn
daughter	*da-d'*	datter
family	*fa-milye*	familie
father	*faa*	far
grandfather	*behsde-fað'*	bestefader
grandmother	*behsde-mooð'*	bestemoder
husband	*man*	mand
mother	*mooð'*	moder
sister	*ser-ð'*	søster
son	*sern*	søn
wife	*koone*	kone

Feelings

I like ...
    yai kan g'd leeðe ...   Jeg kan godt lide ...
I don't like ...
    yai kan eghe leeðe ...   Jeg kan ikke lide ...
(I am) in a hurry.
    (yai haa) hasd-vaRgh   (Jeg har) astværk.
(I am) well.
    (yai haa de) g'd   (Jeg har det) godt.
I am sorry. (condolence)
    de gherR mai ãnd ad her'   Det gør mig ondt at høre.
I am grateful.
    yai ehR taag-nehm-li   Jeg er taknemlig.

I am ...
  yai ehR ...

Jeg er ...

angry	*vrehð*	vred
cold/hot	*k'l/vaam*	kold/varm
happy/sad	*glað/trisd*	glad/trist
hungry/thirsty	*sul-den/terRs-di*	sulten/tørstig
right (correct)	*rehd*	ret
sleepy	*serv-ni*	søvnig
tired (fatigued)	*trehd*	træt
worried	*be-kerm-r'ð*	bekymret

Language Difficulties

Do you speak English?
  tal' dee ehng-elsgh?

Taler De engelsk?

Does anyone speak English?
  ehR de nooen s'm tal' ehng-elsgh?

Er det nogen som taler engelsk?

I speak a little ...
  yai tal' en smoole ...

Jeg taler en smule ...

I don't speak ...
  yai tal' eghe ...

Jeg taler ikke ...

I (don't) understand.
  yai f'-sdor (eghe)

Jeg forstår (ikke).

Could you repeat that?
  kune dee ghehn-ta de?

Kunne De gentage det?

Could you speak more slowly please?
  kune dee tale me' laand-s'md, mã yai beðe?

Kunne De tale mere langsomt, må jeg bede?

How do you say ...?
  vo-dan see' man ð?

Hvordan siger man ...?

What does ... mean?
vað be-tülð ð?   Hva betyder ...?

I speak ...
yai tal' ...   Jeg taler ...

English	*ehng-elsgh*	engelsk
French	*fraansgh*	fransk
German	*tüsgh*	tysk
Italian	*itali-ensgh*	italiensk

Some Useful Phrases

Sure.
sel-sagd   Selvsagt.

Just a minute.
ehd 'je-blegh   Et øjeblikk.

It's (not) important.
de ehr eghe sä vegh-did   Det er (ikke) så vigtigt.

It's (not) possible.
de ehR eghe mu-lid   Det er (ikke) muligt.

Wait!
ven-d!   Vent!

Good luck!
ler-ghe tel!   Lykke til!

Signs

BAGGAGE COUNTER	BAGAGE SKRANKE
CHECK-IN COUNTER	INDCHECKINGS SKRANKE
CUSTOMS	TOLD
EMERGENCY EXIT	NØDUDGANG
ENTRANCE	INDGANG

EXIT	UDGANG
FREE ADMISSION	GRATIS ADGANG
HOT/COLD	VARM/KOLD
INFORMATION	INFORMATION
NO ENTRY	INGEN ADGANG
NO SMOKING	IKKE-RYGERE
OPEN/CLOSED	ÅBEN/LUKKET
PROHIBITED	FORBUDT
RESERVED	RESERVERET
TELEPHONE	TELEFON
TOILETS	TOILETTER

Emergencies

| POLICE | POLITI |
| POLICE STATION | POLITISTATION |

Help!
  yehlb!   Hjælp!
It's an emergency!
  dehde ehR en nerðs-situa-   Dette er en nødssituation!
  shoon!
There's been an accident!
  de haa veh'ð en uler-ghe!   Det har været en ulykke!
Call a doctor!
  reng efd' en leh-e!   Ring efter en læge!
Call an ambulance!
  reng efd' en süe-v'v!   Ring efter en sygevogn!
I've been raped.
  yai haa bleveð v'-taed   Jeg har blevet voldtaget.
I've been robbed.
  yai haa bleveð raneð   Jeg har blevet ranet.

Call the police!
*reng efd' poli-**tee**-eð!* — Ring efter politiet!

Where is the police station?
*vor ehR poli-tee-sda-**shoo**-nen?* — Hvor er politistationen?

Go away!
*f'-**sven**!* — Forsvind!

I'll call the police!
*yai kal' på poli-**tee**-eð!* — Jeg kalder på politiet!

Thief!
tüv! — Tyv!

I am/My friend is ill.
yai ehR/meen ven ehR sü — Jeg er/Min ven er syg.

I am lost.
yai haa gãeð vil — Jeg har gået vild.

Where are the toilets?
*vor ehR toa-**ledene**?* — Hvor er toilettene?

Could you help me please?
kune dee yelbe mai? — Kunne De hjælpe mig?

Could I please use the telephone?
*mã yai fã broo-e tele-**foo**-nen?* — Må jeg få bruge telefonen?

I'm sorry. I apologise.
*be-**klaa** an-sgül* — Beklager. Undskyld.

I didn't realise I was doing anything wrong.
yai vesde eghe ad yai gyoo' nãeð ghald — Jeg vidste ikke at jeg gjorde noget galt.

I didn't do it.
de vaa eghe mai dehR gyoo' de — Det var ikke mig der gjorde det.

I wish to contact my embassy/
consulate.
    *yai **ern-sgh'** ad k'n-**taaghde**   Jeg ønsker at kontakte min
    meen aamba-saðe/mid   ambassade/mit konsulat.
    k'nsu-lad*

I speak English.
    *yai tal' **ehng**-elsgh*   Jeg taler engelsk.

I have medical insurance.
    *yai haa sile-f'-**segh**-reng*   Jeg har sygeforsikring.

My possessions are insured.
    *meene **aayen**-dele ehR*   Mine ejendele er forsikret.
    *f'-**segh**-red*

My ... was stolen.
    mid ... haa bleveð   Mit ... har blevet stjålet.
    sdyā-leð

I've lost ...
    yai haa taabd ...   Jeg har tabt ...

my bags	*meen ba-**gashe***	min bagage
my handbag	*meen h'n-**tasghe***	min håndtaske
my money	*meene **pehng**-e*	mine penge
my passport	*mid pas*	mit pas
my travellers'	*meene raayse-*	mine rejsechecks
cheques	***sheghs***	

Paperwork

name	*naaown*	navn
address	*a-**dras**-se*	adresse
date of birth	*fersels-**dato***	fødselsdato
place of birth	*ferðe-**sdeð***	fødested
age	*al'*	alder
sex	*kern*	køn

DANISH

nationality	*nasho-nali-**ted***	nationalitet
religion	*reli-**ghyoon***	religion
reason for travel	*for-māleð með raaysen*	formålet med rejsen
profession	*profe-**shoon***	profession
marital status	*si-**veel**-sdan*	civilstand
passport	*pas*	pas
passport number	*pas-**nām'***	pasnummer
visa	*veesām*	visum
identification	*leghitima-**shoon***	legitimation
birth certificate	*fersels-**atesd**/**dābs**-atesd*	fødslesattest/dåbsat test
driver's licence	*sehRtifi-**kad***	certifikat
car owner's title	*v'own-**kord***	vognkort
car registration	*v'own-**kord***	vognkort
customs	*t'l*	told
immigration	*imighra-**shoon***	immigration
border	*granse*	grænse

Getting Around

ARRIVALS	ANKOMSTER
BUS STOP	BUSHOLDEPLADS
DEPARTURES	AFGANGER
STATION	STATION
SUBWAY	UNDERGRUNDSBANEN
TICKET OFFICE	BILLETKONTOR
TIMETABLE	KØREPLAN
TRAIN STATION	JERNBANESTATION/ BANEGÅRD

What time does the ... leave/
arrive?

*vo-**nor** gor/an-k'm'* ...		Hvornår går/ankommer ...
(air)plane	*flü-eð*	flyet
boat	*bā-ðen*	båden
bus (city)	*busen*	bussen
bus (intercity)	***rude**-beelen*	rutebilen
train	*tā-weð*	toget
tram	*sbooR-v'ow-nen*	sporvognen

Directions

Where is ...?
  vor ehR ...? Hvor er ...?

How do I get to ...?
  *vo-**dan** k'm' yai tel ð?* Hvordan kommer jeg til ...?

Is it far from here?
  *ehR de langd hehR-**fraa**?* Er det langt herfra?

Is it near here?
  *ehR de ee nehr-**heðen**?* Er det i nærheden?

Can I walk there?
  *kan yai gā dehR-**hen**?* Kan jeg gå derhen?

Can you show me (on the
map)?
  kune dee veese mai (pā Kunne De vise mig (på
  ***kord**-eð)?* kortet)?

Are there other means of
getting there?
  ehR dehR aandr' māð' ad Er der andre måder at
  *k'me dehR-**hen**?* komme derhen?

I want to go to ...
  *yai **ern**-sgh' ad k'me tel* ... Jeg ønsker at komme til ...

DANISH

Go straight ahead.
  gā lee-e-fram — Gå ligefrem.
It's two streets down.
  de ehR too gað' u-na — Det er to gader unna.
Turn left ...
  draaay tel vehns-dr' ... — Drej tel venstre ...
Turn right ...
  draaay tel h'yr' ... — Drej til højre ...
at the next corner
  ve nehsde yerR-ne — ved næste hjørne
at the traffic lights
  ve traa-figh-lü-seð — ved trafiklyset

behind	*ba*	bag
far	*fyehRn*	fjern
near	*nehR*	nær
in front of	*for-an*	foran
opposite	*pā moð-sad seeð a*	på modsat side af

Buying Tickets

Excuse me, where is the ticket office?
  ān-sghül, vor ehR bi-lehd-k'n-too-'ð? — Undskyld, hvor er billetkontoret?
Where can I buy a ticket?
  vor kaa yai ker-be en bi-lehd? — Hvor kan jeg købe en billet?

I want to go to ...
  yai ern-sgh' ad raay-se tel ... — Jeg ønsker at rejse til ...

Do I need to book?
*ehR de nerð-vehn-did ad
be-sdel-le plas?*

Er det nødvendigt at bestille
plads?

You need to book.
*de ehR nerð-vehn-did ad
be-sdel-le plas*

Det er nødvendig at bestille
plads.

I'd like to book a seat to ...
*yai ern-sgh' ad be-sde-le
plas tel ...*

Jeg ønsker at bestille plads
til ...

It is full.
de ehR ful-d

Det er fuldt.

Is it completely full?
ehR de held ful-d?

Er det helt fuldt?

Can I get a stand-by ticket?
*kan yai mä-sghe ker-be en
stand-by be-lehd?*

Kan jeg måske købe en
stand-by billet?

I would like ...
yai vel gaR-ne ha-ve ...

Jeg vil gerne have ...

a one-way ticket	*en eng-gheld-bi-lehd*	en enkeltbillet
a return ticket	*en tooR-re-tooR bi-lehd*	en tur-retur billet
two tickets	*too bi-lehd'*	to billetter
tickets for all of us	*bi-lehd' f' a-le-saa-men*	billetter for allesammen
a student's fare	*sdu-dehnd-ra-bad*	studentrabat
a child's/pensioner's fare	*en berne/paangsho-nisd bi-lehd*	en børne/pension-ist billet
1st class	*fers-de klas-e*	første klasse
2nd class	*anen klas-e*	anden klasse

Air

CHECKING IN LUGGAGE PICKUP REGISTRATION	INDCHECKING BAGAGE AFHENTING REGISTRERING

Is there a flight to ...?
ehR dehR ed flü tel ...?
Er der et fly til ...?

When is the next flight to ...?
*vo-nor gor **nehs**-de flü tel ...?*
Hvornår går næste fly til ...?

How long does the flight take?
*vor lang tið ta' **flüve**-tu'n?*
Hvor lang tid tager flyveturen?

What is the flight number?
*vað ehR flaihd **nā**-m'-'ð?*
Hvad er flight nummeret?

You must check in at ... (time)
*du mā tjeghe en **kl'**-ghen ...*
Du må checke ind klokken ...

airport tax	**lāfd**-haawne-aow-ghifd	lufthavneavgift
boarding pass	*boarding-**kord***	boardingkort
customs	*t'l*	told

Bus

BUS/TRAM STOP	BUS/SPORVOGN HOLDEPLADS

Where is the bus/tram stop?
*vor ehR bus/**sboR**-v'own h'le-plasen?*
Hvor er bus/sporvogns holdepladsen?

Which bus goes to ...?
  vel-ghen bus *gor tel ...?*   Hvilken bus går til ...?
Does this bus go to ...?
  gor dehne bus-sen tel ...?   Går denne bussen til ...?
How often do buses pass by?
  vor 'fde k'm-m' bus-sen   Hvor ofte kommer bussen
  f'-bee?   forbi?
Could you let me know when
we get to ...?
  ku-ne dee la mai veeð nor   Kunne De lade mig vide når
  vi k'm-m' tel ...?   vi kommer til ...?
I want to get off!
  yai vel a!   Jeg vil af!

What time is the ... bus?
  vo-nor gor ... bus?   Hvornår går ... bus?
next   **nehs**-de   næste
first   **fers**-de   første
last   **sis**-de   sidste

Metro

METRO/UNDERGROUND	UNDERGRUNDSBANEN
CHANGE (for coins)	VÆKSEL
THIS WAY TO	DENNE VEJ TIL
WAY OUT	UDGANG

Which line takes me to ...?
  vel-ghen bane gor tel ...?   Hvilken bane går til ...?
What is the next station?
  *vað ehR **nehs**-de sda-*   Hvad er næste station?
  ***shoon**?*

Train

DINING CAR	SPISEVOGN
EXPRESS	EKSPRES
PLATFORM NO	PLATFORM NUMMER
SLEEPING CAR	SOVEVOGN

Is this the right platform
for ...?
   *ehR dehde rehgh-di pa-r'ng
   f' tā-oweð tel ...?*

Er dette rigtig perron for
toget til ...?

The train leaves from
platform ...
   *tā-oweð gor fraa
   pa-r'ng ð*

Toget går fra perron ...

Passengers must change
trains/platforms.
   *pasa-she-'ne mā bü-de
   tā-ow/pa-r'ng*

Passagerene må bytte
tog/perron

dining car	*sbeese-v'own*	spisevogn
express	*ehghs-pras*	ekspres
local	*lo-kal*	lokal
sleeping car	*s'owe-v'own*	sovevogn

Taxi

Can you take me to ...?
   kan du ker' mai tel ...?

Kan du køre mig til ...?

Please take me to ...
*va's'***vehn***-lid ad ker'mai tel ...*

Vær så venligt at køre mig til ...

How much does it cost to go to ...?
*vor ***maa***-yeð kāsd'de ad ker'tel ...?*

Hvor meget koster det at køere til ...?

Instructions

Here is fine, thank you.
sd'b hehR, taagh

Stop her, tak.

The next corner, please.
*veð ***nehs***-de yerR-ne, taagh*

Ved næste hjørne, tak.

Continue!
ford-sehd!

Fortsæt!

The next street to the left/right.
nehs-de gað tel vens-dr'/h'yr'

Næste gade til venstre/højre.

Stop here!
sd'b hehR!

Stop her!

Please slow down.
*va's'***vehn***-li ad kerR laang-s'm-m"*

Vær så venlig at køre langsommere.

Please wait here.
*vehn-lid ***vehn***-d hehR*

Venligt vent her.

Some Useful Phrases

The train is delayed/cancelled.
tā-oweð ehR f'-sen-gheð/en-sdel-eð

Toget er forsinket/indstilt.

How long will it be delayed?
*vor lehnge **blee-v' tä**-oweð f'-sen-gheð?*

Hvor lenge bliver toget forsinket?

There is a delay of ... hours.
de ehR en f'-seng-ghelse pā ... teem'

Det er en forsinkelse på ... timer.

Can I reserve a place?
*ehR de **moo**-lid ad reh-saR-ve' plas?*

Er det muligt at reservere plads?

How long does the trip take?
*vor laang tið taa' **too**-'n?*

Hvor lang tid tager turen?

Is it a direct route?
*ehr de en **di**-raghde f'-ben-else?*

Er det en direkte forbindelse?

Is that seat taken?
*ehr **seed**-ed 'b-taa-eð?*

Er sædet optaget?

I want to get off at ...
*yai **ern**-sgh' ad gā a ved ...*

Jeg ønsker at gå af ved ...

Excuse me.
ān-sghül

Undskyld.

Where can I hire a bicycle?
*vor kan yai **laa**-ye en sü-ghel?*

Hvor kan jeg leje en cykel?

Car

DETOUR	OMKØRSEL
FREEWAY	MOTORVEJ
GARAGE	GARAGE
GIVE WAY	VIGEPLIKT
MECHANIC	MEKANIKER
NO ENTRY	INDKØRSEL FORBUDT

NO PARKING	PARKERING FORBUDT
NORMAL	NORMAL
ONE WAY	ENRETTET FÆRDSEL
REPAIRS	REPARATIONER
SELF SERVICE	SELVBETJENING
STOP	STOP
SUPER	SUPER
UNLEADED	BLYFRIT

Where can I rent a car?
vor kan yai laa-ye en beel?

Hvor kan jeg leje en bil?

How much is it daily/weekly?
vor maa-yeð k's-d' de par da/par ooe?

Hvor meget koster det per dag/per uge?

Does that include insurance/ mileage?
en-klu-de' de f'-segh-reng/ ube-ghran-seð me kilo-me-d'?

Inkluderer det forsikring/ ubegrænset med kilometer?

Where's the next petrol station?
vor ehR nehs-de behn-seen-sda-shoon?

Hvor er næste benzinstation?

Please fill the tank.
ful taanggh, taagh

Fuld tank, tak.

I want ... litres of petrol (gas).
yai ern-sgh' ... lid' me behn-seen

Jeg ønsker ... liter med benzin.

Please check the oil and water.
va' s' vehn-li ad tjehghe olyen ' van-eð

Vær så venlig at checke olien og vandet.

How long can I park here?
vor lehnge kan yai paa-ke' hehR?

Hvor længe kan jeg parkere her?

Does this road lead to ...?
fer' dehne vaay-en tel ...?

Fører denne vejen til ...?

air (for tyres)	*lãfd*	luft
battery	*bade-ree*	batteri
brakes	*bram-s'*	bremser
clutch	*k'b-leng*	kobling
driver's licence	*saR-tifi-kaad*	certifikat
engine	*moo-to*	motor
lights	*lüs*	lys
oil	*olye*	olie
puncture	*pãng-te-Reng*	punktering
radiator	*raadi-aa-to*	radiator
road map	*vaay-kord*	vejkort
tyres	*dehgh*	dæk
windscreen	*f'-rooðe*	forrude

Car Problems

I need a mechanic.
yai haa broo f' en me-ka-nigh'

Jeg har brug for en mekaniker.

What make is it?
vað f' ed maR-ghe ehR de?

Hvad for et mærke er det?

The battery is flat.
bade-ree-eð ehR derð

Batteriet er dødt.

The radiator is leaking.
raadi-ato-on leh-gh'

Radiatoren lækker.

I have a flat tyre.
  yai haa pāng-te-'ð   Jeg har punkteret.
It's overheating. (engine)
  moo-to-on kā-ow' ow'   Motoren koger over.
It's not working.
  dehn viR-gh' eghe   Den virker ikke.

Accommodation

CAMPING GROUND	CAMPINGPLADS
GUESTHOUSE	GJÆSTGIVERI
INN	KRO
HOTEL	HOTEL
MOTEL	MOTEL
YOUTH HOSTEL	VANDREHJEM

I am looking for ...
  yai le-ð' efd' ...   Jeg leder efter ...
Where is a ...?
  vor ehR ed ...?   Hvor er et ...?
cheap hotel   *bi-lid ho-tehl*   billigt hotel
good hotel   *g'd ho-tehl*   godt hotel
nearby hotel *ho-tehl ee nehR-   hotel i nærheden
              heden*

What is the address?
  vað ehR a-dra-sen?   Hvad er adressen?
Could you write the address,
please?
  *ku-ne dee va' s' vehn-li ad   Kunne De være så venlig at
  sghree-ve neð a-dra-sen?*   skrive ned adressen?

At the Hotel

Do you have any rooms
available?
>   *haa ee leðee-e vaR'l-s'?* Har I ledige værelser?

I would like ...
>   *yai ern-sgh'* ... Jeg ønsker ...

a single room	*ed eng-gheld-vaR'l-se*	et enkeltværelse
a double room	*ed d'beld-vaR'l-se*	et dobbeltværelse
a room with a bathroom	*ed vaR'l-se meh bað*	et værelse med bad
to share a dorm	*plas ee en s'owe-saal*	plads i en sovesal
a bed	*en sehng*	en seng

I want a room with a ...
>   *yai ern-sgh' ed vaR'l-se meh* ... Jeg ønsker et værelse med ...

bathroom	*bað*	bad
shower	*broose-bað*	brusebad
TV	*tele-vi-shoon*	television
window	*ven-dooe*	vindue

I'm going to stay for ...
>   *yai blee-v'* ... Jeg bliver ...

one day	*en nad*	en nat
two days	*too nehð'*	to nætter
one week	*en ooe*	en uge

Do you have identification?
>   *haa du leghi-tima-shoon?* Har du legitimation?

Your membership card, please.
>   *yaR-'s mehð-lehms-kord, taagh* Jeres medlemskort, tak.

Sorry, we're full.
be-klaa', de ehR ful-d

Beklager, det er fuldt.

How long will you be staying?
vor lehnge blee-v' du?

Hvor længe bliver du?

How many nights?
vor maang-e nehð'?

Hvor mange nætter?

It's ... per day/per person.
de kāsd' ... par da/par paR-soon

Det koster ... per dag/per person.

How much is it per night/per person?
vor maa-yeð kāsd' de par nad/par paR-soon?

Hvor meget koster det per nat/per person?

Can I see it?
mā yai fāse vaR'l-seð?

Må jeg få se værelset?

Are there any others?
ehR dehR aandr' vaR'l-s'?

Er der andre værelser?

Are there any cheaper rooms?
fen-es dehr bilee-'e vaR'l-s'?

Findes der billigere værelser?

Can I see the bathroom?
mā yai fā se baaðe-vaR'l-seð?

Må jeg få se badeværelset?

Is there a reduction for students/children?
ehR dehR sdu-dehnd-raa-bad/berR-ne-raa-bad?

Er det studentrabat/børnerabat?

Does it include breakfast?
ehR moron-mað en-klu-de'-eð?

Er morgenmad inkluderet?

It's fine, I'll take it.
  de ehR fee-nd, yai taa' de
  Det er fint, jeg tager det.

I'm not sure how long I'm
staying.
  *yai veð eghe vor lehng-e
  yai blee-v'*
  Jeg ved ikke hvor længe jeg
  bliver.

Where is the bathroom?
  vor ehR toa-leh-deð?
  Hvor er toiletet?

Is there somewhere to wash
clothes?
  *ehR dehR ed ehl' aneð
  sdehð f' ad vasghe kle-ð'?*
  Er der et eller andet sted for
  at vaske klæder?

Is there hot water all day?
  *ehR dehR vaamd-van hele
  d'y-neð?*
  Er der varmtvand hele
  døgnet?

Is there a lift?
  ehR dehR ele-vaa-tor?
  Er der elevator?

Can I use the kitchen?
  kan yai broo-e ker-ghe-neð?
  Kan jeg bruge køkkenet?

Can I use the telephone?
  *kan yai be-ner-de tele-foo-
  nen?*
  Kan jeg benytte telefonen?

Requests & Complaints

Please wake me up at ...
  *ku-ne dee veh-ghe mai
  kl'-ghen ...*
  Kunne De vække mig
  klokken ...

The room needs to be cleaned.
  vaR'l-seð mā rü-ðes
  Værelset må ryddes.

Please change the sheets.
  *va' s' vehn-li ad sghif-de
  laay-n'ne*
  Vær så venligt at skifte
  lagnene.

I can't open/close the window.
yai kan eghe ābne/lā-ghe ven-du-eð

Jeg kan ikke åbne/lukke vinduet.

I've locked myself out of my room.
yai haa lā-sd mai ooðe a vaR'l-seð

Jeg har låst mig ude af værelset.

The toilet won't flush.
toa-leh-deð sgher-l' eghe

Toilettet skyller ikke.

I don't like this room.
yai sünes eghe 'm dehde vaR'l-seð

Jeg synes ikke om dette værelset.

It's (too) ...
de ehR (f') ...

Det er (for) ...

small	*li-le*	lille
noisy	*sd'y-ene*	støjende
dark	*morR-ghd*	mørkt
expensive	*düR-d*	dyrt

Some Useful Phrases

I am/We are leaving ...
yai/vi raay-s' ...

Jeg/Vi rejser ...

now/tomorrow
nu/i mor-orn

nu/i morgen

I would like to pay the bill.
yai ern-sgh' ad be-taa-le raay-neng-en

Jeg ønsker at betale regningen.

name	*naown*	navn
surname	*ehfd'-naown*	efternavn
room number	*vaR'l-se-nām'*	værelsenummer

Some Useful Words

address	*a-dra-se*	adresse
air-conditioned	*lā-fd-k'ndi-sho-ne-'ð*	luftkonditionert
balcony	*bal-k'ng*	balkon
bathroom	*bað*	bad
bed	*sehng*	seng
bill	*raay-neng*	regning
blanket	*teh-be*	tæppe
candle	*lüs*	lys
chair	*sdool*	stol
clean	*rehn*	ren
dark	*morRgh*	mørk
dirty	*snaow-seð*	snavset
double bed	*d'beld-sehng*	dobbeltseng
electricity	*elehgh-trisi-teð*	elektricitet
excluded	*ehghsklu-de-eð*	eksluderet
fan	*vef-de*	vifte
included	*enklu-de-'ð*	inkluderet
key	*n'y-le*	nøgle
lift (elevator)	*ele-vaato*	elevator
light bulb	*e-lehgh-trisgh peh'*	elektrisk pære
lock (n)	*lās*	lås
mattress	*ma-dras*	madras
mirror	*sbai-l*	spejl
padlock	*hehnge-lās*	hængelås
pillow	*hooeð-pooðe*	hovedpude
quiet	*sdele*	stille
room (in hotel)	*var'l-se*	værelse
sheet	*laay-en*	lagen
shower	*broose-bað*	brusebad

soap	*sehbe*	sæpe
suitcase	*kā-f'd*	kuffert
swimming pool	*sver-me-ba-seng*	svømmebassin
table	*booR*	bord
toilet	*toa-lehd*	toilet
toilet paper	*toa-lehd-pa-peeR*	toiletpapir
towel	*h'n-klehðe*	håndklæde
water	*van*	vand
cold water	*k'ld van*	koldt vand
hot water	*vaa-md van*	varmt vand
window	*ven-dooe*	vindue

Around Town

I'm looking for ...
    yai ser' ehfd' ...   Jeg søger efter ...

the art gallery	*kān-sd-mu-seheð*	kunstmuseet
a bank	*en bang-gh*	en bank
the church	*kiR-ghen*	kirken
the city centre	*sehn-trām*	centrum
the ... embassy	*dehn ... amba-saa-ðe*	den ... ambassade
my hotel	*mid ho-tehl*	mit hotel
the market	*maa-gheð-ed*	markedet
the museum	*mu-seh-eð*	museet
the police	*poli-tee-eð*	politiet
the post office	*p'sd-k'n-tooR-eð*	postkontoret
a public toilet	*ed 'fend-lid toa-lehd*	et offentligt toilet
the telephone centre	*tele-foon-sehn-traa-len*	telefoncentralen
the tourist information office	*tu-risd-enforma-shoo-nen*	turistinformationen

What time does it open?
vo-nor ābn' de? — Hvornår åbner det?

What time does it close?
vo-nor lā-gh' de? — Hvornår lukker det?

What ... is this?
vað f' en ... ehR dehde? — Hvad for en ... er dette?

street	**gaa-ðe**	gade
suburb	**f'-sdað**	forstad

For directions, see the Getting Around section, page 23.

At the Bank

I want to exchange some
money/traveller's cheques.
yai ern-sgh' ad vehgh-sle noo-le pehng-e/raayse-sheghs — Jeg ønsker at veksle nogle penger/reisechecks.

What is the exchange rate?
vað ehR kuR-sen? — Hvad er kursen?

How many kroner per dollar?
vor maang-e kroo-n' par d'-la? — Hvor mange kroner per dollar?

Can I have money transferred
here from my bank?
kan yai fā pehng-e' ow'-fer' hid fra meen baang-gh? — Kan jeg få penge overført hit fra min bank?

How long will it take to
arrive?
vor laang tið vel de ta ferR de an-k'm'? — Hvor lang tid vil det tage før de ankommer?

Has my money arrived yet?
*haa meene **pehng**-e
an-k'm-eð e-**nu**?*

Har mine penge ankommet endnu?

bank draft	***baang**-gh-an-vee-sneng*	bankanvisning
bank notes	*sehŏ-l'*	sedler
cashier	*ka-**seh**-'*	kasserer
coins	***mern**-d'*	mønter
credit card	***kreh**-did-kord*	kreditkort
exchange	***vehgh**-sle*	veklse
loose change	*smā-**pehng**-e*	småpenge
signature	*sin-ya-**tooR***	signatur

At the Post Office

I would like to send ...
*yai **ern**-sgh' ad seh-ne ...*

Jeg ønsker at sende ...

a letter	*ed brehv*	et brev
a postcard	*ed p'sd-kord*	et postkort
a parcel	*en **pa**-ghe*	en pakke
a telegram	*ed tele-**ghram***	et telegram

I would like some stamps.
*yai vel **gaR**-ne haa-ve
noo-le fri-**maRgh**'*

Jeg vil gerne have nogle frimerker.

How much is the postage?
*vor **maa**-yeð ehR portoo-en?*

Hvor meget er portoen?

How much does it cost to send this to ...?
*vor **maa**-yeð k's-d' de ad
seh-ne dehne tel ...?*

Hvor meget koster det at sende denne til ...?

an aerogram	ed ahRo-*graam*	et aerogram
air mail	lā-fd-p'sd	luftpost
envelope	k'nvo-*lud*	konvolut
mailbox	p'sd-kase	postkasse
parcel	paa-ghe	pakke
registered mail	rehk'-man-de-'ð	rekommanderet
surface mail	ow'-flaað-p'sd	overfladepost

Telephone

I want to ring ...
   yai ern-sgh' ad rehng-e tel ...   Jeg ønsker at ringe til ...
The number is ...
   nām-r'ð ehR ...   Nummeret er ...
I want to speak for three
minutes.
   yai ern-sgh' ad taa-le treh   Jeg ønsker at tale tre
   mi-nud'   minutter.
How much does a three-
minute call cost?
   vor maa-yeð k's-d'de f'   Hvor meget koster det for
   treh mi-nud'?   tre minutter?
How much does each extra
minute cost?
   vor maa-yeð k's-d' vehRd   Hvor meget koster hvert
   mi-nud ehghs-dra?   minutt ekstra?
I would like to speak to Mr
Pedersen.
   yai ern-sgh' ad taa-le meh   Jeg ønsker at tale med Hr
   haR peh-d'-sen   Pedersen.
It's engaged.
   de ehR 'b-taa-eð   Det er optaget.

I want to make a reverse-
charges phone call.
   *yai **ern**-sgh' ad mod-
   taa-'en sgha be-**taa**-le*

Jeg ønsker at modtageren
skal betale.

I've been cut off.
   yai bleh-v aw-brud

Jeg blev afbrudt.

Sightseeing

Do you have a guidebook/
local map?
   *haa ee en **raay**-se-h'n-
   bāow/lo-**kaal**-kord?*

Har I en rejsehåndbog/
lokalkort?

What are the main attractions?
   *vað ehR hoo-veð-atraagh-
   shoo-nene?*

Hvad er hovedattraktionene?

What is that?
   vað ehR de?

Hvad er det?

How old is it?
   *vor **gaa**-mel ehR dehn?*

Hvor gammel er den?

Can I take photographs?
   mā yai fā ta be-leð'?

Må jeg få tage billeder?

What time does it open/close?
   *vo-**nor** ābn'/lā-gh' de?*

Hvornår åbner/lukker det?

ancient	*ehl-gaa-mel*	ældgammel
archaeological	*akeho-loo-isgh*	arkæologisk
beach	*sdran*	strand
building	*bügh-neng*	bygning
castle	*sl'd*	slot

cathedral	kade-**draal**	katedral
church	**kiR**-ghe	kirke
concert hall	k'n-sa**Rd**-saal	koncertsal
library	biblio-**tehgh**	bibliotek
main square	hoo-veð-**torv**	hovedtorv
market	**maa**-gheð	marked
monastery	**kl's**-d'	kloster
monument	monu-**mehnd**	monument
mosque	m'-**sghe**	moské
old city	**gaam**-le büen	gamle byen
opera house	oo-**bera**	opera
palace	pa-**las**	palads
ruins	ru-ee-n'	ruiner
stadium	**sdaa**-di'n	stadion
statues	**sdaa**-too'	statuer
synagogue	süna-**ghooe**	synagoge
temple	**tehm**-bel	tempel
university	uni-va**Rsi-teh**-deð	universitet

Entertainment

What's there to do in the
evenings?
>   vað ehR dehR ad gher''m
>   **aaf**-denen?

Hvad er der at gøre om
aftenen?

Are there any discos?
>   ehR dehR disgh'-**tehgh**'?

Er der disoteker?

Are there places where you
can hear local folk music?
>   **fen**-es dehR sdeh-ð' vor de
>   ehR **moo**-lid ad her' f'**lghe**-
>   mu-sigh?

Findes der steder hvor det
er muligt at høre
folkemusik?

How much does it cost to get in?

vor maa-yeð k's-d' de ad k'm-me en?

Hvor meget koster det at komme ind?

cinema	*bio-ghraaf*	biograf
concert	*k'n-saRd*	koncert
discotheque	*disgh'-tehgh*	diskotek
theatre	*te-aa-d'*	teater

In the Country
Weather

What's the weather like?

vor-dan ehR veh-'ð?

Hvordan er vejret?

The weather is ... today.

de ehR ... ee daa

Det er ... i dag.

Will it be ... tomorrow?

k'm-m' de ad blee-ve ... ee mor-orn?

Kommer det at blive ... i morgen?

cloudy	*ow'-sghü-eð*	overskyet
cold	*k'ld*	koldt
foggy	*tā-weð*	tågede
frosty	*fr'sd*	frost
hot	*hed*	hedt
raining	*raay-n*	regn
snowing	*sne*	sne
sunny	*sool*	sol
windy	*bleh-se-vehR*	blæsevejr

Camping

Am I allowed to camp here?
mā yai fā kaam-peh' hehR?   Må jeg få campere her?

Is there a campsite nearby?
fen-es dehR en kaam-peng-   Findes der en campingplads
plas ee nehR-heðen?   i nærheden?

backpack	*rergh-sehgh*	rygsæk
can opener	*dāse-ābn'*	dåseåbner
compass	*k'm-pas*	kompas
crampons	*kladr'-yaRn*	klatrejern
firewood	*brane*	brænde
gas cartridge	*gas-be-h'l'*	gasbeholder
hammock	*hehnge-k'ye*	hængekøje
ice axe	*ees-erghse*	isøkse
mattress	*ma-dras*	madras
penknife	*l'me-kneev*	lommekniv
rope	*t'w*	tov
sleeping bag	*s'owe-poose*	sovepose
stove	*kaam-peng-'own*	campingovn
tent	*tehld*	telt
tent pegs	*tehld-pehle*	teltpæle
torch (flashlight)	*l'me-lerghde*	lommelygte
water bottle	*fehld-flasghe*	feltflaske

Food

Traditional Danish cooking is dominated, although not to the same extent as the other Scandinavian countries, by smoked, cured, pickled or otherwise preserved food, due to the short growing season and long winters. Regional variations are not great, though proximity to the ocean flavours menus with seafood.

breakfast	*mor-orn-mað*	morgenmad
lunch	*frā-k'sd*	frokost
dinner	*meda*	middag

Table for ..., please.
    ed booR f' ..., taagh — Et bord for ..., tak.
Can I see the menu please?
    mā yai fā seh menūen? — Må jeg få se menuen?
I would like the set lunch,
please.
    yai taa' daaens rad, taagh — Jeg tager dagens ret, tak.
What does it include?
    vað enklu-deh' dehn? — Hvad inkluderer den?
Is service included in the bill?
    ehR ser-vis enklu-deh-'ð ee — Er service inkluderet i
    raay-nengen? — regningen?
Not too spicy please.
    eghe f' krūð-r'ð 'm yai mā — Ikke for krydret, om jeg må
    behðe — bede.

Vegetarian Meals

I am a vegetarian.
    yai ehR veghe-taai-aan' — Jeg er vegetarianer.
I don't eat meat.
    yai sbees' eghe kerð — Jeg spiser ikke kød.
I don't eat chicken, or fish, or
ham.
    yai sbees' eghe kū-leng ehl' — Jeg spiser ikke kylling eller
    fesgh ehl' sgheng-ghe — fisk eller skinke.

ashtray	*asghe-beh'*	askebæger
the bill	*raay-nengen*	regningen
a cup	*en k'b*	en kop
dessert	*deh-sehR*	dessert
a drink	*ed dreh-ghe*	et drikke
a fork	*en ghaa-fel*	en gaffel
fresh	*faRsgh*	fersk
a glass	*ed glas*	et glas
a knife	*en kneev*	en kniv
a plate	*en ta-laR-ghen*	en tallerken
spicy	*krüð-r'ð*	krydret
a spoon	*en sgheh*	en ske
stale	*gaa-mel*	gammel
sweet	*serð*	sød
teaspoon	*teh-sgheh*	teske
toothpick	*tan-sdegh'*	tandstikker

Breakfast

Morgenmad

fried egg (always sunny side up)	*spejlæg*
hardboiled egg	*hårdkogte æg*
oatmeal	*havregrød*
pancakes	*pandekager*
scrambled eggs	*røræg*
scrambled eggs with bacon	*flæskeæggekage*
scrambled eggs with onions, potatoes and bacon	*ægekage*
softboiled egg	*blødkogte æg*
toast	*ristet brød*

Sandwiches   Smørebrød

Danish sandwiches are ornate and tasty. A feast for the eye and a delight to the palate.

Bøftartar
   Beef tartar: raw ground beef topped with a raw egg yolk, onion and capers.
Hakkebøf med løg
   Hamburger covered with fried onions, served cold.
Leverpostej
   Liver paté.
Rejemad
   Small shrimp served with mayonnaise and lemon slices.
Røget ål
   Smoked eel, a delicacy.
Røget laks
   Smoked salmon, served with scrambled eggs.
Røget sild
   Smoked herring on bread with a raw egg yolk and chives
Ost
   Cheese. Denmark is famous for its cheeses, and produces an enormous variety.

bread	*brød*
crusty roll	*rundstykke*
Danish pastry	*wienerbrød*
French bread, baguette	*franskbrød*
rye bread	*rugbrød*
soft roll	*bolle*

Soup   Suppe

Fiskesuppe
  Fish soup, usually creamy.
Grøntsagssuppe
  Vegetable soup.
Hønsekødsuppe
  Chicken soup.
Sødsuppe
  A sweet barley or sago soup with raisins and prunes.
Ølebrød
  A smooth beer and bread soup served with whipped cream.
Ærter gule
  Split pea soup served with pork.

Meat   Kød

Denmark is a major meat exporter, and is best known for its
pork, ham and bacon.

Benløse fugle
  Meatloaf shaped to resemble small game birds.
Bankekød
  Similar to Weinerschnitzel.
Forloren skilpadde
  Imitation turtle stew made with tongue, veal, meatballs and
  fishballs.
Frikadeller med surt
  Meat patties served with potatoes, brown sauce, and pickled
  cucumbers.
Fyldt hvidkålshoved
  Cabbage leaves wrapped around ground beef.

Høns i karri
  Stewed chicken in a curry sauce.
Ruskomsnusk
  Hash made with bits of ham, carrots, potatoes and onions,
  fried in butter.

chicken	*kylling*
hamburger	*hakkebøf*
lamb chops	*lammekoteletter*
roast beef	*oksesteg*
roast lamb	*lammesteg*
roast pork	*flæskesteg*
sausage	*pølse*
steak	*engelsk bøf*

Seafood   Fisk

Ål stegt med stuvede kartofler
  Fried eel with either fried or boiled diced potatoes.
Kogt torsk
  Poached cod in a mustard sauce served with boiled potatoes.
Kryddersild
  Herring pickled in different marinades, onion, mustard,
  tomato, etc.

haddock	*kuller*
halibut	*helleflynde*
herring	*sild*
plaice	*rødspætte*
salmon	*laks*
shrimp	*rejer*
sole	*søtunge*
trout	*forel*

Vegetables — Grøndsager

beets (usually served pickled)	rødbeder
cabbage	kål
carrots	gulerødder
cauliflower	blomkål
celery	bladselleri
cucumber	augurk
lettuce	grøn salat
mashed potatoes	kartoffelmos
mushrooms	champignons
onions	løg
peas	ærter
pickled cucumbers	surt
potato (boiled/baked)	kartoffel (kogt/bagt)
rice	ris
string beans	snittebønner

Condiments — Surt og Sødt

butter	smør
garlic	hvidløg
mustard	sennep
oil	olie
pepper	peber
salt	salt
sugar	sukker
vinegar	eddik

Dessert — Dessert

Bindepige med slør

'Peasant girl with a veil'. Browned breadcrumbs mixed with chocolate and covered with whipped cream.

Chokoladeis/vanilleis
  Chocolate ice cream/Vanilla ice cream.
Kage
  Cake.
Konditorkager
  French pastry.
Rødgrød med fløde
  Red currant or raspberry pudding served with cream or custard.
Pandekager
  Crepes rolled around a jam filling and sprinkled with powdered sugar.

Drinks – Nonalcoholic	**Drikke**
coffee (with cream)	*kaffe (med fløde)*
orange juice	*orangesaft*
skim milk	*skummet mælk*
soft drink, carbonated water	*sodavand*
tea	*te*
water, ice water.	*vand, isvand*
whole milk	*sødmælk*

Drinks – Alcoholic	**Drikke**

øl
  beer, lager.
bajer
  Beer. Specifically means a darker beer more like ale, but is used colloquially to mean any beer.
snapps
  Various kinds of grain alcohol flavoured with different herbs. *Jægermeister, Gammel Dansk*, etc. Traditionally consumed with fatty foods to help digestion.

Shopping

How much is it?
> *vor maa-yeð k's-d' de?* Hvor meget koster det?

bookshop	*bāw-han-el*	boghandel
camera shop	*foto-han-el*	fotohandel
clothing store	*kleh-ð-magha-seen*	klædemagasin
delicatessen	*delika-tehse*	delikatesse
general store, shop	*lan-han-el, bu-tigh*	landhandel, butik
laundry	*vasghe-ree*	vaskeri
market	*maa-gheð*	marked
newsagency	*a-vees-ki-'sgh*	aviskiosk
pharmacy	*aapo-tegh*	apotek
shoeshop	*sgho-t'ys-f'rad-neng*	skotøjsforretning
souvenir shop	*suve-neer-bu-tigh*	souvenirbutik
stationers	*pa-peeR-han-el*	papirhandel
supermarket	*soo-b'-maa-gheð*	supermarked
vegetable shop	*grernd-han-el*	grønthandel

I would like to buy ...
> *yai ern-sgh' ad kerbe ...* Jeg ønsker at købe ...

Do you have others?
> *haa du an-eð?* Har du andet?

I don't like it.
> *dehn kan yai eghe leeðe* Den kan jeg ikke lide.

Can I look at it?
> *mā yai fā ki-ghe pā dehn?* Må jeg få kikke på den?

I'm just looking.
> *yai baa-a ki-gh'* Jeg bare kikker.

Can you write down the price?
  *ku-ne du sghree-ve
  pree-sen?*   Kunne du skrive prisen?

Do you accept credit cards?
  *aagh-sehb-teh'ee kreh-did-
  kord?*   Accepterer I kreditkort?

Can I help you?
  mā yai fā yehl-be dehm?   Må jeg få hjælpe Dem?

Will that be all?
  ehr de de heh-le?   Er det det hele?

Would you like it wrapped?
  *ern-sgh' dee de paa-gheð
  en?*   Ønsker De det pakket ind?

Sorry, this is the only one.
  *des-vaR', dehde ehR dehn
  enesde*   Desværre, dette er den
                                 eneste.

How much/many do you
want?
  *vor maa-yeð/maang-e
  ern-sgh' dee?*   Hvor meget/mange ønsker
                                 De?

Souvenirs

earrings	*er'n-rehnge*	ørenringe
handicraft	*kā-nsd-h'n-vaRgh*	kunsthåndværk
necklace	*hals-b'n*	halsbånd
pottery	*keaa-migh*	keramik
ring	*rehng*	ring
rug	*teh-be*	tæppe

DANISH

Clothing

clothing	*kleh'*	klæder
coat	*fraa-ghe*	frakke
dress	*kyoo-le*	kjole
jacket	*yaa-ghe*	jakke
jumper (sweater)	*sweh-d'*	sweater
shirt	*sghyoR-de*	skjorte
shoes	*sghoo*	sko
skirt	*neð'-dehl*	nederdel
trousers	*bā'-gh-s'*	bukser

It doesn't fit.
  dehn pa-s' eghe   Den passer ikke.

It is too ...
  dehn ehR f'...   Den er for ...

big	*sdooR*	stor
small	*li-le*	lille
short	*kord*	kort
long	*laang*	lang
tight	*traang*	trang
loose	*lers*	løs

Materials

cotton	*bām-ul*	bomuld
handmade	*h'n-laa-veð*	håndlavet
leather	*lehð'*	læder
of brass	*a mehs-eng*	af messing
of gold	*a gul*	af guld
of silver	*a serl*	af sølv
pure alpaca	*rehn al-paaka*	ren alpaka
silk	*sel-ghe*	silke
wool	*ul*	uld

Toiletries

comb	*kaam*	kam
condoms	*k'n-doom-'*	kondomer
deodorant	*deo-do-raand*	deodorant
hairbrush	*hor-borRs-de*	hårbørste
moisturising cream	*fågh-di-heðs-krehm*	fugtighedscreme
razor	*baa-behR-kneev*	barberkniv
sanitary napkins	*ben*	bind
shampoo	*sham-pu*	shampoo
shaving cream	*baa-behR-krehm*	barbercreme
soap	*seh-be*	sæbe
sunblock cream	*sool-krehm*	solcreme
tampons	*taam-p'ng'*	tamponer
tissues	*ranse-sarvi-ehd*	rense-serviet
toilet paper	*toa-lehd-pa-peeR*	toiletpapir
toothbrush	*tan-berRs-de*	tandbørste
toothpaste	*tan-pasda*	tandpasta

Stationery & Publications

map	*kord*	kort
newspaper	*a-vees*	avis
newspaper in English	*en a-vees pā eng-elsgh*	en avis på engelsk
novels in English	*ro-maa-n' pā eng-elsgh*	romaner på engelsk
paper	*pa-peeR*	papir
pen (ballpoint)	*koo-le-pehn*	kuglepen
scissors	*saaghs*	saks

Photography

How much is it to process this film?

vor maa-yeð k's-d' de ad fram-kale dehne fil-men?

Hvor meget koster det at fremkalde denne filmen?

When will it be ready?

vor-nor blee-v' dehn faR-di?

Hvornår bliver den ferdig?

I'd like a film for this camera.

yai ern-sgh' ad ker-be film tel dehde kaa-meraa-eð

Jeg ønsker at købe film til dette kameraet.

B&W (film)	*soRd-við*	sort-hvid
camera	*kaa-meraa*	kamera
colour (film)	*faa-ve*	farve
film	*film*	film
flash	*blids*	blitz
lens	*'b-yehgh-teev*	objektiv
light meter	*lüs-māl'*	lysmåler

Smoking

A packet of cigarettes, please.

en paa-ghe sighaa-rad', taagh

En pakke cigaretter, tak.

Are these cigarettes strong/ mild?

ehR dise sighaa-rad' sdaR-ghe/mile?

Er disse cigaretter stærke/milde?

Do you have a light?

kan yai fā il hās dai?

Kan jeg få ild hos deg?

cigarette papers	*sighaa-rad-pa-peeR*	cigaretpapir
cigarettes	*sigha-rad'*	cigaretter
filtered	*með fil-d'*	med filter
lighter	*fülR-t'y*	fyrtøj
matches	*teh-sde-gh'*	tændstikker
menthol	*mehn-tool*	mentol
pipe	*pee-be*	pibe
tobacco (pipe)	*pee-be-to-baagh*	pibetobak

Colours

black	*soRd*	sort
blue	*blä*	blå
brown	*broon*	brun
green	*grern*	grøn
orange	*o-rang-she*	orange
pink	*roosa*	rosa
purple	*li-la*	lilla
red	*rerð*	rød
white	*við*	hvid
yellow	*gool*	gul

Sizes & Comparisons

small	*li-le*	lille
big	*sdooR*	stor
heavy	*täng*	tung
light	*lehd*	let
more	*mehR*	mer
less	*men-dr'*	mindre
too much/many	*f' maa-yeð/maang-e*	for meget/mange
many	*maang-e*	mange
enough	*n'gh*	nok
also	*'ows'*	også
a little bit	*en li-le smoole*	en lille smule

Health

Where is ...?		Hvor er ...?
vor ehR ...?		
the doctor	*leh-en*	lægen
the hospital	*hosbi-taa-leð*	hospitalet
the chemist	*aapo-teh-gh'*	apoteker
the dentist	*tan-leh-en*	tandlægen

I am sick.
  yai ehR sü   Jeg er syg.

My friend is sick.
  meen vehn ehR sü   Min ven er syg.

Could I see a female doctor?
  mä yai fä seh en kvene-li   Må jeg få se en kvindelig
  leh-e?   læge?

What's the matter?
  vað ehR dehR ee vaay-en?   Hvad er der i vejen?

Where does it hurt?
  vor gerR de änd?   Hvor gør det ondt?

It hurts here.
  de gerR änd hehR   Det gør ondt her.

My ... hurts.
  meen/mid ... gerR änd   Min/mitt ... gør ondt.

Parts of the Body

ankle	*aang-ghel*	ankel
arm	*aam*	arm
back	*rergh*	ryg
chest	*brersd*	bryst
ear	*er'*	øre
eye	*'ye*	øje

finger	*feng-'*	finger
foot	*fooð*	fod
hand	*h'n*	hånd
head	*hooðe*	hoved
heart	*yaR-de*	hjerte
leg	*behn*	ben
mouth	*mān*	mund
ribs	*riben*	ribben
skin	*huð*	hud
stomach	*maave*	mave
teeth	*tehn'*	tænder
throat	*hals*	hals

Ailments

I have ...
   yai haa ...   Jeg har ...

an allergy	*alaR-ghee*	allergi
anaemia	*aneh-mee*	anæmi
a blister	*en vaa-ble*	en vable
a burn	*ed braan-sor*	et brandsår
a cold	*en f'-kerl-else*	en forkølelse
constipation	*f'-sd'b-else*	forstoppelse
a cough	*en hoos-de*	en hoste
diarrhoea	*dia-reh*	diarré
fever	*fe-b'*	feber
a headache	*hoo-ðe-peene*	hovedpine
hepatitis	*hepa-titis*	hepatitis
indigestion	*maa-ve-be-svehR-li-heð'*	mavebesværli-gheder
an infection	*en en-fehgh-shoon*	en infektion
influenza	*en-flu-ehnsa*	influenza
lice	*loos*	lus

DANISH

low/high blood pressure	*laa-vd/h'yd bloð-trergh*	lavt/højt blodtryk
a pain	*en smaR-de*	en smerte
sore throat	*ānd ee hal-sen*	ondt i halsen
sprain	*f'-sdoo-neng*	forstuvning
a stomachache	*ānd ee maaven*	ondt i maven
sunburn	*sool-f'-bran-eng*	solforbrænding
a temperature	*fe-b'*	feber
a venereal disease	*en kerns-sü-d'm*	kønssygdom
worms	*oRm*	orm

Some Useful Words & Phrases

I'm ...
 yai ehR ... Jeg er ...

diabetic	*dia-be-tigh'*	diabetiker
epileptic	*epi-lehb-tisgh*	epileptisk
asthmatic	*asd-maa-tisgh*	astmatisk

I'm allergic to ...
 yai ehR a-laR-ghisgh i-mooð... Jeg er allergisk imod ...

antibiotics	*anti-bi-oo-tikām*	antibiotikum
penicillin	*penisi-leen*	penicillin

I'm pregnant.
 yai ehR graa-við Jeg er gravid.

I'm on the pill.
 yai broo' pe-pelen Jeg bruger p-pillen.

I haven't had my period for ... months.
 yai haa eghe haafd mehns-drua-shoon pā ... māneð' Jeg har ikke haft menstrua-tion på ... måneder.

I have been vaccinated.
yai haa ble-veð vaaghsi-neh-'ð   Jeg har blevet vaccineret.

I have my own syringe.
yai haa meen aayen ka-nüle   Jeg har min egen kanyle.

I feel better/worse.
yai fer-l' mai behðr'/vaR'   Jeg føler mig bedre/værre.

accident	*u-lerghe*	ulykke
addiction	*aaw-hengi-heð*	afhængighed
antibiotics	*anti-bi-oo-tikäm*	antibiotikum
aspirin	*asbi-reen*	aspirin
a bandage	*en ban-daashe*	en bandage
blood test	*bloð-prer-ve*	blodprøve
contraceptive	*prehvehn-teev*	præventiv
medicine	*medi-seen*	medicin
menstruation	*mehnsdrua-shoon*	menstruation
nausea	*kvalme*	kvalme
oxygen	*'ghsü-ghen*	oxygen
vitamins	*vita-mee-n'*	vitaminer

At the Chemist

I need medication for ...
yai be-her-v' ed medika-mehn dee i-mooð...   Jeg behøver et medikament imod ...

I have a prescription.
yai haa reh-sehbd   Jeg har recept.

At the Dentist

I have a toothache.
yai haa tan-peene   Jeg har tandpine.

I've lost a filling.
   yai haa taabd en plām-be   Jeg har tabt en plombe.

I've broken a tooth.
   *yai haa **bra**-gheð en tan*   Jeg har brækket en tand.

My gums hurt.
   *mid **tan**-kerð gorR ānd*   Mit tandkød gør ondt.

I don't want it extracted.
   yai vel eghe haave dehn   Jeg vil ikke have den
   trā-gheð   trukket.

Please give me an anaesthetic.
   mā yai fā en lo-kaal   Må jeg få en lokal
   be-der-velse?   bedøvelse?

Time & Dates

What date is it today?
   vað f' en daato ehR de ee   Hvad for en dato er det i
   daa?   dag?

What time is it?
   *vað ehR **kl'**-ghen?*   Hvad er klokken?

It is ... am/pm.
   ***kl'**-ghen ehR ... 'm*   Klokken er ... om
   mor-nen/aaf-denen   morgenen/aftenen.

in the morning	*'m **mor**-nen*	om morgenen
in the afternoon	*'m **ehfd**'-medaa-en*	om eftermiddagen
in the evening	*'m **aaf**-denen*	om aftenen

Days of the Week

Monday	*man-daa*	mandag
Tuesday	*teers-daa*	tirsdag
Wednesday	*ohns-daa*	onsdag
Thursday	*tors-daa*	torsdag
Friday	*fre-daa*	fredag

| Saturday | *lerR-daa* | lørdag |
| Sunday | *sern-daa* | søndag |

Months

January	*janu-aa*	januar
February	*febru-aa*	februar
March	*maads*	marts
April	*a-preel*	april
May	*maay*	maj
June	*yoo-ni*	juni
July	*yoo-li*	juli
August	*aaw-gāsŏ*	august
September	*sehb-tehm-b'*	september
October	*ogh-too-b'*	oktober
November	*no-vehm-b'*	november
December	*de-sehm-b'*	december

Seasons

summer	*s'm'*	sommer
autumn	*ehfd'-or*	efterår
winter	*ven-d'*	vinter
spring	*f'-or*	foraår

Present

today	*ee daa*	i dag
this morning	*ee mor-ors*	i morges
tonight	*ee nad*	i nat
this week/this year	*dehne ooe/ee or*	denne uge/i år
now	*nu*	nu

Past

yesterday	*ee gor*	i går
day before yesterday	*ee for-ghors*	i forgårs
yesterday morning	*ee gor mor-ors*	i går morges
last night	*ee gor nad*	i går nat
last week/last year	*foree-e ooe/i fyoo-R*	forrige uge/i fjor

Future

tomorrow	*ee mor-orn*	i morgen
day after tomorrow	*ee 'ow'-mor-orn*	i overmorgen
tomorrow morning	*ee mor-orn tiðlid*	i morgen tidligt
tomorrow after-noon/evening	*ee mor-orn ehfd'-medaa/aafden*	i morgen eftermiddag/aften
next week	*nehsde ooe*	næste uge
next year	*nehsde ā*	næste år

During the Day

afternoon	*ehfd'-medaa*	eftermiddag
dawn	*daaow-grü*	daggry
day	*daa*	dag
early	*tiðli*	tidlig
midnight	*mið-nad*	midnat
morning	*mor-orn*	morgen
night	*nad*	nat
noon	*mið-daa*	middag
sundown	*sool-neð-ghaang*	solnedgang
sunrise	*sool-'b-ghaang*	solopgang

Numbers & Amounts

0	*nål*	nul
1	*en*	en
2	*too*	to
3	*treh*	tre
4	*fee'*	fire
5	*fehm*	fem
6	*sehghs*	seks
7	*süw*	syv
8	*åde*	otte
9	*nee*	ni
10	*tee*	ti
11	*ehlve*	elve
12	*t'l*	tolv
13	*traden*	tretten
14	*fyoRden*	fjorten
15	*fehmden*	femten
16	*saaysden*	seksten
17	*serden*	sytten
18	*aden*	atten
19	*neden*	nitten
20	*tüve*	tyve
21	*en-'-tüve*	enogtyve
30	*traðve*	tredve
40	*for'*	fyrre
50	*hal-***trehs**	halvtreds
60	*trehs*	tres
70	*hal-fyaRs*	halvfjedrs
80	*fiRs*	firs
90	*hal-fehms*	halvfems
100	*hun-r'ðe*	hundrede

1000	*tu-sene*	tusinde
one million	*en mili-oon*	en million
1st	*forRsd*	først
2nd	*anen*	anden
3rd	*trehð-ye*	tredje
¼	*en fyeh'-del*	en fjerdedel
⅓	*en trehð-ye-del*	en tredjedel
½	*en hal*	en halv
¾	*treh fyeh'-dele*	tre firedele

Some Useful Words

a little (amount)	*en li-le smoole*	en lille smule
double	*d'b-eld*	dobbelt
a dozen	*ed du-seen*	et dusin
Enough!	*n'gh*	Nok!
few	*fā*	få
less	*mendr'*	mindre
many	*maang-e*	mange
more	*me'*	mere
once	*en-ghaang*	engang
a pair	*ed paa*	et par
percent	*pro-sehnd*	procent
some	*noo-le*	nogle
too much	*f' maay-eð*	for meget
twice	*to ghaange*	to gange

Abbreviations

0800/2000	am/pm
a/s	Ltd., Inc.
BZ – besittere	squatters

DSB – Danske Statsbaner	the Danish National Railways
DUH – Danske Ungdomsherberger	Danish Youth Hostel Association
DVH – Danske Vandrehjem	Danish Youth Hostel Association
dagl. – dagligt	daily (Monday to Saturday)
e.kr./f.kr.	AD/BC
EF – Europæiske Fellesmarked	EEC, the Common Market
FN	UN
frk. – frøken	Miss
fr – fredag	Friday
fru	Mrs
Gd/V	St/Rd/etc
hel. – hellig	holy (as in holiday)
hlp. – holdeplass	bus/tram stop
Hr. – herr	Mr/Sir
jb – jernbane	railway
jrbst – jernbane station	railway station
Kbhvn – København	Copenhagen
KDAK	the Royal Danish Automobile Association
kgl. – kongelig	royal
kl. – klasse	class (on trains and airplanes)
km/t – kilometer pr. time	kilometres per hour
kr – krone	crown (Danish monetary unit)
lø – lørdag	Saturday

m. – med	with
ma – mandag	Monday
moms	VAT, sales tax (included in the price on all goods and services)
ndf. – nedenfor	below (used in notices, timetables, etc)
Ndr. – nordre	to the north (pertaining to place names)
on – onsdag	Wednesday
SAS	Scandinavian Airline System
Sdr. – søndre	to the south (pertaining to place names)
sø – søndag	Sunday
t.h. – til høire	to the right (used in addresses)
ti – tirsdag	Tuesday
tlf – telefon	telephone
to – torsdag	Thursday
t.v. – til venstre	to the left (used in addresses)
x, excl. – eksklusive	excluded, except

FINNISH

Finnish

Introduction

Finnish, or *suomi* as it is called in Finland, is almost unique. It is not closely related to any language other than Estonian and Karelian and a handful of other rare languages. Linguistically, Finnish belongs to the Finnic (or more widely, Finno-Ugric) group of languages. Hungarian is the most widely spoken of the Finno-Ugric languages, but similarities with Finnish are extremely few.

Finnish is spoken by some five million people. It is not related to any Indo-European languages. There are, however, many loan words from Baltic, Slavonic and Germanic languages, and many words that derive from French and, especially, English.

The main difficulties with Finnish are the suffixes added to noun and verb roots, which often alter in this process, and the habit of constructing long words by putting several small words together.

Outside the big towns of Finland, few people speak fluent English, so it is advisable to learn some phrases in Finnish to make your visit more rewarding. Finns appreciate any effort made by a non-native speaker and are eager to help further. Finnish is by no means an easy language to master, but it is easy to read out loud and the phonetics are not difficult – and mistakes made by foreigners are usually disregarded. There is also a notable Swedish-speaking minority in Finland, and all Finns do learn Swedish in school, so you may need your Swedish vocabulary in Finland from time to time.

Pronunciation
Vowels

Finnish has eight vowels. The alphabet also includes Swedish *å* which is pronounced as the 'au' in 'caught'. It's probably worth noting that the **å**, **ä** and **ö** are the last three letters of the alphabet. So, while *Aatami* would be one of the first entries in a telephone book, *Äänehodi* would be one of the last.

a	as the 'u' in 'sun'
e	as the 'e' in 'fell'
i	as 'i' in 'in'
o	as the 'o' in 'pot'
u	as the 'u' in 'pull'
y	as the German *ü*
ä	as the 'a' in 'act'
ö	as the 'e' in 'summer'

Vowel Harmony

Finnish divides vowels into two groups: those formed 'in the front of the mouth' (**e, i, y, ä, ö**) and those formed 'in the back of the mouth' (**a, o, u**). This distinction is very important when forming words with suffixes, because the vowels in the suffixes must be of the same type as the vowels in the root word. For example, *koulussa*, 'in school', is formed by adding *-ssa*, not *-ssä*, to the root.

Double Vowels

Double vowels are tricky to pronounce, so follow the pronunciation guide carefully. You will find that some double vowels are pronounced as one sound within one syllable, others as diphthongs, and some as separate syllables.

For example, **ää** is pronounced as a long **a**, as in American

FINNISH

'fast', but **aa** is pronounced as in British 'can't'. To indicate the difference, **ää**, as one syllable, is written *ÿ* in the pronunciation guide in this chapter.

Consonants

There are only 13 consonants in Finnish, although the alphabet includes English consonants. The letter **x** can be written as **ks**, and **z** can be written, and is pronounced, as **ts**. Finns consider **v** and **w** more or less as the same letter, and in phone books you will find both under 'V'. In literature of a certain type, **w** makes a word look 'older'. *Vanha* is 'old', but *wanha* is 'definitely old'.

h	weak, except at end of a 'closed' syllable, when it is almost as strong as the German *ch* in *machen*
j	as the 'y' in 'yellow'
k	soft, as the 'k' in 'skate'
p	soft, as the 'p' in 'spirit'
r	rolled
s	weak
t	soft, as the 't' in 'steak'
v	as in 'vain'

Double Consonants

Double consonants like **kk** in *viikko*, 'week', or **mm** in *summa*, 'sum', are held longer, and they always split the word into two syllables. Note that **ng** and **nk** both make two syllables, and are pronounced as **-ng-ng-** and **-ng-k-** . For example, vangit, 'prisons', is *vahng-ngit*. Note also that **np** is pronounced as **mp**, as in olenpa, *o-lehm-pah*, 'I am'.

Greetings & Civilities

Finns use *Päivää!*, literally 'Day!', as a general greeting during most of the day.

Top Useful Phrases

Hello.
   hay, tehr-veh (moy)   Hei, terve. (Moi. – inf)
Goodbye.
   na-keh-meen (moy)   Näkemiin. (Moi. – inf)
Excuse me.
   ahn-teehk-si   Anteeksi.
May I? Do you mind?
   sai-sin-ko?   Saisinko?
Sorry.
   o-lehn pah-hoyl-lah-ni (so-ri)   Olen pahoillani. (Sori. – inf)
Thank you.
   kee-toss (keet-ti)   Kiitos. (Kiitti. – inf)
Many thanks.
   pahl-yon kee-tok-si-ah   Paljon kiitoksia.
That's fine. You're welcome.
   o-leh hü-va (ay-pa kehs-ta)   Ole hyvä. (Eipä kestä – inf)

There isn't any frequently used word in Finnish for 'please'. Often *kiitos* is used. Another useful expression is 'could you', *voisitteko*, plus a verb. If you assume equality, or generally deal with informal situations, you are free to use less formal expressions. If you speak to a young clerk at a ticket booth or in a bank, you can say *voitko*, or even *voitsä*, 'are you able to', whereas an elderly lady would like to hear *voisitteko*, 'could you'. When buying a pack of cigarettes or a beer, you just state the merchandise. *Pitkä!* means 'Could you give me a large glass of beer, please!'

FINNISH

Greetings

Good morning.

hü-vÿ hu-o-mehn-tah		Hyvää huomenta.
hu-o-mehn-tah		Huomenta. (inf)

Good afternoon.

hü-vÿ pa-i-vÿ		Hyvää päivää.
pa-i-vÿ		Päivää. (inf)

Good evening/night.

hü-vÿ il-taa/ü-er-ta	Hyvää iltaa/yötä.

How are you?

mi-ta koo-loo?	Mitä kuuluu?

Well, thanks.

kee-toss hü-vÿ	Kiitos hyvää.

Forms of Address

Madam/Mrs	*rohv-vah*	Rouva
Sir/Mr	*hehr-rah*	Herra
Miss	*nay-ti*	Neiti
companion, friend	*üs-ta-va* *kah-veh-ri*	ystävä kaveri (inf)

Small Talk

When you ask for a favour, use the most polite word: *Te* ('you' in the plural). Thus you place yourself below the person you are speaking to. Traditionally Finns had to make a deal, *sinunkaupat*, to call each other *sinä* instead of *Te*. The deal involved an exchange of names and a formal handshake, after which you were friends forever.

Minä means 'I', *sinä* is 'you'. Not everyone uses these words, however. In southern Finland, especially in Helsinki, most people say *mä* and *sä*. In Turku, Tampere and Oulu it is *mää*, for 'I', and *sää* for 'you' (*nää* in Oulu). In southern Savo they say *mie* and *sie*. In Helsinki it would be better to use *mä* instead of *minä*, to express that you don't place yourself above the other. In northern Savo and places in Karelia, people still use *minä* – elsewhere you may sound rather egoistic if you use it. There is an asterisk (*) in cases when you could consider using some other form, as you tour Finland. *Minä* is still the only correct word for 'I'.

Meeting People
What is your name?

mi-ka tay-dan ni-mehn-neh on?   Mikä Teidän nimenne on?

mi-ka sun ni-mi on?   Mikä sun nimi on? (inf)

My name is ...

mi-nun ni-mehn-ni on ...   Minun nimeni on ...

mun ni-mi on ...   Mun nimi on ... (inf)

I'd like to introduce you to ...

hah-lu-ai-sin eh-si-tehl-la si-nut ...   Haluaisin esitellä sinut ...-lle

I'm pleased to meet you.

hows-kah tah-vah-tah   Hauska tavata.

Nationalities
Where are you from?

mis-ta si-na o-leth ko-toy-sin?   Mistä sinä* olet kotoisin?

I am from ...

o-lehn ...   Olen ...

Australia	*owst-rah-li-ahs-tah*	Australiasta
Canada	*kah-nah-dahs-tah*	Kanadasta

England	*ehng-lahn-nis-tah*	Englannista
Finland	*su-o-mehs-tah*	Suomesta
Ireland	*ir-lahn-nis-tah*	Irlannista
New Zealand	*oo-dehs-tah*	Uudesta-
	seeh-lahn-nis-tah	Seelannista
Scotland	*scot-lahn-nis-tah*	Skotlannista
the USA	*üch-düs-vahl-loys-tah/*	Yhdysvalloista/
	ah-meh-ri-kahs-tah	Amerikasta
Wales	*wayl-sis-ta*	Walesistä

Age

How old are you?
ku-in-kah **vahn**-hah si-na
o-leht?　　　　　　　　　Kuinka vanha sinä* olet?

I am ... years old.
o-lehn ... **vu**-o-ti-ahs　　　　Olen ...-vuotias.

Occupations

What work do you do?
mi-ta si-na **teeht** tüh-erk-
seh-si?　　　　　　　　　Mitä sinä* teet työksesi?

I am (a/an) ...
o-lehn ...　　　　　　　　Olen ...

artist	*tai-tay-li-yah*	taiteilija
businessperson	*lee-keh-mi-ehs*	liikemies
engineer	*in-si-ner-ri*	insinööri
farmer	*maan vil-yeh-li-ja*	maanviljelijä
journalist	*yohr-nah-lis-ti/*	journalisti/lehtim-
	lech-ti mi-ehs	ies
lawyer	*yu-ris-ti/lah-ki mi-ehs*	juristi/lakimies
manual worker	*tü-er-la-i-nehn*	työläinen

mechanic	*meh-kaa-nik-ko*	mekaanikko
doctor	*lÿ-ka-ri*	lääkäri
nurse	*sai-raan hoy-tah-yah*	sairaanhoitaja
office worker	*toy-mis-to tü-ern teh-ki-ya*	toimistotyöntekijä
scientist	*tut-ki-yah/ti-eh-deh mi-ehs*	tutkija/tiedemies
student	*o-pis-keh-li-yah*	opiskelija
teacher	*o-peht-tah-yah*	opettaja
waiter	*tahr-yoy-li-yah*	tarjoilija
writer	*kihr-yai-li-yah*	kirjailija

FINNISH

Religion

What is your religion?

mi-ka on si-nun us-kon-to-si?   Mikä on sinun uskontosi?

I am not religious.

ehn o-leh us-kon-nol-li-nehn/us-ko-vai-nehn   En ole uskonnollinen/uskovainen.

I am (a/an) …

o-lehn …   Olen …

Buddhist	*bud-hah-lai-nehn*	buddhalainen
Catholic	*kah-to-li-nehn*	katolinen
Christian	*kris-tit-tü*	kristitty
Hindu	*hin-du-lai-nehn*	hindulainen
Jewish	*yoo-tah-lai-nehn*	juutalainen
Lutheran	*lu-teh-ri-lai-nehn*	luterilainen
Muslim	*mus-li-mi*	muslimi

Family

Are you married?

o-leht-ko nai-mi-sis-sah?   Oletko naimisissa?

FINNISH

I am single. I am married.
   o-lehn nai-mah-ton   Olen naimaton.
   o-lehn nai-mi-sis-sah   Olen naimisissa.

How many children do you have?
   ku-in-kah mon-tah   Kuinka monta lasta sinulla
   lahs-tah sul-lah on?   on?

I don't have any children.
   mul-lah ay o-leh lahp-si-ah   Minulla ei ole lapsia.

I have a daughter/a son.
   mul-lah on tü-tar   Minulla on tytär (tyttö – inf)/
   (tüt-ter)/poy-kah   poika.

How many brothers/sisters do you have?
   ku-in-kah mon-tah vehl-   Kuinka monta veljeä/siskoa
   yeh-a/sis-ko-ah si-nul-lah   sinulla on?
   on?

Is your husband/wife here?
   on-ko si-nun mi-eh-heh-si/   Onko sinun miehesi/
   vai-mo-si tÿl-la?   vaimosi täällä?

Do you have a boyfriend/ girlfriend?
   on-ko sul-lah poy-kah   Onko sinulla poikaystävää/
   üs-ta-vÿ/üt-ter üs-ta-vÿ?   tyttöystävää?

brother	*veh-li*	veli
children	*lahp-set*	lapset
daughter	*tü-tar*	tytär
family	*pehr-heh*	perhe
father	*i-sa*	isä
grandfather	*i-so i-sa/vaa-ri/uk-ki*	isoisä/vaari/ukki

grandmother	*i-so a-i-ti*/**mum-mi**	isoäiti/mummi
husband	*ah-vi-o* **mi-es**	aviomies
mother	*a-i-ti*	äiti
sister	*sis-ko*	sisko
son	*poy-kah*	poika
wife	*vai-mo*	vaimo

Feelings

I like ...
　pi-dan ...-sta/stah　　　　Pidän ...-sta/stä.

I don't like ...
　ehn pi-da ...-sta/stah　　En pidä ...-sta/stä.

I am cold/hot.
　mi-nul-lah on kül-ma/　　Minulla on kylmä/kuuma.
　koo-mah

I am hungry/thirsty.
　mi-nun on nal-ka/yah-no　Minun on nälkä/jano.

I am in a hurry.
　mi-nul-lah on kee-reh　　Minulla on kiire.

I am right.
　o-lehn oy-keh-ahs-sah　　Olen oikeassa.

I am sleepy.
　o-lehn u-ni-nehn　　　　Olen uninen.

I am angry.
　o-lehn vi-hai-nehn　　　Olen vihainen.

I am happy/sad.
　o-lehn i-loy-nehn/su-rul-li-　Olen iloinen/surullinen.
　nehn

I am tired.
　o-lehn va-sü-nüt　　　　Olen väsynyt.

FINNISH

I am well.
  voyn hü-vin   Voin hyvin.
I am worried.
  o-lehn hu-o-lis-sah-ni   Olen huolissani.
I am sorry. (condolence)
  o-tahn o-saa, o-lehn   Otan osaa, olen pahoillani.
  pah-hoyl-lah-ni
I am grateful.
  o-lehn kee-tol-li-nehn   Olen kiitollinen.

Language Difficulties
Do you speak English?
  pu-hut-ko ehng-lahn-ti-ah?   Puhutko englantia?
Does anyone speak English?
  pu-hoo-ko ku-kaan   Puhuuko kukaan englantia?
  ehng-lahn-ti-ah?
I speak a little …
  pu-hun va-han …   Puhun vähän …
I don't speak …
  ehn pu-hu …   En puhu …
I understand.
  üm-mar-ran   Ymmärrän.
I don't understand.
  ehn üm-mar-ra   En ymmärrä.
Could you speak more slowly
please?
  voy-sit-ko pu-hu-ah   Voisitko puhua hitaammin?
  hi-taam-min?
Could you repeat that?
  voyt-ko toys-taa   Voitko toistaa.

How do you say …?
mi-tehn sah-no-taan …?   Miten sanotaan …?

What does … mean?
mi-ta … tahr-koyt-taa?   Mitä … tarkoittaa?

I speak …
pu-hun …   Puhun …

English	*ehng-lahn-ti-ah*	englantia
Finnish	*su-o-meh-ah*	suomea
French	*rahns-kaa*	ranskaa
German	*sahk-saa*	saksaa

Some Useful Phrases

Just a minute.
heth-ki-nehn   Hetkinen.

It's (not) important.
seh on (ay o-leh) tar-keh-ÿ   Se on (ei ole) tärkeää.

It's (not) possible.
seh on (ay o-leh) mahch-dol-lis-tah   Se on (ei ole) mahdollista.

Wait!
o-do-tah!   Odota!

Good luck!
on-neh-ah (lükh-kü-a tüh-ker)   Onnea! (Lykkyä tykö!)

Signs

BAGGAGE COUNTER	MATKATAVARAT
CHECK-IN COUNTER	LÄHTÖSELVITYS
CUSTOMS	TULLI

FINNISH

EMERGENCY EXIT	VARAULOSKÄYNTI
ENTRANCE	SISÄÄN
EXIT	ULOS
FREE ADMISSION	VAPAA PÄÄSY
HOT/COLD	KUUMA/KYLMÄ
INFORMATION	OPASTUS, NEUVONTA
NO ENTRY	PÄÄSY KIELLETTY
NO SMOKING	TUPAKOINTI KIELLETTY
OPEN/CLOSED	AUKI/SULJETTU
PROHIBITED	KIELLETTY
RESERVED	VARATTU
TELEPHONE	PUHELIN
TOILETS	WC

Emergencies

| POLICE | POLIISI |
| POLICE STATION | POLIISIASEMA |

Help!
ah-pu-ah!   Apua!

It's an emergency!
ta-ma on ha-ta-tah-pows!   Tämä on hätätapaus!

There's been an accident!
nüt on tah-pah-tu-nut   Nyt on tapahtunut
on-neht-to-moos!   onnettomuus!

Call a doctor!
kut-su-kaa lü-ka-ri!   Kutsukaa lääkäri!

Call an ambulance!
soyt-tah-kaa ahm-bu-   Soittakaa ambulanssi!
lahns-si!

I've been raped.
mi-nut on rais-kaht-tu — Minut on raiskattu.

I've been robbed.
mi-nut on rü-ers-teht-tü — Minut on ryöstetty.

Call the police!
soyt-tah-kaa po-lee-si! — Soittakaa poliisi!

Where is the police station?
mis-sa on po-lee-si ah-seh-mah? — Missä on poliisiasema?

Go away!
meh-neh poys (ha-i-vü)! — Mene pois! (Häivy! – inf)

I'll call the police!
mi-na kut-sun po-lee-sin! — Minä* kutsun poliisin!

Thief!
vah-rahs! — Varas!

I am/My friend is ill.
mi-na o-lehn/mun üs-ta-va on sai-rahs — Minä* olen/Minun ystäväni on sairas.

I am lost.
mi-na o-lehn ehk-sük-sis-sa — Minä* olen eksyksissä.

Where are the toilets?
mis-sa on vehs-sah? — Missä on vessa?

Could you help me please?
voyt-teh-ko (voyt-ko) owt-taa — Voitteko (voitko) auttaa.

Could I please use the telephone?
saan-ko ka-üt-tÿ pu-heh-lin-tah? — Saanko käyttää puhelinta?

FINNISH

I'm sorry. I apologise.
   oh-lehn pah-hoyl-lah-ni.   Olen pahoillani. Pyydän
   püü-dan ahn-teehk-si   anteeksi.
I didn't realise I was doing
anything wrong.
   ehn tah-yun-nut teh-keh-   En tajunnut tekeväni mitään
   va-ni mi-tÿn vÿ-rin   väärin.
I didn't do it.
   ehn teh-nüt si-ta   En tehnyt sitä.
I wish to contact my
embassy/consulate.
   hah-lu-ahn ot-taa üch-teh-üt-   Haluan ottaa yhteyttä suurlä-
   ta soor-la-heh-tüs-ter-ni/   hetystööni/konsulaattiin.
   kon-su-laat-teen
I speak English.
   pu-hun ehng-lahn-ti-ah   Puhun englantia.
I have medical insurance.
   mul-lah on vah-koo-tus   Minulia on vakuutus.
My possessions are insured.
   mun tah-vah-raht on vah-   Minun tavarat on vakuutettu.
   koo-teht-tu

My ... was stolen.
   mul-tah on vah-rahs-teht-tu   Minulta on varastettu ...
I've lost ...
   mi-na o-lehn hu-kahn-nut ...   Minä* olen hukannut ...

my bags	*lowk-ku-ni*	laukkuni
my handbag	*ka-si lowk-ku-ni*	käsilaukkuni
my money	*rah-hah-ni*	rahani
my travellers' cheques	*maht-kah shehk-ki-ni*	matkashekkini
my passport	*pahs-si-ni*	passini

Paperwork

name	*ni-mi*	nimi
address	*o-soy-teh*	osoite
date of birth	*sün-tü-ma ai-kah/ hen-ki-ler tun-nus*	syntymäaika/ henkilötunnus
place of birth	*sün-tü-ma paik-kah*	syntymäpaikka
age	*i-ka*	ikä
sex	*su-ku pu-o-li*	sukupuoli
nationality	*kahn-sah-lai-soos*	kansalaisuus
religion	*us-kon-to*	uskonto
reason for travel	*maht-kahn tahr-koy-tus*	matkan tarkoitus
profession	*ahm-maht-ti*	ammatti
marital status	*si-vee-li sÿ-tü*	siviilisääty
passport	*pahs-si*	passi
passport number	*pahs-sin nu-meh-ro*	passin numero
visa	*vee-su-mi*	viisumi
identification	*hehn-ki-ler pah-peh-rit*	henkilöpaperit
birth certificate	*sün-tü-ma to-dis-tus*	syntymätodistus
driver's licence	*ah-yo-kort-ti*	ajokortti
car registration	*ow-ton mehrk-ki*	auton merkki
customs	*tul-li*	tulli
border	*rah-yah*	raja

FINNISH

FINNISH

Getting Around

As you look for places, visit them and leave them, you will use different words in each case, and a little grammar is needed to gain understanding on how words are constructed. Finnish grammar is extremely complicated. With all possible suffixes and meanings, you can construct over 450 different words from any noun root.

- *-ssa* or *-ssä*, 'in something': *koulu-ssa*, 'in school'
- *-sta* or *-stä*, 'from something': *koulu-sta*, 'from school'
- -double vowel plus *n*, 'to something': *koulu-un*, 'to school'
- *-lla* or *-llä*, 'on', 'at' or 'in something' or 'somebody': *koulu-lla*, 'at school'
- *-lta* or *-ltä*, 'from something' or 'somebody': *koulu-lta*, 'from school'
- *-lle*, 'to something' or 'somebody': *koulu-lle*, 'to school'

Consider following examples of expressing 'in ...', and 'to ... a town':

- *Helsinki: Helsingi-ssä, Helsinki-in*
- *Turku: Turu-ssa, Turku-un*
- *Varkaus: Varkaude-ssa, Varkaute-en*
- *Tampere: Tampere-lla, Tampere-lle*
- *Rovaniemi: Rovanieme-llä, Rovanieme-lle* (and others ending *-niemi*)
- *Seinäjoki: Seinäjoe-lla, Seinäjoe-lle* (and others ending *-joki*)
- *Kemijärvi: Kemijärve-llä, Kemijärve-lle* (and others ending *-järvi*)

To express being inside a vehicle, hotel etc, the *-ssa* suffix is used for 'in', and a double vowel plus **n** for 'to': *juna-ssa/juna-an, hotelli-ssa/hotelli-in*. When you use a vehicle, you use the *-lla* suffix, as *matkustaa juna-lla*, 'to travel by train'.

FINNISH

ARRIVALS	SAAPUVAT
BUS STOP	PYSÄKKI
DEPARTURES	LÄHTEVÄT
STATION	ASEMA
SUBWAY	ALIKULKUKÄYTÄVÄ
TICKET OFFICE	LIPPUTOIMISTO
TIMETABLE	AIKATAULU
TRAIN STATION	RAUTATIEASEMA

What time does …leave/ arrive?
  mi-hin ai-kaan …   Mihin aikaan …
  lach-teeh/saa-poo?   lähtee/saapuu?

the (air)plane	*lehn-to ko-neh*	lentokone
the boat	*lai-vah*	laiva
the bus (city)	*bus-si*	bussi
the bus (intercity)	*bus-si/lin-yah ow-to*	bussi/linjauto
the train	*yu-nah*	juna
the tram	*rai-ti-o vow-nu*	raitiovaunu
	(rait-sik-kah)	(raitsikka)

Directions
Where is …?
  mis-sa on …?   Missä on …?
How do I get to …?
  mi-ten mi-na pÿ-sen …?   Miten minä* pääsen …?

Is it far from/near here?
on-ko seh kow-kah-nah/ la-hehl-la?
Onko se kaukana/lähellä?

Can I walk there?
voy-ko sin-neh ka-vehl-la?
Voiko sinne kävellä?

Can you show me (on the map)?
voyt-ko na-üt-tÿ mul-leh (kahr-tahs-tah)?
Voitko näyttää minulle (kartasta)?

Are there other means of getting there?
pÿ-seeh-ker sin-neh yol-lah-kin mool-lah tah-vahl-lah?
Pääseekö sinne jollakin muulla tavalla?

I want to go to ...
hah-lu-ahn men-na ...
Haluan mennä ...

Go straight ahead.
kul-yeh su-o-raan
Kulje suoraan.

It's two blocks down.
seh on kahch-den kort-teh-lin pÿs-sa
Se on kahden korttelin päässä.

Turn left ...
kÿn-nü vah-sehm-paan ...
Käänny vasempaan ...

Turn right ...
kÿn-nü oy-keh-aan ...
Käänny oikeaan ...

at the next corner
seh-u-raa-vahs-tah kah-dun kul-mahs-tah
seuraavasta kadunkulmasta

at the traffic lights
lee-kehn-neh vah-loys-sah
liikennevaloissa

behind	...-n tah-kah-nah	...-n takana
far	kow-kah-nah	kaukana
near	la-hehl-la	lähellä
in front of	eh-dehs-sa	en edessä
opposite	vahs-tah pÿ-ta ... ta/tah	vastapäätä ... -ta/-tä

Buying Tickets

Excuse me, where is the ticket office?

ahn-teehk-si, mis-sa on lip-pu toy-mis-to?

Anteeksi, missä on lipputoimisto?

Where can I buy a ticket?

mis-ta voy os-taa li-pun?

Mistä voi ostaa lipun?

I want to go to ...

ha-lu-ahn men-na ...

Haluan mennä ...-lle/ ...vowel + n

Do I need to book?

ta-ü-tüü-ker vah-rah-tah?

Täytyykö varata?

You need to book.

si-nun ta-ü-tüü vah-rah-tah

Sinun täytyy varata.

I would like to book a seat to ...

ha-lu-ai-sin vah-rah-tah is-tu-mah pai-kahn ...

Haluaisin varata istumapaikan ...lle/...vowel + n

I would like ...

saan-ko ...

Saanko ...

a one-way ticket	meh-no li-pun	menolipun
a return ticket	meh-no pa-loo li-pun	menopaluulipun
two tickets	kahk-si lip-pu-ah	kaksi lippua
tickets for all of us	li-put mayl-leh	liput meille
	kai-kil-leh	kaikille

FINNISH

a student's fare	*o-pis-keh-li-ya li-pun*	opiskelijalipun
a child's/pen-sioner's fare	*lahs-tehn li-pun/eh-la-keh-la-is-tehn li-pun*	lastenlipun/eläke-läisten lipun
1st class	*en-sim-ma-i-nehn lu-ok-kah*	ensimmäinen luokka
2nd class	*toy-nehn lu-ok-kah*	toinen luokka

It is full.
   seh on ta-ün-na   Se on täynnä.
Is it completely full?
   on-ko se ai-vahn ta-ün-na?   Onko se aivan täynnä?
Can I get a stand-by ticket?
   voyn-ko saa-dah li-pun il-mahn paik-kah-vah-rows-tah?   Voinko saada lipun ilman paikkavarausta?

Air

CHECKING IN	LÄHTÖSELVITYS

Is there a flight to …?
   on-ko … len-to-ah?   Onko …-lle/…(vowel + n) lentoa?

When is the next flight to …?
   mil-loyn on seh-u-raa-vah len-to …?   Milloin on seuraava lento …vowel + n/ …-lle?
How long does the flight take?
   kow-ahn-ko len-to kehs-tÿ?   Kauanko lento kestää?
What is the flight number?
   mi-ka on len-non nu-meh-ro?   Mikä on lennon numero?

You must check at …
    tay-dan (sun) taü-tüü cheh-kah-tah … -la
    Teidän (sun) täytyy tsekata …-lla

airport tax	*lehn-to kehnt-ta veh-ro*	lentokenttävero
boarding pass	*tahr-kahs-tus kort-ti*	tarkastuskortti
customs	*tul-li/tul-li tahr-kahs-tus*	tulli/tullitarkastus

FINNISH

Bus

BUS/TRAM STOP	PYSÄKKI

Where is the bus/tram stop?
    mis-sa on bus-si/rait-sik-kah pü-sak-ki?
    Missä on bussi/raitsikka-pysäkki?

Does this bus go to …?
    meh-neeh-ker ta-ma bus-si …?
    Meneekö tämä bussi … vowel + n / …lle?

How often do buses pass by?
    ku-in-kah u-sayn tas-ta kul-keeh bus-si?
    Kuinka usein tästä kulkee bussi?

Could you let me know when we get to …?
    voyt-ko sah-no-ah, mil-loyn on jü-ta-va poys …-n lu-o-nah?
    Voitko sanoa, milloin on jäätävä pois …-n luona?

I want to get off!
    mi-na hah-lu-ahn jü-da poys!
    Minä* haluan jäädä pois!

What time is the ... bus?
mi-hin ai-kaan on ...   Mihin aikaan on ... bussi?
bus-si?

next   *seh-u-raa-vah*   seuraava
first   *ehn-sim-ma-i-nehn*   ensimmäinen
last   *vee-may-nehn*   viimeinen

Train

DINING CAR	RAVINTOLA
EXPRESS	PIKAJUNA
PLATFORM NO	RAIDE
SLEEPING CAR	MAKUUVAUNU
LONG-DISTANCE	KAUKOLIIKENNE
TRAFFIC	
LOCAL TRAIN TICKETS	LÄHILIIKENNELIPPUJA
TRAVEL SERVICE	VR MATKAPALVELU
LOST AND FOUND	LÖYTÖTAVARAT

Is this the right platform
for ...?
on-ko ta-ma oy-keh-ah   Onko tämä oikea raide ...
rai-deh ...?   vowel + n/...lle?
Passengers must ...
maht-kus-tah-yi-ehn on ...   Matkustajien on ...
change trains
vaich-deht-tah-vah yu-naa   vaihdettava junaa
The train leaves from
platform ...
yu-nah lach-teeh   Juna lähtee raiteelta ...
rai-teehl-tah ...

dining car	*rah-vin-to-lah vow-nu*	ravintolavaunu
express	*pi-kah yu-nah*	pikajuna
local	*pai-kahl-lis yu-nah*	paikallisjuna
sleeping car	*mah-koo vow-nu*	makuuvaunu

Metro

CHANGE (for coins)	KOLIKOT
PLATFORM AREA (for ticket check)	LAITURIALUE
WAY OUT	ULOS

Which direction takes me to …?
> *kum-paan soon-taan pÿ-seeh …?*

Kumpaan suuntaan pääsee …lle / vowel + n?

What is the next station?
> *mi-ka on seh-u-raa-vah ah-seh-mah?*

Mikä on seuraava asema?

Taxi

People usually just say their destination without any civilities.

Can you take me to …?
> *voyt-teh-ko vi-eh-da mi-nut …?*

Voitteko viedä minut …?

How much does it cost to go to …?
> *pahl-yon-ko mahk-saa maht-kah …?*

Paljonko maksaa matka …vowel + n/…lle?

Instructions

Here is fine, thank you!
> *tas-sa on hü-va, kee-toss!*

Tässä on hyvä, kiitos!

The next corner, please.
seh-u-raa-vaan ris-teh-ük-seehn
Seuraavaan risteykseen.

Continue!
yaht-kah vi-eh-la!
Jatka vielä!

The next street to the left/right.
seh-u-raa-vaa kah-tu-ah vah-sehm-mahl-leh/oy-keh-ahl-leh
Seuraavaa katua vasemmalle/oikealle.

Stop here!
pü-sa-ü-ta tas-sa!
Pysäytä tässä!

Please slow down.
hi-das-tah va-han
Hidasta vähän.

Please wait here.
voyt-ko o-dot-taa tas-sa va-han
Voitko odottaa tässä vähän.

Some Useful Phrases

The train is delayed/cancelled.
yu-nah on mü-er-has-sa/peh-roo-teht-tu
Juna on myöhässä/peruutettu.

How long will it be delayed?
kow-ahn-ko seh on mu-er-has-sa?
Kauanko se on myöhässä?

There is a delay of ... hours.
seh on ... tun-ti-ah mu-er-has-sa
Se on ... tuntia myöhässä.

Can I reserve a place?
voyn-ko vah-rah-tah pai-kahn?
Voinko varata paikan?

FINNISH

How long does the trip take?
kow-ahn-ko maht-kah kehs-tÿ?
Kauanko matka kestää?

Is it a direct route?
on-ko se su-o-rah rayt-ti?
Onko se suora reitti?

Is that seat taken?
on-ko toy paik-kah vah-raht-tu?
Onko tuo paikka varattu?

I want to get off at ...
mi-na jÿn poys ...-ssa/lla
Minä* jään pois ...-ssa/-lla.

Excuse me.
ahn-teehk-si
Anteeksi.

Where can I hire a bicycle?
mis-ta mi-na voyn vu-ok-rah-tah pol-ku pü-er-ran?
Mistä minä* voin vuokrata polkupyörän?

Is there room for the bicycle?
mach-too-ko pol-ku pü-er-ra?
Mahtuuko polkupyörä?

Car

BAD ROAD	KELIRIKKO
DETOUR	KIERTOTIE
FREEWAY	MOOTTORITIE
GARAGE	HUOLTOASEMA
MECHANIC	KORJAAMO
NO ENTRY	KIELLETTY AJOSUUNTA
NO PARKING	PYSÄKÖINTI KIELLETTY
NORMAL LEADED	97 OKTAANIA
ONE WAY	YKSISUUNTAINEN
	AJOTIE
REPAIRS	TIETYÖ
ICE ON ROAD	JÄÄTIE

FINNISH

SELF SERVICE	ITSEPALVELU
STOP	STOP
SUPER LEADED	99 OKTAANIA
UNLEADED	LYIJYTÖN 95E

Where can I rent a car?
   mis-ta mi-na voy-sin
   vu-ok-rah-tah ow-ton?

Mistä minä* voisin
vuokrata auton?

daily/weekly
   pehr pa-i-va/pehr veek-ko

per päivä/per viikko

Does that include insurance/
mileage?
   koo-loo-ko see-hen vah-
   koo-tus/rah-yoyt-tah-mah-
   ton ki-lo-meht-ri mÿ-ra?

Kuuluuko siihen
vakuutus/rajoittamaton
kilometrimäärä?

Where's the next petrol
station?
   mis-sa on la-hin ben-sah
   ah-seh-mah?

Missä on lähin bensäsema?

Please fill the tank.
   tahnk-ki ta-ü-teehn,
   kee-toss

Tankki täyteen, kiitos.

I want ... litres of petrol (gas).
   mi-na hah-lu-ai-sin ...
   lit-raa ben-saa

Minä* haluaisin ... litraa
bensaa.

Please check the oil and water.
   voyt-ko tahr-kis-taa erl-yün
   ya yÿch-dü-tüs nehs-teehn

Voitko tarkistaa öljyn ja
jäähdytysnesteen.

How long can I park here?
   kow-ahn-ko tas-sa saa
   park-keeh-rah-tah?

Kauanko tässä saa
parkkeerata?

Does this road lead to …?
meh-neeh-ker ta-ma
ti-eh …?

Meneekö tämä tie …
vowel + n / …lle?

air (for tyres)	**il-mah**	ilma
battery	**ahk-ku**	akku
brakes	**yahr-rut**	jarrut
clutch	**küt-kin**	kytkin
driver's licence	**ah-yo kort-tih**	ajokortti
engine	**mort-to-ri, ko-neh**	moottori, kone
lights	**vah-lot**	valot
oil	**erl-yü**	öljy
puncture	**rehng-ngahs rik-ko**	rengasrikko
radiator	**yüch-dü-tin**	jäähdytin
road map	**ti-eh-kahrt-tah**	tiekartta
tyres	**rehn-kaat**	renkaat
windscreen	**too-li lah-si**	tuulilasi

Car Problems

I need a mechanic.
mi-na tar-vin kor-yaa-yaa
Minä* tarvitsen korjaajaa.

What make is it?
mi-ta mehrk-ki-a se on?
Mitä merkkiä se on?

The battery is flat.
ahk-ku on tüch-ya
Akku on tyhjä.

The radiator is leaking.
yüch-dü-tin vu-o-taa
Jäähdytin vuotaa.

I have a flat tyre.
rehng ngahs on tüch-ja
Rengas on tyhjä.

It's overheating.
seh koo-meh-neh lee-kaa
Se kuumenee liikaa.

It's not working.
seh ay toy-mi
Se ei toimi.

Accommodation

CAMPING GROUND	LEIRINTÄALUE
GUESTHOUSE	MATKAILIJAKOTI
HOTEL	HOTELLI
MOTEL	MOTELLI
YOUTH HOSTEL	RETKEILYMAJA

I am looking for ...
   mi-na eht-sin   Minä* etsin ...
Where is ...?
   mis-sa o-li-si ...?   Missä olisi ...?
a cheap hotel   *hahl-pah ho-tehl-li*   halpa hotelli
a good hotel   *hü-va ho-tehl-li*   hyvä hotelli
a nearby hotelli   *la-hin ho-tehl-li*   lähin hotelli

What is the address?
   mi-ka on o-soy-teh?   Mikä on osoite?
Could you write the address,
please?
   voy-sit-teh-ko kir-joyt-taa   Voisitteko kirjoittaa osoit-
   o-soyt-teen   teen.

At the Hotel
Do you have any rooms
available?
   on-ko tayl-la vah-paa-tah   Onko teillä vapaata
   hu-o-neht-tah?   huonetta?

I would like …
ha-lu-ai-sin …   Haluaisin …

a single room	*üch-dehn hehng-*	yhden hengen
	ngehn hu-o-neehn	huoneen
a double room	*kahch-dehn hehng-*	kahden hengen
	ngehn hu-o-neehn	huoneen
a room with a	*hu-o-neehn kül-pü*	huoneen
bathroom	*hu-o-neehl-lah*	kylpyhuoneella
to share a dorm	*mah-koo sah-lin*	makuusalin
	san-kü pai-kahn	sänkypaikan
a bed	*sang-ngün*	sängyn

I want a room with a …
mi-na hah-lu-ahn hu-o-   Minä* haluan huoneen …
neehn …

bathroom	*kül-pü hu-o-neehl-lah*	kylpyhuoneella
shower	*su-ih-kul-lah*	suihkulla
television	*yos-sah on teh-leh-*	jossa on televisio
	vi-si-o	
window	*yos-sah on ik-ku-nah*	jossa on ikkuna

I'm going to stay for …
mi-na ai-on vee-pü-a …   Minä* aion viipyä …

one day	*üch-dehn pai-van*	yhden päivän
two days	*kahk-si pai-vÿ*	kaksi päivää
one week	*vee-kon*	viikon

Do you have identification?
on-ko tayl-la (sul-lah)   Onko Teillä (sulla – inf)
hehn-ki-ler pah-peh-ray-tah?   henkilöpapereita?

Your membership card, please.
saan-ko ya-sehn kort-tin — Saanko jäsenkortin.

Sorry, we're full.
vah-li-teht-tah-vahs-ti mayl-la on ta-üt-ta — Valitettavasti meillä on täyttä.

How long will you be staying?
ku-in-kah kow-ahn si-na ai-ot vee-pü-a? — Kuinka kauan sinä* aiot viipyä?

How many nights?
ku-in-kah mon-tah u-er-ta? — Kuinka monta yötä?

It's ... per day/per person.
se on ... pa-i-val-ta/hehng-ngehl-ta — Se on ... päivältä/hengeltä.

How much is it per night/per person?
pahl-yon-ko seh on ü-erl-ta/hehng-ngehl-ta? — Paljonko se on yöltä/hengeltä?

Can I see it?
voyn-ko mi-na nach-da sehn? — Voinko minä* nähdä sen?

Are there any others?
on-ko mi-tÿn mu-i-tah? — Onko mitään muita?

Are there any cheaper rooms?
on-ko hahl-vehm-paa hu-o-neht-tah? — Onko halvempaa huonetta?

Can I see the bathroom?
voyn-ko mi-na nach-da kül-pü hu-o-neehn? — Voinko minä* nähdä kylpyhuoneen?

Is there a reduction for
students/children?
*saa-ko o-pis-keh-li-yah/
lahp-si ah-lehn-nus-tah?*

Saako opiskelija/lapsi
alennusta?

Does it include breakfast?
*koo-loo-ko aa-mi-ai-nehn
hin-taan?*

Kuuluko aamiainen hintaan?

It's fine, I'll take it.
*se on hü-va, mi-na o-tahn
sen*

Se on hyvä, minä* otan sen.

I'm not sure how long I'm
staying.
*mi-na ehn ti-eh-da ku-in-
kah kow-ahn mi-na o-lehn
tÿl-la*

Minä* en tiedä kuinka
kauan minä* olen täällä.

Is there a lift?
on-ko tÿl-la his-si-a?

Onko täällä hissiä?

Where is the bathroom?
*mis-sa on kül-pü hu-o-neh
(vehs-sah)?*

Missä on kylpyhuone
(vessa)?

Is there hot water all day?
*on-ko koo-maa veht-ta
ko-ko pai-van?*

Onko kuumaa vettä koko
päivän?

Do you have a safe where I
can leave my valuables?
*on-ko taal-la yos-sain
pehs-ta vaat-tat-tah*

Onko teillä säilytyslokeroa
arvotavaralle?

Is there somewhere to wash
clothes?
*voy-ko tÿl-la yos-sain
pehs-ta vaat-tay-tah?*

Voiko täällä jossain pestä
vaatteita?

Can I use the kitchen?
*voyn-ko ka-üt-tÿ
kayt-ti-er-ta?*
Voinko käyttää keittiötä?

Can I use the telephone?
voyn-ko ka-üt-tÿ pu-heh-lin-tah?
Voinko käyttää puhelinta?

Is your sauna warm?
*on-ko tay-dan sow-nah
lam-pi-ma-na?*
Onko teidän sauna
lämpimänä?

Do you have a smoke sauna?
*on-ko tayl-la sah-vu
sow-naa?*
Onko teillä savusaunaa?

Requests & Complaints

Please wake me up at ...
*voyt-teh-ko heh-rat-tÿ
mi-nut kehl-lo ...*
Voitteko herättää minut
kello ...

The room needs to be cleaned.
*hu-o-neh ta-ü-tü-i-si
see-vo-tah*
Huone täytyisi siivota.

Please change the sheets.
*voyt-teh-kö vaich-taa
lah-kah-naht*
Voitteko vaihtaa lakanat.

I can't open/close ...
ehn saa ... ow-ki/keen-ni   En saa ... auki/kiinni.
window   *ik-ku-naa*   ikkunaa
door   *o-veh-ah*   ovea
heating   *paht-teh-ri-ah* patteria

FINNISH

I left my key in the room.
  mun a-vain ya-i hu-o-neeh-seehn — Minun avain jäi huoneeseen.
The toilet won't flush.
  vehs-sah ay veh-da — Vessa ei vedä.
I don't like this room.
  mi-na ehn oy-kayn pi-da tas-ta hu-o-neehs-tah — Minä* en oikein pidä tästä huoneesta.
It's too small.
  se ohn lee-ahn pi-eh-ni — Se on liian pieni.
It's noisy.
  si-ehl-la on meh-lu-ah — Siellä on melua.
It's too dark.
  se ohn lee-ahn pi-meh-a — Se on liian pimeä.
It's expensive.
  se ohn kahl-lis — Se on kallis.

Some Useful Words & Phrases

I am/We are leaving …
  mi-na lah-dehn/meh lach-deh-tyn … — Minä* lähden/Me läh-detään …
now/tomorrow
  nüt/hu-o-mehn-nah — nyt/huomenna
I would like to pay the bill.
  mi-na mahk-sai-sin lahs-kun — Minä* maksaisin laskun.

name	*ni-mi*	nimi
given names	*eh-tu ni-meht*	etunimet
surname	*su-ku ni-mi*	sukunimi
room number	*hu-o-neehn nu-meh-ro*	huoneen numero

address	*o-soy-teh*	osoite
air-conditioned	*il-mahs-toy-tu*	ilmastoitu
balcony	*pahr-veh-keh*	parveke
bathroom	*kül-pü hu-o-neh*	kylpyhuone
bed	*san-kü*	sänky
bill	*lahs-ku*	lasku
blanket	*payt-to*	peitto
candle	*künt-ti-la*	kynttilä
chair	*tu-o-li*	tuoli
clean	*puh-dahs*	puhdas
cupboard	*kaap-pi*	kaappi
dark	*pi-meh-a*	pimeä
dirty	*li-kai-nehn*	likainen
double bed	*kahk-soys vu-o-deh*	kaksoisvuode
electrity	*sach-ker*	sähkö
excluded	*ay koo-lu hin-taan*	ei kuulu hintaan
included	*koo-loo hin-taan*	kuuluu hintaan
key	*ah-vain*	avain
lift (elevator)	*his-si*	hissi
light bulb	*heh-ku lahmp-pu/*	hehkulamppu/
	lahmp-pu	lamppu
lock (n)	*luk-ko*	lukko
mattress	*paht-yah*	patja
mirror	*pay-li*	peili
padlock	*mu-nah luk-ko*	munalukko
pillow	*tüü-nü*	tyyny
quiet	*hil-jai-nehn*	hiljainen
room (in hotel)	*hu-o-neh/ho-tehl-li*	huone/
	hu-o-neh	hotellihuone
sauna	*sow-nah*	sauna
sheet	*lah-kah-nah*	lakana

shower	*su-ih-ku*	suihku
soap	*saip-pu-ah*	saippua
suitcase	*maht-kah lowk-ku*	matkalaukku
swimming pool	*u-i-mah ahl-lahs*	uima-allas
table	*per-ü-ta*	pöytä
toilet	*veeh-seeh/vehs-sah*	WC/vessa
toilet paper	*vehs-sah pah-peh-ri*	vessapaperi
towel	*püü-heh*	pyyhe
(some) water	*veht-ta*	vettä
cold water	*kül-mah vesi...*	kylmä vesi
hot water	*koo-mah vettÿ*	kuumaa vettää
window	*ik-ku-nah*	ikkuna

Around Town

I'm looking for .../
Where is ...?

| *mi-na eht-sin/mis-sa on ...?* | Minä* etsin .../Missä on ...? |

the art gallery	*tai-deh gahl-leh-ri-aa/tai-deh gahl-leh-ri-ah*	taidegalleriaa/tai-degalleria
a bank	*pahnk-ki-ah/pahnk-ki*	pankkia/pankki
the church	*kirk-ko-ah/kirk-ko*	kirkkoa/kirkko
the city centre	*kehs-kus-taa/kehs-kus-tah*	keskustaa/keskusta
the ...embassy	*soor la-heh-tüs-ter-a/soor la-heh-tüs-ter*	...-n suurlähety-stöä/suurlähetystö
my hotel	*mi-nun ho-tehl-li-ah/mi-nun ho-tehl-li*	minun hotellia/minun hotelli
a mail box	*pos-ti laa-tik-ko-ah/pos-ti laa-tik-ko*	postilaatikkoa/posti laatikko
the market	*to-ri-ah/to-ri*	toria/tori

the museum	*mu-seh-o-tah/mu-seh-o*	museota/museo
the police	*po-lee-si-ah/po-lee-si*	poliisia/poliisi
the post office	*pos-ti-ah/pos-ti*	postia/posti
a public toilet	*ü-lays-ta vehs-saa/ ü-lay-nehn vehs-sah*	yleistä vessaa/ yleinen vessa
the telephone centre	*pu-heh-lin-tah/ pu-heh-lin*	puhelinta/puhelin
the tourist information office	*maht-kay-lu toy-mis-to-ah*	matkailutoimistoa/ matkailutoimisto

What time does it open?

   mil-loyn seh ah-vah-taan?   Milloin se avataan?

What time does it close?

   mil-loyn seh sul-jeh-taan?   Milloin se suljetaan?

What ... is this?

   mi-ka ... ta-ma on?   Mikä ... tämä on?

street	*kah-tu*	katu
suburb	*kow-pung-ngin o-sah/ eh-si kow-pung-ki*	kaupunginosa/ esikaupunki

For directions, see the Getting Around section, page 89.

At the Bank

I want to exchange some money/traveller's cheques.

   hah-lu-ai-sin vaich-taa rah-haa/maht-kah shehk-keh-ja   Haluaisin vaihtaa rahaa/matkashekkejä.

What is the exchange rate?

   mi-ka on vah-loot-tah kurs-si?   Mikä on valuuttakurssi?

How many marks per dollar?
   pahl-yon-ko dol-lah-ril-lah saa mahrk-ko-yah?

Paljonko dollarilla saa markkoja?

Can I have money transferred here from my bank?
   voyn-ko mi-na saadah rah-haa seer-reht-tü-a o-mahs-tah pahn-kis-tah-ni?

Voinko minä* saada rahaa siirrettyä omasta pankistani?

How long will it take to arrive?
   kow-ahn-ko sehn tu-lo kehs-tÿ?

Kauanko sen tulo kestää?

Has my money arrived yet?
   on-ko mi-nun rah-hah-ni saa-pu-nut vi-eh-la?

Onko minun rahani saapunut vielä?

(some) banknotes	*seh-teh-leh-i-ta*	seteleitä
cashier	*kahs-sah*	kassa
some coins	*ko-li-koy-tah*	kolikoita
credit card	*lu-ot-to kort-ti*	luottokortti
exchange	*rah-hahn vaich-to*	rahanvaihto
loose change	*pik-ku rah-haa, vaich-to rah-haa*	pikkurahaa, vaihtorahaa
money transfer	*ti-li seer-to*	tilisiirto
signature	*ahl-leh kir-yoy-tus*	allekirjoitus

At the Post Office

I would like to send …
   hah-lu-ai-sin la-heht-tÿ …

Haluaisin lähettää …

a fax	*fahk-sin*	faksin
a letter	*kir-yeehn*	kirjeen
a postcard	*pos-ti kor-tin*	postikortin

| a parcel | **pah-keh-tin** | paketin |
| a telegram | **sach-keehn** | sähkeen |

I would like some stamps.
   hah-lu-ai-sin pos-ti   Haluaisin postimerkkejä.
   mehrk-keh-ja
How much is the postage?
   pahl-yon-ko on pos-ti   Paljonko on postimaksu?
   mahk-su?
How much does it cost to
send this to …?
   pahl-yon-ko mahk-saa   Paljonko maksaa lähettää
   la-heht-tÿ ta-ma …?   tämä …vowel + n?

an aerogram	**ah-eh-ro-grahm-mi**	aerogrammi
air mail	**lehn-to pos-ti-nah**	lentopostina
envelope	**kir-jeh**	kirje
parcel	**pah-keht-ti**	paketti
registered mail	**kir-jaht-tu kir-jeh**	kirjattu kirje
surface mail	**maa pos-ti-nah**	maapostina

Telephone

I want to ring …
   hah-lu-ai-sin soyt-taa …   Haluaisin soittaa …
The number is …
   pu-heh-lin nu-meh-ro on …   Puhelinnumero on …
I want to speak for three
minutes.
   hah-lu-ahn pu-hu-ah   Haluan puhua kolme
   kol-meh mi-noot-ti-ah   minuuttia.

How much does a three-
minute call cost?
   pahl-yon-ko **mahk**-*saa kol-
   mehn* **mi**-*noo-tin pu-heh-lu?*
How much does each extra
minute cost?
   pahl-yon-ko **mahk**-*saa jo-
   kai-nehn li-sa* **mi**-*noot-ti?*
I would like to speak to Mr
Nieminen.
   *hah-lu-ai-sin pu-hu-ah
   * **hehr**-*rah ni-eh-mi-sehn
   * **kahns**-*sah*
I want to make a reverse-
charges phone call.
   *hah-lu-ahn soyt-taa
   vahs-tah pu-heh-lun*
It's engaged.
   seh on vah-raht-tu
I've been cut off.
   pu-heh-lu **kaht**-*keh-si*

Paljonko maksaa kolmen
minuutin puhelu?

Paljonko maksaa jokainen
lisäminuutti?

Haluaisin puhua herra
Nieminen kanssa.

Haluan soittaa vastapuhelun.

Se on varattu.

Puhelu katkesi.

Sightseeing
Do you have a guidebook/
local map?
   on-ko si-nul-lah **maht**-*kah
   o-pahs-tah/* **kahrt**-*taa?*
What are the main attractions?
   mit-ka o-vaht **tar**-*kaym-mat
   nach-ta-vüü- deht?*

Onko sinulla
matkaopasta/karttaa?

Mitkä ovat tärkeimmät
nähtävyydet?

What is that?
   mi-ka tu-o on?   Mikä tuo on?
How old is it?
   ku-in-kah vahn-hah seh on?   Kuinka vanha se on?
Can I take photographs?
   voyn-ko mi-na ot-taa vah-lo   Voinko minä* ottaa
   ku-vi-ah?   valokuvia?
What time does it open/close?
   mil-loyn seh ow-keh-aa/   Milloin se aukeaa/suljetaan?
   sul-yeh-taan?

ancient	*vahn-hah*	vanha
archaeological	*ahr-keh-o-lo-gi-nehn*	arkeologinen
beach	*u-i-mah rahn-tah*	uimaranta
building	*rah-kehn-nus*	rakennus
castle	*lin-nah*	linna
cathedral	*tu-o-mi-o kirk-ko,*	tuomiokirkko,
	kah-tehd-raa-li	katedraali
church	*kirk-ko*	kirkko
concert hall	*kon-sehrt-ti hahl-li*	konserttihalli
library	*kir-jahs-to*	kirjasto
main square	*kehs-kus to-ri*	keskustori
market	*to-ri/kowp-pah to-ri/*	tori, kauppatori,
	mahrk-ki-naht	markkinat
monastery	*lu-os-tah-ri*	luostari
monument	*mu-is-to mehrk-ki/*	muistomerkki/
	mo-nu-mehnt-ti	monumentti
mosque	*mos-kay-yah*	moskeija
old city	*vahn-hah kow-pun-ki*	vanhakaupunki
palace	*pah-laht-si*	palatsi
opera house	*orp-peh-rah tah-lo*	oopperatalo

ruins	*row-ni-ot*	rauniot
stadium	*stah-di-on*	stadion
some statues	*paht-sai-tah*	patsaita
synagogue	*sü-nah-gor-gah*	synagooga
temple	*tehmp-peh-li*	temppeli
university	*ü-li o-pis-to, kor-keh-ah koh-lu*	yliopisto, korkeakoulu

FINNISH

Entertainment

What's there to do in the evening?

mi-ta tÿl-la voy teh-da il-tai-sin?

Mitä täällä voi tehdä iltaisin?

Are there any discos?

on-ko tÿl-la üch-tÿn dis-ko-ah?

Onko täällä yhtään diskoa?

Are there places where you can hear local folk music?

voy-ko tÿl-la mis-sÿn kool-lah pai-kal- lis-tah kahn-sahn mu-seek-ki-ah?

Voiko täällä missään kuulla paikallista kansanmusiikkia?

How much does it cost to get in?

pahl-yon-ko on pÿ-sü mahk-su?

Paljonko on pääsymaksu?

cinema	*eh-lo-ku-vah teh-aht-teh-ri*	elokuvateatteri
concert	*kon-sehrt-ti*	konsertti
discotheque	*dis-ko*	disko
theatre	*teh-aht-teh-ri*	teatteri

FINNISH

In the Country
Weather

What's the weather like?

mi-ka on sÿ ti-lah,	Mikä on säätila?
mil-lai-nehn sÿ on?	Millainen sää on?

The weather is ... today.

ta-nÿn on ...	Tänään on ...

Will it be ... tomorrow?

on-ko hu-o-mehn-nah?	Onko huomenna... ?

cloudy	*pil-vis-ta*	pilvistä
cold	*kül-mÿ*	kylmää
foggy	*su-mu-is-tah*	sumuista
forest fire alert	*meht-sa pah-lo vah-roy-tus*	metsäpalovaroitus
frosty	*pahk-kahs-tah*	pakkasta
hot	*koo-mah*	kuuma
raining	*sah-deht-tah*	sadetta
snowing	*lun-tah/lu-mih sah-deht-tah*	lunta/lumisadetta
summer night frost	*hahl-laa*	hallaa
sunny	*ow-rin-koys-tah*	aurinkoista
thunderstorm	*uk-kos-tah*	ukkosta
wet snowfall	*ran-tÿ*	räntää
windy	*too-lihs-tah*	tuulista

Camping

Am I allowed to camp here?

saa-ko tÿl-la lay-ri-ü-tü-a?	Saako täällä leiriytyä?

Is there a campsite nearby?
on-ko tÿl-la yos-sain la-hehl-la?

Onko täällä jossain lähellä leirintäaluetta?

backpack	*rehp-pu*	reppu
can opener	*pur-kin ah-vaa-yah*	purkinavaaja
compass	*kom-pahs-si*	kompassi
some firewood	*polt-to poo-tah*	polttopuuta
foam mattress	*mah-koo ah-lou-tah*	makuualusta
gas cartridge	*kaa-su sa-i-li-er*	kaasusäiliö
hammock	*reep-pu maht-to*	riippumatto
mattress	*paht-yah*	patja
penknife	*link-ku vayt-si*	linkkuveitsi
rope	*ker-ü-si*	köysi
tent	*tehlt-tah*	teltta
torch (flashlight)	*tahs-ku lahmp-pu*	taskulamppu
sleeping bag	*mah-koo pus-si*	makuupussi
stove	*reht-ki kay-tin*	retkikeitin
water bottle	*veh-si pul-lo*	vesipullo

Food

breakfast	*aa-mi-ai-nehn*	aamiainen
lunch	*loh-nahs*	lounas
early/late dinner	*pa-i-val-li-nehn/ il-lahl-li-nehn*	päivällinen/ illallinen

Table for ..., please.
saa-daan-ko meh per-ü-ta ...?

Saadaanko me pöytä ...lle?

Can I see the menu please?
voyn-ko mi-na nach-da meh-nun?

Voinko minä* nähdä menun?

FINNISH

I would like the set lunch,
please.
   saan-ko pa-i-van loh-naan   Saanko päivän lounaan.
What does it include?
   mi-ta see-hehn koo-loo?   Mitä siihen kuuluu?
Service is included in the bill.
   tahr-yoy-lu koo-loo   Tarjoilu kuuluu hintaan.
   hin-taan

Some Useful Words

ashtray	*tuh-kah kup-pi*	tuhkakuppi
the bill	*lahs-ku*	lasku
a cup	*kup-pi*	kuppi
dessert	*yal-ki ru-o-kah*	jälkiruoka
a drink	*yu-o-mah*	juoma
a fork	*haa-ruk-kah*	haarukka
fresh	*tu-o-reh*	tuore
a glass	*lah-si*	lasi
a knife	*vayt-si*	veitsi
a plate	*low-tah-nehn*	lautanen
spicy	*mows-teht-tu*	maustettu
spoiled	*pi-laan-tu-nut*	pilaantunut
a spoon	*lu-sik-kah*	lusikka
sweet	*mah-keh-ah*	makea
teaspoon	*teeh lu-sik-kah*	teelusikka
toothpick	*hahm-mahs tik-ku*	hammastikku

Vegetarian Meals

I am a vegetarian.
   o-lehn kahs-vis-sü-er-ya   Olen kasvissyöjä.
I don't eat meat.
   ehn sü-er li-haa   En syö lihaa.

I don't eat chicken, fish, or
ham.

> **ehn sü-er kah-naa, kah-laa** En syö kanaa, kalaa enkä
> **ehn-ka kink-ku-ah** kinkkua.

Staples
bread	*leipä*
cheese	*juusto*
macaroni	*makaroni*
oats	*kaura*
rice	*riisi*
rye	*ruis*

Meat
chicken	*kana/broileri*
beef	*naudan/härkä*
ham	*kinkku*
liver	*maksa*
meat	*liha*
minced meat	*jauheliha*
pork	*porsaan/possun*
reindeer	*poron*
sausage	*makkara*
steak	*pihvi*

Seafood
Baltic herring	*silakka*
fish	*kala*
herring	*silli*
salmon	*lohi*
seafood (not fish)	*äyriäis*
shrimp	*katkarapu*

FINNISH

Vegetables

cabbage	*kaali*
carrot	*porkkana*
garlic	*valkosipuli*
mushroom	*sieni*
onion	*sipuli*
pea	*herne*
potato	*peruna*
swede	*lanttu*
tomato	*tomaatti*
vegetable	*vihannes*
vegetable/vegetarian	*kasvis*

Prepared Food

berry or fruit soup	*kiisseli*
filled bread	*kukko*
minced vegetables and/or meat, baked in an oven	*laatikko*
omelette	*munakas*
open sandwich	*voileipä*
pan-fried food	*pannu*
pie	*piiras*
porridge	*puuro*
roll	*sämpylä*
salad	*salaatti*
sauce	*soosi/kastike*
scalloped food or pie	*paistos*
soup	*keitto/soppa*
thin barley bread, like chappati	*rieska*
titbit	*herkku*

Grilli Food

Grilli can also be called *katukeittiö*, *snägäri* or *nakkikioski*.
Enormously popular, they prepare real junk food by order till
early hours when everything else is closed. You can also find
local specialities, such as *mikkeliläinen* in Mikkeli.

atomi	Meat pie with ham or fried egg.
camping	Sausage.
hampurilainen	Hamburger.
kalapuikot	Finger-shaped fried fish.
kebakko	Finger-shaped meat ball
kuumakoira	Hot dog.
lihapiirakka	Pie with meat & rice filling.
makkaraperunat	Sausage with French fries.
munakukkaro	Hamburger with fried egg.
nakki/nakit	Small sausage.
nakkipiiras	Small sausage inside a pie.
porilainen	Thick *lauantai* sausage in a burger bread.
publiski	Kind of hot dog.
ranskalaiset	French fries.
reissumies	Two slices of rye bread with filling.
vety	Meat pie with ham and eggs.

Other Meals

janssonin kiusaus	Potato and herring prepared in oven.
kaalikääryleet	Minced meat covered with cabbage leaves.
kesäkeitto	Vegetable soup/'summer soup'.
lihamureke	Seasoned minced meat prepared in oven.
lihapullat	Meatballs.
lipeäkala	Lutefish.

FINNISH

metsästäjänpihvi	'Hunter's steak' – minced meat with mushroom sauce.
pyttipannu	Ham and potatoes fried in butter.

Local Specialities

karjalanpiirakka	Rye pie with rice, barley or potato filling. (Eastern)
lanttusupikas	Kind of rye pita bread with swede filling. (Savo)
lörtsy	Thin pancake-shaped doughnut with apple or meat filling. (Eastern)
kukko	Large rye bread loaf with filling, either pork and vegetable, such as swede, *lanttukukko,* or potato, *perunakukko;* or pork and fish, *kalakukko,* specifically small whitefish, *muikkukukko,* or perch, *ahvenkukko.* (Eastern)
kukkonen	Rice porridge on bread. (Karelian)
leipäjuusto	Cheese bread. (Pohjanmaa & Kainuu)
loimulohi	Salmon prepared at open fire. (Eastern)
mustamakkara	Rice-filled black sausage. (Tampere)
muurinpohjalettu	Thin large fried pancake. (Eastern)
neulamuikut	Small whitefish. (Karelian)
poronkäristys	Reindeer casserole. (Lapland)
sultsina	Kind of chappati bread stuffed with porridge. (Karelian)
rönttönen	Round pie with filling made of rye, potato and lingon. (Kuhmo)
vatruska	Thick pancake made of mashed potato and wheat flour. (Karelian)

Methods of Cooking & Preparation

BBQ'd	*grillattu*
cooked	*keitetty*
cutlet	*leike*
dipped in flour & fried	*paneerattu*
fried	*käristetty*
frozen	*pakastettu/jäädyke*
gravy-salted	*graavisuolattu*
heated in microwave oven	*kuumennettu mikrossa*
prepared in oven	*paistettu*
salted	*suolattu*
smoked	*savustettu*
steamed	*höyrytetty*
stuffed	*täytetty*
sugar added	*sokeroitu*
sweetened or malted	*imelletty*

Fruit

blueberry	*mustikka*
cranberry	*puolukka*
pineapple	*ananas*
strawberry	*mansikka* .

Drinks – Nonalcoholic

A *kahvila* is a normal café, whereas a *kahvio* serves coffee in say, a fuel station or a supermarket, but basically these two are similar places, also called *kuppila*.

A *baari* serves beer and soft drinks, no strong alcohol, and is also called *kapakka*. Restaurants, *ravintola*, that have permission to serve strong alcohol have *A-oikeudet*, or 'full rights'. With *B-oikeudet* you have less choice.

berry drink	*mehu*
coffee	*kahvi*
drinking water	*juomavesi*
fresh juice	*tuoremehu*
hot chocolate	*kaakao*
ice water	*jäävesi*
milk	*maito*
soft drink	*limonadi/limu/limppari/limsa*
soft drink, literally 'refreshing drink'	*virvoitusjuoma*
sour milk	*piimä*
tea	*tee*
water	*vesi*

Drinks – Alcoholic

drinkki	Cocktail drink.
huurteinen	Cold beer, literally 'frosty'.
kossu	Another name for strong Koskenkorva spirit.
kotikalja	Literally 'home-brewed malt drink'.
lonkero	Another name for a long gin.
pitkä	Literally 'long', large glass of strong beer.

beer	*olut*
beer, literally 'malt drink'	*kalja*
light beer	*I-olut/ykkös olut*
medium strong beer	*keskikalja/kolmonen/III-olut*
red wine	*punaviini*
strong alcohol, vodka	*viina*
strong beer	*IV A-olut/nelos olut*
white wine	*valkoviini*
wine	*viini*

Shopping

How much is it?
pahl-yon-ko seh mahk-saa?   Paljonko se maksaa?

bookshop	*kir-yah kowp-pah*	kirjakauppa
camera shop	*vah-lo ku-vows lee-keh*	valokuvausliike
clothing store	*vaa-teh kowp-pah*	vaatekauppa
delicatessen	*hehrk-ku kowp-pah*	herkkukauppa
general store, shop	*kowp-pah*	kauppa
laundry	*peh-su-lah*	pesula
market	*kowp-pah to-ri/ mahrk-ki-naht/ bah-saa-ri*	kauppatori/mark-kinat/basaari
newsagency/ stationers	*lech-ti ki-os-ki/pah-peh-ri kowp-pah*	lehtikioski/paperika uppa
pharmacy	*ahp-teehk-ki*	apteekki
shoeshop	*kehn-ka kowp-pah*	kenkäkauppa
souvenir shop	*maht-kah mu-is-to müü-ma-la*	matkamuisto-myymälä
supermarket	*su-pehr mahr-keht*	supermarket
vegetable shop	*vi-hahn-nehs kowp-pah*	vihanneskauppa

I would like to buy …
hah-lu-ai-sin os-taa …   Haluaisin ostaa …
Do you have others?
on-ko tayl-la mu-i-tah?   Onko teillä muita?
I don't like it.
ehn oy-kayn pi-da see-ta   En oikein pidä siitä.

FINNISH

Can I look at it?
voyn-ko mi-na kaht-so-ah si-ta? Voinko minä* katsoa sitä?

I'm just looking.
mi-na vain kaht-seh-lehn Minä* vain katselen.

Can you write down the price?
voyt-teh-ko kir-yoyt-taa hin-nahn? Voitteko kirjoittaa hinnan?

Do you accept credit cards?
voy-ko mahk-saa lu-ot-to-kort-til-lah? Voiko maksaa luottokortilla?

Could you lower the price?
voyt-ko lahs-keh-ah hin-taa? Voitko laskea hintaa?

I don't have much money.
mul-lah ay o-leh pahl-yon rah-haa. Mulla ei ole paljon rahaa.

Can I help you?
voyn-ko owt-taa? Voinko auttaa?

Will that be all?
yah tu-leeh-ko moo-tah? Ja tuleeko muuta?

Would you like it wrapped?
pis-teh-tyn-ker pah-keht-teen? Pistetäänkö pakettiin?

Sorry, this is the only one.
ta-ma on may-dan ai-no-ah Tämä on meidän ainoa.

How much/many do you want?
pahl-yon-ko si-na hah-lu-aht/ku-in-kah mon-tah pis-teh-tyn? Paljonko sinä* haluat?/ Kuinka monta pistetään?

Souvenirs

some earrings	*kor-vah ko-ru-yah*	korvakoruja
some handicrafts	*ka-si ter-i-ta*	käsitöitä
necklace	*kow-lah ko-ru*	kaulakoru
pottery	*keh-rah-meek-kah*	keramiikka
ring	*sor-mus*	sormus
rug	*maht-to, raa-nu*	matto, raanu

Clothing

clothing	*vaat-teeht*	vaatteet
coat	*tahk-ki*	takki
dress	*pu-ku*	puku
jacket	*tahk-ki*	takki
jumper (sweater)	*pu-seh-ro/yump-peh-ri*	pusero/jumpperi
shirt	*pai-tah*	paita
shoes	*kehng-ngat*	kengät
skirt	*hah-meh*	hame
trousers	*hoh-sut*	housut

It doesn't/They don't fit.

   ta-ma/na-ma ay mahch-du   Tämä/Nämä ei mahdu.

It is too …

   seh on lee-ahn …   Se on liian …

big/small	*i-so/pi-eh-ni*	iso/pieni
short/long	*lü-hüt/peet-ka*	lyhyt/pitkä
tight/loose	*ki-reh-a/ler-ü-sa*	kireä/löysä

FINNISH

FINNISH

Materials

cotton	*poo-vil-laa*	puuvillaa
handmade	*ka-sin teh-tüh/ka-si-tü-er-ta*	käsintehty/käsityötä
leather	*nahch-kaa*	nahkaa
of brass	*mehs-sin-ki-a*	messinkiä
of gold	*kul-taa*	kultaa
of silver	*ho-peh-aa*	hopeaa
flax	*pehl-lah-vaa*	pellavaa
pure alpaca	*ahl-pahk-kaa*	alpakkaa
silk	*silk-ki-a*	silkkiä
wool	*vil-laa*	villaa

Toiletries

comb	*kahm-pa*	kampa
some condoms	*kon-do-meh-yah*	kondomeja
deodorant	*deh-o-do-rahnt-ti*	deodorantti
hairbrush	*hi-us hahr-yah*	hiusharja
moisturising cream	*kos-te-us voy-deh*	kosteusvoide
razor	*pahr-tah teh-ra*	partaterä
sanitary napkins	*tehr-veh-üs si-deh/ pik-ku hoh-sun su-o-yah*	terveysside/ pikkuhousunsuoja
shampoo	*shahmp-por*	shampoo
shaving cream	*pahr-tah vaah-to*	partavaahto
some tampons	*tahm-po-neh-yah*	tamponeja
tissues	*neh-na lee-nah*	nenäliina
toilet paper	*vehs-sah pah-peh-ri*	vessapaperi
toothbrush	*hahm-mahs hahr-yah*	hammasharja
toothpaste	*hahm-mahs tah-nah*	hammastahna

Stationery & Publications

map	*kahrt-tah*	kartta
newspaper	*sah-no-mah lech-ti*	sanomalehti
newspaper in English	*ehng-lahn-nin ki-eh-li-nehn sah-no-mah lech-ti*	englannin kieli-nen sanomalehti
novels in English	*ehng-lahn-nin ki-eh-li-si-a ro-maa-neh-yah*	englannin kielisiä romaaneja
paper	*pah-peh-ri*	paperi
pen (ballpoint)	*kü-na (koo-lah kü-na)*	kynä (kuulakynä)
scissors	*sahk-seht*	sakset

Photography

How much is it to process this film?

pahl-yon-ko mahk-saa keh-hit-tÿ ta-ma fil-mi?

Paljonko maksaa kehittää tämä filmi?

When will it be ready?

kos-kah seh on vahl-mis?

Koska se on valmis?

I'd like a film for this camera.

mi-na hah-lu-ai-sin fil-min ta-han kah-meh-raan

Minä* haluaisin filmin tähän kameraan.

B&W (film)	*mus-tah vahl-koy-nehn*	mustavalkoinen
camera	*kah-meh-rah*	kamera
colour (film)	*va-ri fil-mi*	värifilmi
film	*fil-mi*	filmi
flash	*sah-lah-mah*	salama
lens	*ob yehk tee vi/lins-si*	objektiivi/linssi
light meter	*vah-lo-tus mit-tah-ri*	valotusmittari

FINNISH

Smoking

A packet of cigarettes, please.

saan-ko tu-pahk-kah ahs-kin, kee-toss

Saanko tupakka-askin, kiitos.

Are these cigarettes strong/mild?

o-vaht-ko na-ma tu-pah-kaht vach-vo-yah/mi-eh-to-yah?

Ovatko nämä tupakat vahvoja/mietoja?

Do you have a light?

on-ko sul-lah tul-tah?

Onko sinulla tulta?

cigarette papers	*sah-vu-keh pah-peh-ri-ah*	savukepaperia
some cigarettes	*tu-pahk-kaa*	tupakkaa
filtered	*filt-teh-ri*	filtteri
lighter	*sü-tü-tin*	sytytin
	süt-ka	sytkä (inf)
matches	*tu-li ti-kut*	tulitikut
	ti-kut	tikut (inf)
menthol	*menth-tor-li*	menthol
pipe	*peep-pu*	piippu
tobacco	*tu-pahk-kah*	tupakka

Colours

black	*mus-tah*	musta
blue	*si-ni-nehn*	sininen
brown	*rus-keeh*	ruskea
green	*vih-reeh*	vihreä
orange	*o-rahns-si*	oranssi
pink	*vaa-leh-ahn pu-nai-nehn (pink-ki)*	vaaleanpunainen (pinkki)

purple	*vi-o-leht-ti*	violetti
red	*pu-nah-nehn*	punainen
white	*vahl-ko-nehn*	valkoinen
yellow	*kel-tah-nehn*	keltainen

FINNISH

Sizes & Comparisons

small	*pi-eh-ni*	pieni
big	*soo-ri/i-so*	suuri/iso
heavy	*pai-nah-vah*	painava
light	*keh-vüt*	kevyt
more	*eh-neh-man*	enemmän
less	*va-hehm-man*	vähemän
too much/many	*lee-kaa/lee-ahn mon-tah*	liikaa/liian monta
many	*mon-tah*	monta
enough	*tahr-peehk-si*	tarpeeksi
also	*mü-ers*	myös
a little bit	*va-han*	vähän

Health

Where is …?
  mis-sa on …?   Missä on …?

the doctor	*la-a-ka-ri*	lääkäri
the hospital	*sai-raa-lah*	sairaala
the chemist	*ahp-teehk-ki*	apteekki
the dentist	*hahm-mahs lÿ-ka-ri*	hammaslääkäri

I am sick.
  o-lehn sai-rahs   Olen sairas.
My friend is sick.
  üs-ta-va-ni on sai-rahs   Ystäväni on sairas.

Could I see a female doctor?
on-ko mahch-dol-lis-tah tah- Onko mahdollista tavata
*vah-tah **nais** lÿ-ka-ri?* naislääkäri?
What's the matter?
mi-ka on ha-ta-na? Mikä on hätänä?
Where does it hurt?
*mis-ta **saht-too**?* Mistä sattuu?
It hurts here.
saht-too tÿl-ta Sattuu täältä.
My ... hurts.
mi-nun ... on ki-peh-a Minun ... on kipeä.

Parts of the Body

ankle	*nilk-kah*	nilkka
arm	*ka-si*	käsi
back	*sehl-ka*	selkä
chest	*rin-tah/rin-tah keh-ha*	rinta/rintakehä
ear	*kor-vah*	korva
eye	*sil-ma*	silmä
finger	*sor-mi*	sormi
foot	*yahl-kah*	jalka
hand	*ka-si*	käsi
head	*pÿ*	pää
heart	*sü-dan*	sydän
leg	*sÿ-ri*	sääri
mouth	*soo*	suu
nose	*neh-na*	nenä
ribs	*kül-ki loot*	kylkiluut
skin	*i-ho*	iho
stomach	*vaht-sah/mah-hah*	maha/vatsa
teeth	*hahm-paat*	hampaat
throat	*kurk-ku*	kurkku

Ailments

I have …
mul-lah on …   Minulla on …

an allergy	*ahl-lehr-gi-ah*	allergia
anaemia	*ah-neh-mi-ah*	anemia
a blister	*rahk-ko*	rakko
a burn	*pah-lo vahm-mah*	palovamma
a cold	*fluns-sah*	flunssa
constipation	*um-meh-tus-tah*	ummetusta
a cough	*üs-ka*	yskä
diarrhoea	*ri-pu-li*	ripuli
fever	*koo-meht-tah*	kuumetta
a headache	*pÿn sar-kü*	päänsärky
hepatitis	*mahk-sah tu-leh-dus*/*heh-pah-teet-ti*	maksatulehdus/hepatiitti
indigestion	*roo-ahn su-lah-tos ha-i-ri-er*	ruuansulatushäiriö
an infection	*tu-leh-dus*	tulehdus
influenza	*in-flu-ehns-sah*	influenssa
lice	*ta-i-ta*	täitä
low/high blood pressure	*mah-tah-lah*/*kor-keh-ah veh-rehn pai-neh*	matala/korkea verenpaine
sore throat	*kurk-ku ki-peh-a*	kurkku kipeä
sprain	*nilk-kah nür-yach-ta-nüt*	nilkka nyrjähtänyt
a stomachache	*mah-hah ki-pu*	mahakipu
sunburn	*i-ho pah-lah-nut*	iho palanut
a venereal disease	*su-ku pu-o-li tow-ti*	sukupuolitauti
worms	*mah-to-yah*	matoja

FINNISH

FINNISH

Some Useful Words & Phrases

I'm pregnant.
o-lehn rahs-kaa-nah   Olen raskaana.

I'm on the pill.
o-lehn lÿ-keh koo-ril-lah   Olen lääkekuurilla.

I haven't had my period for
... months

  mul-lah ay o-leh ol-lut koo-   Minulla ei ole ollut
  kow-ti-si-ah ... koo-kow-   kuukautisia ...vowel + n
  teehn   kuukauteen.

I have been vaccinated.
  mut on ro-ko-teht-tu   Minut on rokotettu.

I have my own syringe.
  mul-lah on o-mah ru-is-   Minulla on oma ruiskeneula.
  keh neh-u-lah

I feel better/worse.
  voyn-ti-ni on pah-rehm-   Vointini on
  pi/hu-o-nom-pi   parempi/huonompi.

I'm ...
  o-lehn ...   Olen ...

diabetic	*di-ah-beeh-tik-ko*	diabeetikko
epileptic	*eh-pi-lehp-tik-ko*	epileptikko
asthmatic	*ahst-maa-tik-ko*	astmaatikko

I'm allergic to ...
  mi-na o-lehn ahl-lehr-gi-   Minä* olen allerginen ...
  nehn ...

antibiotics	*ahn-ti-bi-or-tayl-leh*	antibiooteille
penicillin	*peh-ni-sil-lee-nil-leh*	penisilliinille

accident	*on-neht-to-moos*	onnettomuus
addiction	*reep-pu-voos*	riippuvuus
some antibiotics	*ahn-ti-bi-ort-teh-yah*	antibiootteja
antiseptic	*ahn-ti-sehp-ti-nehn*	antiseptinen
aspirin	*ahs-pi-ree-ni*	aspiriini
bandage	*si-deh*	side
blood test	*veh-ri ko-eh*	verikoe
contraceptive	*ech-ka-i-sü va-li-neh*	ehkäisyväline
injection	*ru-is-keh*	ruiske
injury	*vahm-mah*	vamma
medicine	*lü-keh*	lääke
menstruation	*koo-kow-ti-seht*	kuukautiset
nausea	*pah-hoyn voyn-ti*	pahoinvointi
oxygen	*hahp-pi*	happi
some vitamins	*vi-tah-mee-neh-yah*	vitamiineja

FINNISH

At the Chemist
I need medication for …
   tahr-vit-sen lü-ki-tüs-ta …   Tarvitsen lääkitystä …-a/ä
   -ah/a vahr-tehn   varten.
I have a prescription.
   mi-nul-lah on reh-sehp-ti   Minulla on resepti.

At the Dentist
I have a toothache.
   mun hahm-mahs-tah   Minun hammasta särkee.
   sar-keeh
I've lost a filling.
   mi-nul-tah on ir-ron-nut   Minulta on irronnut paikka.
   paik-kah

I've broken a tooth.
mi-nul-tah on loh-yehn-nut   Minulta on lohjennut
hahm-mahs   hammas.

My gums hurt.
i-keh-ni-a sar-keeh   Ikeniä särkee.

I don't want it extracted.
ehn hah-lu-ah eht-ta hahm-   En halua, että hammas
mahs poys-teh-taan   poistetaan.

Please give me an anaesthetic.
voyt-teh-ko poo-dut-taa   Voitteko puuduttaa.

Time & Dates

What date is it today?
mi-ka pa-i-va ta-nÿn on?   Mikä päivä tänään on?

What time is it?
pahl-yon-ko kehl-lo on?   Paljonko kello on?

It is ...
kehl-lo on ...   Kello on ...

in the morning	*aa-mul-lah*	aamulla
in the afternoon	*il-tah pa-i-val-la*	iltapäivällä
in evening	*il-lahl-lah*	illalla

Days of the Week

Monday	*maa-nahn-tai*	maanantai
Tuesday	*tees-tai*	tiistai
Wednesday	*kehs-ki veek-ko*	keskiviikko
Thursday	*tors-tai*	torstai
Friday	*pehr-yahn-tai*	perjantai
Saturday	*low-ahn-tai*	lauantai
Sunday	*sun-nun-tai*	sunnuntai

FINNISH

Months

January	*tahm-mi-koo*	tammikuu
February	*hehl-mi-koo*	helmikuu
March	*maa-lis-koo*	maaliskuu
April	*huh-ti-koo*	huhtikuu
May	*toh-ko-koo*	toukokuu
June	*keh-sa-koo*	kesäkuu
July	*hay-na-koo*	heinäkuu
August	*eh-lo-koo*	elokuu
September	*süüs-koo*	syyskuu
October	*lo-kah-koo*	lokakuu
November	*mahr-rahs-koo*	marraskuu
December	*yoh-lu-koo*	joulukuu

Seasons

summer	*keh-sa*	kesä
autumn	*sük-sü*	syksy
winter	*tahl-vi*	talvi
spring	*keh-vat*	kevät

Present

today	*ta-nÿn*	tänään
this morning	*ta-na aa-mu-nah*	tänä aamuna
tonight	*ta-na il-tah-nah*	tänä iltana
this week	*tal-la vee-kol-lah*	tällä viikolla
this year	*ta-na vu-on-nah*	tänä vuonna
now	*nüt*	nyt

Past

yesterday	*ay-lehn*	eilen
day before yesterday	*toys-sah pa-i-va-na*	toissapäivänä

yesterday morning	*ay-lehn aa-mul-lah*	eilen aamulla
last night	*vee-meh ü-er-na*	viime yönä
last week	*vee-meh vee-kol-lah*	viime viikolla
last year	*vee-meh vu-on-nah*	viime vuonna

Future

tomorrow	*hu-o-mehn-nah*	huomenna
day after tomorrow	*ü-li hu-o-mehn-nah*	ylihuomenna
tomorrow morning	*hu-o-mehn aa-mu-nah*	huomenaamuna
tomorrow afternoon/evening	*hu-o-mehn-nah il-tah pa-i-val-la/hu-o-mehn il-tah-nah*	huomenna iltapäivällä/huomen iltana
next week	*ehn-si vee-kol-lah*	ensi viikolla
next year	*ehn-si vu-on-nah*	ensi vuonna

During the Day

afternoon	*il-tah pa-i-val-la*	iltapäivällä
dawn, very early morning	*aa-mun koyt-to, aa-mul-lah vahr-hain*	aamunkoitto, aamulla varhain
day	*pa-i-va*	päivä
early	*ai-kai-sin*	aikaisin
midnight	*kehs-ki ü-er*	keskiyö
morning	*aa-mu*	aamu
night	*ü-er*	yö
noon	*kehs-ki pa-i-va*	keskipäivä
sundown	*ow-ring-ngon lahs-ku*	auringonlasku
sunrise	*ow-ring-ngon noh-su*	auringonnousu

Numbers & Amounts

0	*nol-lah*	nolla
1	*ük-si*	yksi (yks – inf)
2	*kahk-si*	kaksi (kaks – inf)
3	*kol-meh*	kolme
4	*nehl-ya*	neljä
5	*vee-si*	viisi (viis – inf)
6	*koo-si*	kuusi (kuus – inf)
7	*sayt-seh-man*	seitsemän
		(seittemän – inf)
8	*kahch-dehk-sahn*	kahdeksan
		(kaheksan – inf)
9	*üch-dehk-san*	yhdeksän
		(yheksän – inf)
10	*küm-meh-nehn*	kymmenen
11	*ük-si toys-tah*	yksitoista
12	*kahk-si toys-tah*	kaksitoista
13	*kol-meh toys-tah*	kolmetoista
14	*nehl-ya toys-tah*	neljätoista
15	*vee-si toys-tah*	viisitoista
20	*kahk-si küm-mehn-ta*	kaksikymmentä
30	*kol-meh küm-mehn-ta*	kolmekymmentä
40	*nehl-ya küm-mehn-ta*	neljäkymmentä
50	*vee-si küm-mehn-ta*	viisikymmentä
60	*koo-si küm-mehn-ta*	kuusikymmentä
70	*sayt-seh-man küm-mehn-ta*	seitsemänkym-mentä
80	*kahch-dehk-sahn-küm-mehn-ta*	kahdeksankym-mentä
90	*üch-dehk-san-küm-mehn-ta*	yhdeksänkym-mentä

FINNISH

FINNISH

100	*sah-tah*	sata
1000	*tu-haht*	tuhat
one million	*mihl-yor-nah*	miljoona
1st	*ehn-sin-ma-i-nehn*	ensimmäinen
	eh-kah	(eka – inf)
2nd	*toy-nehn*	toinen
	to-kah	(toka – inf)
3rd	*kol-mahs*	kolmas
¼	*nehl-yas o-sah/*	neljäsosa/
	nehl-yan-nehs	neljännes
⅓	*kol-mahs o-sah/*	kolmasosa/
	kol-mahn-nehs	kolmannes
½	*pu-o-leht*	puolet
¾	*kol-meh nehl-yas*	kolme neljäsosaa
	o-saa	

Some Useful Words

a little	*va-han*	vähän
double	*tup-laht*	tuplat
a dozen	*tu-si-nah*	tusina
Enough!	*yo reet-tÿ*	Jo riittää!
few	*hahr-vah*	harva
less	*va-hehm-man*	vähemmän
many	*mon-tah/mo-ni-ah*	monta/monia
more	*eh-nehm-man*	enemmän
once	*kehr-rahn*	kerran
a pair	*pah-ri*	pari
percent	*pro-sehnt-ti*	prosentti
some	*yo-tah-kin/va-han/*	jotakin/vähän/
	yon-kin vehr-rahn	jonkin verran

| too much | *lee-kaa/lee-ahn pahl-yon* | liikaa/liian paljon |
| twice | *kahch-dehs-ti/ kahk-si kehr-taa* | kahdesti/kaksi kertaa |

FINNISH

Abbreviations

ALE – alennusmyynti	sale
ark – arkisin	on weekdays (Monday to Saturday)
as. – asema	station
eiL – ei lauantaisin	not on Saturdays
EP – erikoispikajuna	special express train
EY – Euroopan Yhteisöt	European Communities(EC)
Hki	Helsinki
k. – katu	Street
ke – keskiviikko	Wednesday
-kj. – -kuja	alley
kpl – kappaletta	amount of something, or pieces
la – lauantai	Saturday
ma – maanantai	Monday
mk – markka*	Finnish marks (currency)
n:o, nro – numero	number
pe – perjantai	Friday
PL – Postilokero	PO Box
puh., p. – puhelinnumero	telephone number
-t. – -tie	Road
SF – Suomi Finland	Finland – Official abbreviation of Finland, in Finnish and Swedish

SRM – Suomen Retkeilymajajärjestö	Finnish YHA
SS	(in timetables only) when there are two consecutive holidays, buses run on the second holiday only
su – sunnuntai	Sunday
ti – tiistai	Tuesday
Tku	Turku
to – torstai	Thursday
Tre	Tampere
v. – vuonna	year
VR – Valtion Rautatiet	National Railways

ICELANDIC

Icelandic

Introduction

Icelandic is a North Germanic language. Iceland was settled primarily by Norwegians in the 9th and 10th centuries. By the 14th century Icelandic (Old Norse) and Norwegian had grown apart considerably. This was due to changes in Norwegian, whereas Icelandic remained largely unchanged. In fact, it has an unbroken literary tradition, dating from about 1100, and the language has changed remarkably little through the centuries. The treasures of the *Sagas* and the poetic *Edda*, written about 700 years ago, can be enjoyed by a modern-day speaker of Icelandic.

Icelanders are proud of their literary heritage. They are particulary conservative when it comes to the written word; borrowed vocabulary is ill tolerated and the policy of keeping the language pure is very strong. After all, Icelandic is spoken by a mere 250,000 people, and outside pressures on the language, in these times of easy travel and worldwide communications, are enormous.

The practice of creating neologisms (new words), instead of adopting foreign words is well established in Iceland. Neologisms, such as *útvarp*, 'radio', *sjónvarp*, 'television', *tölva*, 'computer', and *þota*, 'jet', are just a few that have become part of the Icelandic vocabulary in the last 50 years.

Icelandic is a highly inflected language. Nouns are inflected in four cases: nominative, accusative, dative and genitive, in singular and plural. Most pronouns and adjectives are also inflected. Prepositions and certain verbs determine cases. Nouns change their endings with each case. The plural is formed with still different endings.

There are three genders; masculine, feminine and neuter. Objects may be defined as any of the three.

Icelandic has no indefinite article ('a/an' in English), only a definite article ('the'). The article changes according to gender. *Hinn* (masculine), *hin* (feminine), *hið* (neuter). It is normally attached to the end of a noun. When attached to a noun it drops the *h*: *maðurinn*, 'the man'. The definite article also declines with the noun. Verbs are inflected in three persons (1st, 2nd, and 3rd), singular and plural.

Icelanders are a rather informal people. A person is very rarely addressed by title and/or surname. Family names are illegal in Iceland, unless they were adopted before the Personal Names Act which was passed by Iceland's parliament, *Alþing*, in 1925. Icelanders use the ancient patronymic system, where *son*, 'son' or *dóttir*, 'daughter' is attached to the genitive form of the father's or, less commonly, the mother's, first name. The telephone book entries are listed according to first names.

All this will, no doubt, be quite daunting to an outsider. As one might expect, most Icelanders speak English, and often as many as three or four other languages, although among themselves they only converse in Icelandic. Your efforts to speak Icelandic will most certainly be met with great enthusiasm.

Pronunciation

Stress is generally on the first syllable. Double consonants are pronounced as such. The Icelandic alphabet consists of 33 letters: a, á, b, d, ð, e, é, f, g, h, i, í, j, k, l, m, n, o, ó, p, r, s, t, u, ú, v, x, y, ý, z, þ, æ, ö.

Icelandic	Pronunciation Guide	Sounds
a	*aa*	as the 'a' in 'father'
a	*ah*	as in the Italian *pasta*
e	*ea*	as in 'fear'
e	*eh*	as in 'get', 'bet'
i, y	*i*	as the 'e' in 'pretty'
í, ý	*ee*	as the 'e' in 'see', 'evil'
o	*o*	as in 'pot'
u	*ü*	there is no equivalent sound in English. It sounds a bit like the vowel sound in the French word *peur*. The pronunciation guide is *ü*, although it is not a good phonetic translation for this sound. The u in *Guð* 'God', is always pronounced as 'v'.
ú	*u*	as the 'o' in 'moon', 'woman'
ö	*er*	as in 'fern', 'turn', but without a trace of 'r'

Diphthongs

á	*ow*	as in 'out'
ei, ey	*ay*	as in 'paid', 'day'
ó	*oh*	as in 'note'
æ	*ai*	as in 'eye', 'dive'
au	*eü*	there is no equivalent sound in English

Semiconsonants

é	*yeh*	as in 'yet', 'yes'

Consonants

ð	*ð*	as in 'lather'
f	*f*	as in English. When between vowels or at the end of a word it is pronounced as 'v'. When followed by l or n it is pronounced as 'b'.

g	*g*	as in 'good'. When between vowels or before r or ð, (*sagt*, 'said'), it has a guttural sound as in the Scottish *loch*, rendered as *gh* in pronunciation guide
h	*h*	as in English, except when followed by 'v', when it is pronounced as 'k'
j	*y*	as in 'yes', 'yellow'
l	*l*	as in English, except when double 'l' occurs, when it is pronounced as 'dl' (*kalla*, 'call')
n	*n*	as in English, except when double 'n' forms an end to a word, when it is pronounced as 'dn', (*einn*, 'one'), but never when double 'n' forms part of the article *hinn*
p	*p*	as in English, except before 's' or 't', when it is pronounced as 'f' (skipta, *skift-ah*, 'exchange')
r	*r*	always trilled
þ	*th*	as in 'thin', 'three'

ICELANDIC

Greetings & Civilities
Top Useful Phrases
Hello.
    hahl-loh   Halló.

Goodbye.
    blehs   Bless.

Yes.
    yow   Já.

No.
    nay   Nei.

Excuse me. (forgive me)
    ahf-saak-ið   Afsakið.

Sorry.
   myehr thi-kir thaað layt   Mér þykir það leitt.
Please.
   gyer-ðü svo veal   Gjörðu svo vel.
Thank you.
   tahk fir-ir   Takk fyrir.
That's fine.
   ahlt ee lai-i   Allt í lagi
You're welcome.
   ehk-ehrt aað thahk-ah   Ekkert að þakka.

Greetings

Good morning.
   gohð-ahn dai-in   Góðan daginn.
Good afternoon.
   gohð-ahn dai-in   Góðan daginn.
Good evening/night.
   ghot kverld/ghoh-ð-ah noht   Gott kvöld.

How are you?
   kvehrn-ikh heahv-ür thu   Hvernig hefur þú það?
   thaað?
Well, thanks.
   ghot, tahk   Gott, takk.

Forms of Address

Madam/Mrs	*froo*	Frú
Sir/Mr	*hehr-rah*	Herra
Miss	*frer-kehn*	Fröken
companion,	*vin-ür*	vinur (m)
friend	*vin-ko-nah*	vinkona (f)

Small Talk
Meeting People
What is your name?
kvaað hay-tir-thu? Hvað heitir þú?

My name is ...
yehgh hay-ti ... Ég heiti ...

I'm pleased to meet you.
kon-dü saidl/sail Kondu sæll (m)/sæl (f).

Nationalities
Where are you from?
kvaað-ahn ehrt thu? Hvaðan ert þú?

I am from ...
yehgh ehr frow ... Ég er frá....

Australia	*owst-rah-lee-ü*	Ástralíu
Canada	*kaaa-naa-dah*	Kanada
England	*ayngh-laan-di*	Englandi
Ireland	*eer-laan-di*	Írlandi
New Zealand	*nee-aa syow-laan-di*	Nýja Sjálandi
Scotland	*skot-laan-di*	Skotlandi
the USA	*baand-ah-ree-kyü-*	Bandaríkjunum
	nüm	

Age
How old are you?
kvaað ehr-dü gaam-ahdl/ Hvað ertu gamall (m)/
ger-mül? gömul?(f)

I am ... years old.
yehgh ehr ... ow-rah Ég er ... ára.

ICELANDIC

Occupations

What do you do?

kvaað geh-ir thu? Hvað gerir þú?

I am (a/an) ...

yehgh ehr ... Ég er ...

business person/ in business	*keüp-sees-lü-maað-r/ ee við-skift-üm*	kaupsýslumaður/ í viðskiptum (in business)
journalist	*fryeht-ah-maað-ür*	fréttamaður
manual worker	*vehrk-ah-maað-ür*	verkamaður
nurse	*hyook-rün-ahr-fraið-ing-ür*	hjúkrunarfræðingur
office worker	*skrif-stof-ü-maað-ür*	skrifstofumaður
scientist	*vee-sin-dah-maað-ür*	vísindamaður
student	*nowms-maað-ür*	námsmaður
teacher	*kehn-ah-ri*	kennari
waiter	*thyohdn/thyohn-üs-dü-stul-kah*	þjónn/þjónus-tustúlka
writer	*rit-herf-ünd-ür*	rithöfundur

Religion

What is your religion?

kvehr-ahr tru-ahr ehrt thu? Hverrar trúar ert þú?

I am not religious.

yehgh ehr ehk-i Ég er ekki trúaður (m)/
tru-aað-ür/tru-üð trúúð (f)

I am ...

yehgh ehr ... Ég er ...

Buddhist	*bu-dah-tru-ahr*	Búddatrúar
Catholic	*Kaa-thohl-skür*	Kaþólskur (m)
	Kaa-tholsk	Kaþólsk (f)

Christian	*krist-in-ahr tru-ahr*	Kristinnar trúar.
Hindu	*hin-du tru-ahr*	Hindú trúar.
Jewish	*gið-ing-ür*	Gyðingur
Muslim	*mu-haa-meðs-tru-ahr*	Múhameðstrúar

Family

Are you married?
   ehrt-ü gift-ür/gift? — Ert þú giftur (m)/gift (f)?

I am single. I am married.
   yehgh ehr ayn-hlayp- — Ég er einhleypur (m)/
   ür/ayn-hlayp. — einhleyp (f).
   yehgh ehr gift-ür/gift — Ég er giftur (m)/gift (f).

How many children do you have?
   kvaað owt thu merg berdn? — Hvað átt þú mörg börn?

I don't have any children.
   yehgh ow ayn-gin berdn — Ég á engin börn.

Is your husband/wife here?
   ehr maað-ür-in thin/ — Er maðurinn þinn/konan þín
   kon-ahn theen hyehr? — hér?

Do you have a boyfriend/girlfriend?
   owt thu kair-ahs-dah/kair- — Átt þú kærasta/kærustu?
   üs-dü?

brother	*broh-ðir*	bróðir
children	*berdn*	börn
daughter	*doht-ir*	dóttir
family	*fyerl-skil-dah*	fjölskylda
father	*faað-ir*	faðir
grandfather	*aa-vi*	afi

ICELANDIC

grandmother	*aam-mah*	amma
husband	*ay-in-maað-ür*	eiginmaður
mother	*mohð-ir*	móðir
sister	*sist-ir*	systir
son	*son-ür*	sonur
wife	*ay-in-ko-nah*	eiginkona

Feelings

I (don't) like ...
    yehgh ehr (ehk-i) hri-vin   Ég er (ekki) hrifinn af ...
    av ...

I am ...
    myehr ehr ...   Mér er ...

cold/hot	*kahlt/hayt*	kalt/heitt
sleepy	*siv-yaað-ür*	syfjaður

I am ...
    yehgh ehr ...   Ég er ...

angry	*rayð-ür/rayð*	reiður (m)/reið (f)
grateful	*thahk-law-tür*	þakklátur (m)
	thahk-lowt	þakklát (f)
happy	*aw-naighð-ür*	ánægður (m)
	ow-naighð	ánægð(f)
hungry	*svown-gür*	svangur (m)
	sveüngh	svöng (f)
sad	*hrig-gür*	hryggur (m)
	hrig	hrygg (f)
tired	*thrayt-ür/thrayt*	þreyttur (m)
		þreytt (f)
well	*frees-gür*	frískur (m)
	freesk	frísk (f)

I am worried.
yehgh heaf ow-hig-yür

Ég hef áhyggjur.

I am sorry. (condolence)
myehr thik-ir layt

Mér þykir leitt.

Language Difficulties

Do you speak English?
taa-laar thu ean-skü?

Talar þú ensku?

Does anyone speak English?
taa-laar ayn-kvehr ean-skü?

Talar einhver ensku?

I speak a little Icelandic.
*yehgh taa-lah svo lit-lah
ees-lehn-skü*

Ég tala svolitla íslensku.

I don't speak ...
yehgh taa-lah ...

Ég tala ...

I (don't) understand.
yehgh skil ehk-i

Ég skil ekki.

Could you speak more slowly
please?
*gai-tir thu taa-lahð
svo-lee-tið haigh-ahr?*

Gætir þú talað svolítið
hægar?

Could you repeat that?
*gai-tir thu ean-dür-tehk-ið
theht-ah?*

Gætir þú endurtekið þetta?

How do you say ...?
*kvehr-nigh say-ir
maað-ür ...?*

Hvernig segir maður ...?

What does ... mean?
kvaað theeð-ir?

Hvað þýðir ...?

ICELANDIC

I speak ...
yehgh taa-lah ...   Ég tala ...

English	*ean-skü*	ensku
French	*frern-skü*	frönsku
German	*thees-kü*	þýsku
Italian	*ee-terl-skü*	ítölsku
Spanish	*spern-skü*	spönsku

Some Useful Phrases

Sure.
    viss-ü-leagh-ah   Vissulega.

Just a minute.
    Bee-dü aað-ayns   Bíddu aðeins.

Good luck!
    gown-gi theehr veahl   Gangi þér vel!

Signs

BAGGAGE COUNTER	FARANGUR
CHECK-IN COUNTER	INNRITUN
CUSTOMS	TOLLUR
EMERGENCY EXIT	NEYÐARÚTGANGUR
ENTRANCE	INNGANGUR or INN
EXIT	ÚTGANGUR or ÚT
FREE ADMISSION	ÓKEYPIS
HOT/COLD	HEITT/KALT
INFORMATION	UPPLÝSINGAR
NO ENTRY	AÐGANGUR BANNAÐUR
NO SMOKING	REYKINGAR BANNAÐAR
OPEN/CLOSED	OPIÐ/LOKAÐ

PROHIBITED	BANNAÐ
RESERVED	FRÁTEKIÐ
TELEPHONE	SÍMI
TOILETS	SNYRTING
LADIES/GENTLEMEN	KONUR/KARLAR

Emergencies

POLICE	LÖGREGLA
POLICE STATION	LÖGREGLUSTÖÐ

Help!
   hyowlp! — Hjálp!

There's been an accident!
   thaað hehf-ür orð-ið slis! — Það hefur orðið slys!

Call a doctor!
   now-ið ee laik-ni! — Náið í lækni!

Call an ambulance!
   now-ið ee syuk-rah beel! — Náið í sjúkrabíl!

I've been raped.
   myehr vaar neüð-gaað — Mér var nauðgað.

I've been robbed!
   yehgh vaar rain-dür/raind! — Ég var rændur (m)/rænd (f)!

Call the police!
   nowið ee lerg-rehgl-ün-ah! — Náið í lögregluna!

Where is the police station?
   kvaar ehr lergh-rehgh-lü-sterð-in? — Hvar er lögreglustöðin?

Go away!
   faar-ðü! — Farðu!

ICELANDIC

Thief!
thyoh-vür!　　　　　　　　Þjófur!

I am/My friend is ill.
yehgh ehr/vin-ür min ehr　　Ég er/vinur minn er veikur.
vay-kür

I am lost.
yehgh erh vilt- ür　　　　　Ég er villtur.

Where are the toilets?
kvaar ehr snirt-ingh-in?/　　Hvar er snyrtingin?/Hvar er
kvaar ehr kloh-seht-ið?　　　klósettið?

Could you help me please?
gai-tir thu hyowlp-ahð　　　Gætir þú hjálpað mér?
myehr?

Could I please use the
telephone?
gai-ti yehgh fayn-ghið ahð　　Gæti ég fengið að hringja?
hrin-gyah?

I'm sorry.
myehr thik-ir thaað layt　　　Mér þykir það leitt.

I didn't realise I was doing
anything wrong.
yehgh vi-si ehk-i ahð yehgh　　Ég vissi ekki að ég væri að
vai-ri ahð gea-rah row-nt　　　gera rangt.

I didn't do it.
yehgh gyer-ði thaað ehk-i　　　Ég gerði það ekki.

I wish to contact my
embassy/consulate.
yehgh vil haa-vah saam-　　　Ég vil hafa samband við
baand við sehndi-rowð　　　　sendiráð mitt/ræðismann
mit/raið-is-mahn min　　　　　minn.

I speak English.
yehgh taa-lah ean-skü Ég tala ensku.

I have medical insurance.
yehgh hehf syuk-raa-trigh-ing-ü Ég hef sjúkratryggingu.

My possessions are insured.
aygh-ür meen-aar ehr-ü trighð-ahr Eigur mínar eru tryggðar.

... was stolen.
... vaar sto-lið ... var stolið.

I've lost ...
yehgh teen-di Ég týndi ...

my bags	*ter-skü-nüm mee-nüm*	töskunum mínum
my handbag	*haand-tersk-ün-i mi-ni*	handtöskunni minni
my money	*pehn-ing-ün-üm mee-nüm*	peningunum mínum
my travellers' cheques	*ferð-aa-tye-kü-nüm mee-nüm*	ferðatékkunum mínum
my passport	*vehg-aa-breef-in-ü mee-nü*	vegabréfinu mínu

Paperwork

name	*nahbn*	nafn
address	*hay-mil-is-fowng*	heimilisfang
date of birth	*faið-ing-ahr-daagh-ür*	fæðingardagur
place of birth	*faið-ing-aar-staað-ür*	fæðingarstaður
age	*aald-ür*	aldur
sex	*kin*	kyn

nationality	*thyohð-ehr-ni*	þjóðerni
religion	*tru*	trú
reason for travel	*ow-staið-ah fehrð-ah-laaghs-ins*	ástæða ferðalagsins
profession	*aat-vin-ah*	atvinna
passport	*veagh-ah-bryehv*	vegabréf
passport number	*veagh-ah-bryehvs-nu-mehr*	vegabréfsnúmer
visa	*veagh-ah-bryehvs-ow-rit-ün*	vegabréfsáritun
tourist card	*fehrð-ah-mahn-ah-spyaald*	ferðamannaspjald
identification	*skil-ree-ki*	skilríki
birth certificate	*faið-ing-ahr-vot-orð*	fæðingarvottorð
driver's licence	*er-kü-skeer-tay-ni*	ökuskýrteini
car owner's title	*ayg-nahr-voth-orð*	eignarvottorð
car registration	*biv-rayð-ah-skoð-ün*	bifreiðaskoðun
customs	*todl-skoð-ü*	tollskoðun
immigration	*vehgh-ah-bryehvs-skoð-ün*	vegabréfsskoðun

Getting Around

ARRIVALS	KOMA
BUS STOP	BIÐSTÖÐ
DEPARTURES	BROTTFÖR
STATION	STÖÐ
TICKET OFFICE	MIÐASALA
TIMETABLE	TÍMAÁÆTLUN
TRAIN STATION	LESTARSTÖÐ

What time does ...
leave/arrive?

kveh-nayr....fehr/keh-mür		Hvenær .....fer/kemur?
the aeroplane	*flügh-vyehl-in*	flugvélin
the boat	*bow-tür-in*	báturinn
the bus	*vahgn-in*	vagninn (city bus)
the train	*lehst-in*	lestin
the tram	*spor-vahgn-in*	sporvagninn

Directions

Where is ...?
kvaar ehr ...?　　　　　　　hvar er ...?

How do I get to ...?
kvehr-nigh kehmst yehgh　　Hvernig kemst ég til ...?
til ...?

Is it far from/near here?
ehr thaað lowngt hyehð-　　Er það langt héðan?
ahn?

Can I walk there?
ehr thaað ee gern-gü fai-ri?　Er það í göngufæri?

Can you show me (on the map)?
geh-tür thu seent myer (ow　Getur þú sýnt mér (á
kort-in-ü)?　　　　　　　　kortinu)?

I want to go to ...
migh lown-gahr aað faa-　　Mig langar að fara til ...
rah til ...

Go straight ahead.
faar-ðü baynt aav eügh-üm　Farðu beint af augum.

It's two blocks down.
   thaað ehr tvaym-ür gert-üm   Það er tveimur götum neðar.
   nehð-ahr
Turn left ...
   baygh-ðü til vinst-ri ...   Beygðu til vinstri.
Turn right ...
   baygh-ðü til haigh-ri ...   Beygðu til hægri ...
at the next corner
   við nais-dah hordn   við næsta horn
at the traffic lights
   við üm-fehrð-aar-ljohs-in   við umferðarljósin

behind	*fir-ir ahft-ahn*	fyrir aftan
in front of	*fir-ir fraam-ahn*	fyrir framan
far	*lownght ee bür-dü*	langt í burtu
near	*now-laight*	nálægt
opposite	*ow moh-ti*	á móti

Buying Tickets

Where is the ticket office?
   kvaar ehr mið-ah-saal-ahn?   Hvar er miðasalan?
Where can I buy a ticket?
   kvaar geht yehgh kayft   Hvar get ég keypt miða?
   mið-ah?
I want to go to ...
   yehgh vil faa-rah til ...   Ég vil fara til ...
Do I need to book?
   thaarf yehgh aað pahn-tah?   Þarf ég að panta?
You need to book.
   thu thahrft aað pahn-tah   Þú þarft að panta.

I'd like to book a seat to ...
gai-ti yehgh pahn-tahð faar til ... Gæti ég pantað far til ...

I would like ...
gai-ti yehgh fayn-ghið ... Gæti ég fengid ...

a one-way ticket	*mið-ah, aað-rah layð-in-ah*	miða, aðra leiðina
a return ticket	*mið-ah, bowð-ahr layð-ir*	miða, báðar leiðir
two tickets	*tvo mið-ah*	tvo miða
tickets for all of us	*mið-ah fir-ir ok-ür erdl*	miða fyrir okkur öll
a student's fare	*nowms-mahn-ah-mið-ah*	námsmannamiða
1st class	*first-ah faar-reem-i*	fyrsta farrými
2nd class	*ahn-aað faar-reem-i*	annað farrými

It is full.
thaað ehr fült Það er fullt.

Is it completely full?
ehr aal-vehgh fült? Er alveg fullt?

Can I get a stand-by ticket?
gyeht yehgh fayn-gið for-fahd-lah-mið-ah? Get ég fengið forfallamiða?

Can I have a refund?
gyeht yehgh fayn-gið ehnd-ür-grayðs-lü? Get ég fengið endurgreiðslu?

Bus

BUS STOP	STRÆTISVAGN/BIÐSTÖÐ

ICELANDIC

Where is the bus stop?
kvaar ehr bið-sterð-in?   Hvar er biðstöðin?
Which bus goes to ...?
kvaað-ah vaaghn fehr til ...?   Hvaða vagn fer til ...?
Does this bus go to ...?
fehr theh-si vaagn til ...?   Fer þessi vagn til ...?
How often do buses pass by?
kvaað ko-mah vahgn-aar-   Hvað koma vagnarnir oft?
nir oft?
What time is the ... bus?
kveh-nair kehm-ür ... vaagn-in?   Hvenær kemur ... vagninn?

next	*naist*	næst
first	*first*	fyrst
last	*seeð-ahst*	síðast

Could you let me know when
we get to ...?
gai-tir thu lqw-tið migh
vi-tah thehgh-aar við   Gætir þú látið mig vita
kom-üm til ...   þegar við komum til ...?
I want to get off!
yehgh vil faa-rah ut ur!   Ég vil fara út úr!

Taxi
Please take me to ...
gai-tir thoo ekið myehr til ...   Gætir þú ekið mér til ...?
How much does it cost to go
to ...?
kvaað kost-ahr að faa-rah   Hvað kostar að fara til ...?
til ...?

Instructions

Here is fine, thank you.
   heehr-nah ehr ow-gait, tahk   Hérna er ágætt, takk.
The next corner, please.
   nais-tah hodn, tahk   Næsta horn, takk.
Continue.
   hahl-dü ow-frahm   Haltu áfram.
The next street to the left/right.
   nais-tah gaa-tah til   Næsta gata til vinstri/hægri.
   vinst-ri/haigh-ri
Stop here!
   staan-sah hyehr-nah!   Stansa hérna!

Car

GARAGE	VERKSTÆÐI
GIVE WAY	BIÐSKYLDA
MECHANIC	VÉLVIRKI
NO ENTRY	ALLUR AKSTUR
	BANNAÐUR
NO PARKING	ENGIN BÍLASTÆÐI
NORMAL	EÐLILEGT
ONE WAY	EINSTEFNA
REPAIRS	VIÐGERÐIR
SELF SERVICE	SJÁLFSAFGREIÐSLA
STOP	STANS
SUPER	SUPER
UNLEADED	BLÝLAUST

ICELANDIC

Where's the next petrol
station?
> *kvaar ehr nais-dah*
> *behn-seen-sterð?*

Hvar er næsta bensínstöð?

Please fill the tank.
> *gyer-ið svo vehl aað fid-lah*
> *town-kin*

Gjörið svo vel að fylla
tankinn.

I want ... litres of petrol (gas).
> *yehgh thaarf ... leet-rah aaf*
> *behn-seen-i*

Ég þarf ... lítra af bensíni.

Please check the oil and water.
> *gyer-ið svo vehl aað aat-*
> *hugh-ah o-lee-ü ogh vahtn*

Gjörið svo vel að athuga
olíu og vatn.

air (for tyres)	*loft (ee dehk)*	loft (í dekk)
battery	*raaf-gay-mir*	rafgeymir
brakes	*brehm-sür*	bremsur
clutch	*kup-leeng*	kúplíng
driver's licence	*er-kü-skeer-tay-ni*	ökuskírteini
engine	*vyehl*	vél
lights	*lyohs*	ljós
radiator	*vahss-kahss-i*	vatnskassi
road map	*vehgh-ah-kort*	vegakort
tyres	*dehk*	dekk
windscreen	*fraam-ruð-ah*	framrúða

Car Problems

The battery is flat.
> *gaym-ir-in ehr*
> *raav-mahgns-leüs*

Geymirinn er rafmagnslaus.

The radiator is leaking.
> *vahss-kahss-in leh-kür*

Vatnskassinn lekur.

I have a flat tyre.
thaað ehr sprun-ghið hyow myer
Það er sprungið hjá mér.

It's overheating.
hahn heh-vür of-hit-nað
Hann hefur ofhitnað.

It's not working.
hahn virk-ahr ehk-i
Hann virkar ekki.

Accommodation

CAMPING GROUND	TJALDSTÆÐI
GUESTHOUSE	GISTIHEIMILI
HOTEL	HÓTEL
MOTEL	GISTIHÚS
YOUTH HOSTEL	FARFUGLAHEIMILI

I am looking for ...
yehgh ehr aað lay-tah aað ...
Ég er að leita að ...

Where is a... hotel?
kvaar ehr ... ho-tehl?
Hvar er ... hótel?

cheap	*oh-deert*	ódýrt
nearby	*now-laight*	nálægt
clean	*hraynt*	hreint

What is the address?
kvaað ehr hay-mil-is-fown-gið?
Hvað er heimilisfangið?

ICELANDIC

Could you write the address, please?

gai-tir thu skrif-aað nið-ür hay-mil-is fown-gið?	Gætir þú skrifað niður heimilisfangid?

At the Hotel

Do you have any rooms available?

ehr-ü hehr-behr-ghi leüs?	Eru herbergi laus?

I would like ...

gai-ti yehgh fayn-ghið ...		Gæti ég fengid ...
a single room	*ayn-stahk-lings-hehr-behr-ghi*	einstaklingsher-bergi
a double room	*tveh-yaa-mahn-ah-hehr-behr-gi*	tveggjamannaher bergi
a room with a bathroom	*hehr-behr-ghi mehð baað-i*	herbergi með baði.
to share a dorm	*aað day-lah hehr-behr-ghi meað erð-rüm*	að deila herbergi með öðrum
a bed	*rum*	rúm

I'm going to stay for ...

yehgh vehrð ee ...		Ég verð í ...
one day	*aydn daagh*	einn dag
two days	*tvo daagh-ah*	tvo daga
one week	*ay-nah vi-kü*	eina viku

Do you have identification?

ehrt thu mehð skil-ree-ki?	Ert þú með skilríki?

Sorry, we're full.
meer thi-kir thaað layt,
thaað ehr füdl boh-kahð

Mé þykir það leitt, það er
fullbókað.

How long will you be staying?
kvaað ait-lahr thu aað
veh-ra layn-gi?

Kvað ætlar þú að vera lengi?

How many nights?
kvaað maar-gahr nai-tür?

Hvað margar nætur?

It's ... per day/per person.
thaað kost-ahr ... ow daagh
fir-ir mahn-in

Það kostar ... á dag fyrir
manninn.

How much is it per night/per
person?
kvaað kost-ahr noht-in
fir-ir mahn-in?

Hvað kostar nóttin fyirir
manninn?

Can I see it?
mow yehgh syow thaað?

Má ég sjá það?

Are there any others?
eh-rü nok-ür ern-ür?

Eru nokkur önnur?

Are there any cheaper rooms?
eh-rü nok-ür oh-deer-ah-ri
hehr-behr-gi?

Eru nokkur ódýrari
herbergi?

Can I see the bathroom?
mow yehgh syow baað-
hehr-behr-gið?

Má ég sjá herbergið?

Is there a reduction for
students/children?
ehr ahf-slowt-ür fir-ir
nowms-mehn/berdn?

Er afsláttur fyrir
námsmenn/börn?

Does it include breakfast?
ehr morgh-ün-maat-ür in-i-faal-in?
Er morgunmatur innifalinn?

It's fine, I'll take it.
thaað er ow-gait, yehgh fai thaað
Það er ágætt, ég fæ það.

I'm not sure how long I'm staying.
yehgh ehr ehk-i viss üm kvaað yehgh vehð layn-gi
Ég er ekki viss um hvað ég verð lengi.

Where is the bathroom?
kvaar ehr baað-hehr-behr-gið?
Hvar er baðherbergið?

Is there hot water all day?
ehr hayt vahtn ahd-lahn dai-in?
Er heitt vatn allan daginn?

May I leave these in your safe?
mow yehgh gay-mah theh-dah ee er-igh-is-hohl-vi?
Má ég geyma þetta í öryggishólfi?

Is there somewhere to wash clothes?
ehr ayn-kvehrs-staað-ahr haight aað thvo thvot?
Er einhversstaðar hægt að þvc þvott?

Can I use the kitchen?
mow yehgh no-tah ehld-hu-sið?
Má ég nota eldhúsið?

Can I use the telephone?
mow yehgh no-tah see-mahn?
Má ég nota símann?

Some Useful Words & Phrases

We are leaving now/tomorrow.

*við ehr-üm aað faa-rah
nu-nah/ow mor-gun*

Við erum að fara núna/á
morgum.

I would like to pay the bill.

*yehgh vil bor-ghah
raykn-ingh-in*

Ég vil borga reikninginn.

bathroom	*baað-hehr-behr-gi*	baðherbergi
bed	*rum*	rúm
bill	*raykn-ingh-ür*	reikningur
blanket	*teh-bi*	teppi
candle	*kehr-di*	kerti
clean	*hraydn*	hreinn
dirty	*ow-hraydn*	óhreinn
double bed	*tvee-brayt rum*	tvíbreitt rúm
electricity	*raav-mahgn*	rafmagn
excluded	*fir-ir üt-ahn*	fyrir utan
fan	*vif-dah*	vifta
included	*in-i-faal-ið*	innifalið
key	*li-kidl*	lykill
lift (elevator)	*lif-dah*	lyfta
light bulb	*lyow-sah-peh-rah*	ljósapera
lock (n)	*lows*	lás
mirror	*spay-idl*	spegill
pillow	*kod-di*	koddi
quiet	*hlyoht*	hljótt
sheet	*laak*	lak
shower	*stür-dah*	sturta
soap	*sow-pah*	sápa
toilet	*kloh-seht/saal-ehr-ni*	klósett/salerni

ICELANDIC

toilet paper	*klow-seht-pah-peer*	klósettpappír
towel	*haand-klai-ði*	handklæði
water	*vahtn*	vatn
cold water	*kahlt vahtn*	kalt vatn
hot water	*hayt vahtn*	heitt vatn
window	*ghlü-ghi*	gluggi

Around Town

I'm looking for ...
  yehgh ehr aað lay-tah aað ...   Ég er að leita að ...

a bank	*bown-kah*	banka
the city centre	*mið-bai-nüm*	miðbænum
the ... embassy	*sehn-di-row-ði-nü*	sendiráðinu
my hotel	*hoh-tehl-i-nü mee-nü*	hótelinu mínu
the market	*mahrk-aað-nüm*	markaðnum
the police	*lergh-rehgl-ü-ni*	lögreglunni
the post office	*pohst-hus-i-nü*	pósthúsinu
a public toilet	*aal-mehn-inghs-saal-ehr-ni*	almenningssalerni
the telephone centre	*seem-sterðin-i*	símstöðinni
the tourist information office	*üp-lees-een-gah-thjohn-üst-ü fir-ir fehrð-ah-fohlk*	upplýsingaþjónustu fyrir ferðafólk

What time does it open?
  kveh-nair ehr op-nahð?   Hvenær er opnað?
What time does it close?
  kveh-nair ehr lo-kahð?   Hvenær er lokað?

What street/suburb is this?
kvaað-ah gaa-tah/kvehr-vi ehr theh-dah?

Hvaða gata/hverfi er þetta?

For directions, see the Getting Around section, page 157.

At the Bank
I want to exchange some money/traveller's cheques.
yehgh thaarf aað skif-dah pehn-ingh-üm/fehrð-ah-tyehk-üm.

Ég þarf að skipta peningum/ferðatékkum.

What is the exchange rate?
kvehrt ehr skift-ah-hlüt-fahdl-ið?

Hvert er skiptahlutfallið?

How many kronas per dollar?
kvaað ehr-ü maar-gahr krohn-ür ee dol-ah-raa-nüm?

Hvað eru margar krónur í dollaranum?

bank notes	*sehð-lahr*	seðlar
cashier	*gyaald-kehr-i*	gjaldkeri
coins	*smow-mint*	smámynt
credit card	*grayð-slü-kort*	greiðslukort
exchange	*skif-dah*	skipta
loose change	*rayð-ü-fyeh*	reiðufé
signature	*ün-dir-skrift*	undirskrift

At the Post Office
I would like to send ...
yehgh ait-lah aað sehn-dah ...

Ég ætla að senda ...

a letter	*breef*	bréf
a postcard	*kort*	kort
a parcel	*pahk-ah*	pakka
a telegram	*skay-ti*	skeyti

I would like some stamps.
 yehgh aid-lah aað fow Ég ætla að fá nokkur
 nok-ür free-mehr-gi   frímerki.
How much is the postage?
 kvaað kos-dahr mi-kið Hvað kostar mikið undir
 ün-dir theh-dah   þetta?
How much does it cost to
send this to ...?
 kvaað kos-dahr aað sehn- Hvað kostar að senda þetta
 dah theh-dah til ...?   til ...?

an aerogram	*flügh-breef*	flugbréf
air mail	*flugh-pohst-ür*	flugpóstur
envelope	*üm-slaagh*	umslag
mail box	*pohst-kahss-i*	póstkassi
parcel	*pah-gi*	pakki
registered mail	*ow-birð-ahr-pohst-ür*	ábyrgðar póstur
surface mail/sea mail	*syoh-pohst-ür*	sjópóstur

Telephone

I want to ring ...
 yehgh thaarv aað hreen- Ég þarf að hringja ...
 gya ...
The number is ...
 nu-mehr-ið ehr ...   Númerið er ...

I want to speak for three minutes.

yehgh ait-lah aað taa-lah ee thryowr meen-ut-ür

Ég ætla að tala í þrjár mínútur.

How much does a three-minute call cost?

kvaað kos-dahr thri-ghjah-meen-ut-nah sahm-taal?

Hvað kostar þriggja mínútna samtal?

How much does each extra minute cost?

kvaað kos-dahr kvehr meen-u-tah?

Hvað kostar hver mínúta?

I would like to speak to Jón Pálsson.

gai-ti yehgh fayn-gið aað taalah við yohn powls-sohn

Gæti ég fengið að tala við Jón Pálsson?

I want to make a reverse-charges phone call.

yehgh ait-lah að hreen-ghyah ogh við-taak-ahn-di bor-gaar

Ég ætla að hringja og viðtakandi borgar.

It's engaged.

thaað ehr ow taa-li

Það er á tali.

I've been cut off.

thaað slit-naað-i

Það slitnaði.

Sightseeing

Do you have a guidebook/local map?

owt-ü fehrð-ah-haand-bohk/kort aav staað-nüm?

Áttu ferðahandbók/kort af staðnum?

What are the main attractions?
kvaað ehr mahrk-vehrt aað syow?
Hvað er markvert að sjá?

What is that?
kvaað ehr theh-dah?
Hvað er þetta?

How old is it?
kvaað ehr thaað gaam-ahlt?
Hvað er það gamalt?

Can I take photographs?
mow yehgh taa-kah mind-ir?
Má ég taka myndir?

What time does it open/close?
klük-ahn kvaað op-nahr/lok-ahr?
Klukkan hvað opnar/lokar?

In the Country
Weather

What's the weather like?
kvehr-nigh ehr vehð-rið?
Hvernig er veðrið?

The weather is ... today.
vehð-rið ehr ... ee daagh
Veðrið er ... í dag.

Will it be ... tomorrow?
thaað vehrð-ür ... ow mor-ghün
Það verður ... á morgun.

cloudy	*skee-ahð*	skýjað
cold	*kahlt*	kalt
hot	*hayt*	heitt
raining	*righ-ningh*	rigning
snowing	*snyoh-ahr*	snjóar
sunny	*sohl-skin*	sólskin
windy	*kvahst*	hvasst

Camping

Am I allowed to camp here?
mow yehgh tyaal-dah hyehr? — Má ég tjalda hér?

Is there a campsite nearby?
ehr tyaald-staið-i hyehr now-laight? — Er tjaldstæði hér nálægt?

backpack	*baak-po-ki*	bakpoki
can opener	*doh-sah-op-naa-ri*	dósaopnari
compass	*owt-ah-vi-ti*	áttaviti
firewood	*ehld-i-við-ür*	eldiviður
gas cartridge	*gaas-ku-tür*	gaskútur
mattress	*dee-nah*	dýna
penknife	*vaa-sah-hneev-ür*	vasahnífur
rope	*snai-ri*	snæri
tent	*tyaald*	tjald
tent pegs	*tyaald-hai-lahr*	tjaldhælar
torch (flashlight)	*vaa-sah-lyohs*	vasaljós
sleeping bag	*svehbn-po-ki*	svefnpoki
stove	*ehld-ah-veehl*	eldavél
water bottle	*vahs-flahs-ga*	vatnsflaska

Food

breakfast	*mor-gün-maa-tür*	morgunmatur
lunch	*how-day-is-maat-ür*	hádegismatur
dinner	*kverld-maat-ür*	kvöldmatur

Table for ..., please.
gyeht yehgh fayn-gið ..., mah-nah borð? — Get ég fengið ..., manna borð?

ICELANDIC

Can I see the menu please?
gyeht-yehgh fayn-gið aað
syow maat-sehð-il-in?

Get ég fengið að sjá matseðilinn?

I would like the set lunch, please.
gai-ti yehgh fayn-gið maat daagh-sins?

Gæti ég fengið mat dagsins?

What does it include?
kvaað ehr in-i-faal-ið?

Hvað er innifalið?

Is service included in the bill?
ehr thyoh-nüs-dah in-i-faal-in?

Er þjónusta innifalin?

Not too spicy please.
eh-ki of kri-dahð, tahk

Ekki of kryddað, takk.

ashtray	*ers-kü-bah-ghi*	öskubakki
the bill	*rayk-ningh-ür-in*	reikningurinn
a cup	*bod-li*	bolli
a drink	*drik-ür*	drykkur
a fork	*ghahf-adl*	gaffall
a glass	*ghlaas*	glas
a knife	*hnee-vür*	hnífur
a plate	*disk-ür*	diskur
a spoon	*skayð*	skeið
teaspoon	*teh-skayð*	teskeið

Vegetarian Meals

I am a vegetarian.
yehgh ehr grain-meht-is-ai-tah

Ég er grænmetisæta.

I don't eat meat.
yehgh bor-ðah ehk-i kyert

Ég borða ekki kjöt.

Staple Foods & Condiments

bread	*brauð*
butter	*smjör*
cheese	*ostur*
cream	*rjómi*
eggs	*egg*
fish	*fiskur*
fruit	*ávextir*
ham	*skinka*
honey	*hunang*
jam	*sulta*
ketchup	*tómatsósa*
lemon	*sítróna*
marmalade	*marmelaði*
meat	*kjöt*
milk	*mjólk*
mustard	*sinnep*
omelette	*eggjakaka*
pepper	*pipar*
potatos	*kartöflur*
rice	*hrísgrjón*
salad	*salat*
salt	*salt*
sandwich	*samloka*
sauce	*sósa*
sausage	*pylsa*
seasonings	*bragðefni*
sugar	*sykur*
vegetables	*grænmeti*
water	*vatn*

ICELANDIC

Meat & Poultry	Kjöt og Fuglar
beef	*nautakjöt*
chicken	*kjúklingur*
lamb	*lambakjöt*
pork	*svínakjöt*
reindeer	*hreindýrakjöt*
turkey	*kalkúnn*

Fish	Fiskur
cod	*þorskur*
haddock	*ýsa*
halibut	*lúða*
herring	*síld*
lobster	*humar*
salmon	*lax*
scallop	*hörpudiskur*
shrimp	*rækja*

Fruit	Ávextir
apples	*epli*
apricots	*apríkósur*
bananas	*bananar*
blueberries	*bláber*
crowberries	*kræikber*
grapes	*vínber*
oranges	*appelsínur*
peaches	*ferskjur*
pears	*perur*
pineapple	*ananas*
strawberries	*jarðaber*

ICELANDIC

Vegetables	**Grænmeti**
cabbage	*hvítkál*
cauliflower	*blómkál*
carrots	*gulrætir*
cucumber	*gúrka*
garlic	*hvítlaukur*
green peas	*grænar baunir*
green pepper	*græn paprika*
lettuce	*salat*
mushrooms	*sveppir*
onion	*laukur*
potatoes	*kartöflur*

Traditional Icelandic Food

Hangikjöt

Smoked lamb, leg or shoulder. Served hot or cold, with potatoes in béchamel sauce and green peas. Also popular as a luncheon meat.

Svið

Singed sheep heads. Eaten hot or cold, with either plain boiled potatoes, mashed potatos or swede turnips. The pressed and gelled variety is popular for packed lunches.

Saltkjöt

Salted lamb/mutton, served with potatoes or swede turnips and often accompanied by split pea soup.

Bjúgu

Smoked minced meat sausage. Served hot or cold with potatoes in white sauce.

Slátur

Blood and liver puddings. Prepared in the months of September and October, when slaughtering is at its peak. The blood pudding is called *Blóðmör* and the liver pudding *Lifrarpylsa*.

ICELANDIC

Eaten hot or cold, sliced. Traditionally, the *Slátur* that could not be eaten fresh, was pickled in whey and enjoyed throughout the winter months.

Harðfiskur

Dried fish; haddock, cod or catfish. It does not require cooking, but is enjoyed as snack food. Often spread with a little butter.

Skyr

A dairy product similar to yoghurt. It is very low in fat content. Eaten as dessert with sugar and milk and with fresh berries, when in season.

Seytt rúgbrauð

Cooked rye bread, moist and chewy. Popular with *Hangikjöt*.

Flatkökur

Rye pancakes, also popular with *Hangikjöt*.

Kjötsúpa

Soup, made of a small quantity of vegetables, large quantity of lamb meat and rice. Always served hot.

Methods of Cooking

baked	*bakað*
boiled	*soðið*
chopped	*saxað*
fried	*steikt*
grilled	*grillað*
jellied	*í hlaupi*
mashed	*stappað*
smoked	*reykt*
steamed	*gufusoðið*

Desserts — **Ábætir**

biscuits	*smákökur/kex*
cake	*kaka*
fruit	*ávextir*
ice cream	*ís/rjómaís*
pancakes	*pönnukökur*
pudding	*búðingur*
schocolate	*súkkulaði*
stewed fruit	*ávaxtagrautur*

Drinks – Nonalcoholic

coffee/white/black	*kaffi/með mjólk/svart*
fruit juice	*ávaxtasafi*
milk	*mjólk*
ice	*klaki*
soft drinks	*gosdrykkir*
tea	*te*
water	*vatn*

Drinks – Alcoholic

aqua vitae (brandy)	*brennivín*
beer	*bjór*
cognac	*koníak*
liqeur	*líkjör*
whisky	*whisky*
wine: red/white	*vín: rauðvín/hvítvín*

Shopping

general store, shop	*buð*	búð
laundry	*thvo-dah-hus*	þvottahús
market	*mahr-kaað-ür*	markaður

ICELANDIC

newsagency/ stationers	*blaa-ðaa-saa-lah/ boh-kah-buð*	blaðasala/bókabúð
pharmacy	*aap-oh-tehk*	apótek
supermarket	*stohr-mahr-kaað-ür*	stórmarkaður
vegetable shop	*grain-meht-is-buð*	grænmetisbúð

I would like to buy ...
migh lown-ghahr aað keü-pah ... Mig langar að kaupa ...

Can you write down the price?
gyeht-ür-ü skri-vaað nið-ür verðið Gætir þú skrifað niður verðið?

Toiletries

comb	*gray-ðah*	greiða
condoms	*smok-ahr*	smokkar
deodorant	*svi-tah-likt-ahr-ay-ðir*	svitalyktareyðir
razor	*raak-veehl*	rakvél
sanitary napkins	*der-mü-bin-di*	dömubindi
shampoo	*syaam-poh*	sjampó
shaving cream	*raak-krehm*	rakkrem
soap	*sow-pah*	sápa
tampons	*vaht-tahp-ahr/ tahm-poh-nahr*	vatttappar/ tampónar
tissues	*breehf-thür-kür*	bréfþurkur
toilet paper	*kloh-seht-pah-peer*	klósettpappír
toothbrush	*tahn-büs-di*	tannbursti
toothpaste	*tahn-krehm*	tannkrem

Stationery & Publications

map	*kort*	kort
newspaper	*daagh-blaað*	dagblað
newspaper in English	*dagh-blaað ow ean-skü*	dagblað á ensku
paper	*pah-peer*	pappír
pen (ballpoint)	*pehn-ni/ku-lü-pehn-ni*	penni/kúlupenni

Smoking

A packet of cigarettes, please.
aydn see-gaar-eh-dü-pahk-ah, tahk — Einn sígarettupakka, takk.

Do you have a light?
ow-dü ehld? — Áttu eld?

cigarette papers	*see-gaar-eh-dü-breehf*	sígarettubréf
cigarettes	*see-gaar-eh-dür*	sígarettur
filtered	*mehð see-ü/mehð feel-tehr*	með síu/með fílter
lighter	*kvay-kyah-ri*	kveikjari
matches	*ehld-speet-ür*	eldspýtur
menthol	*mehnt-ohl*	mentól
tobacco	*toh-baak*	tóbak

Colours

black	*svahrt*	svart
blue	*blowt*	blátt
brown	*brunt*	brúnt
green	*graint*	grænt
red	*reüt*	rautt
white	*kveet*	hvítt
yellow	*gült*	gult

ICELANDIC

Sizes & Comparisons

small	*lee-tið*	lítið
big	*stohrt*	stórt
heavy	*thunt*	þúngt
light	*lyeht*	létt
more	*may-rah*	meira
less	*mi-nah*	minna
too much/many	*ov mi-kið/maar-gir*	of mikið/margir

Health

Where is ...?
  kvaar ehr ...?   Hvar er?

a doctor	*laik-nir*	læknir
a hospital	*syuk-rah-hus*	sjúkrahús
a chemist	*aa-po-tehk*	apótek
a dentist	*tahn-laik-nir*	tannlæknir

Could I see a female doctor?
  gay-ti yehgh fayn-gið aað   Gæti ég fengið að tala við
  taa-lah við kvehn layk-ni?   kvenlækni?

What's the matter?
  kvaað ehr aað?   Hvað er að?

Where does it hurt?
  kvaar fin-ür thu til?   Hvar finnur þú til?

It hurts here.
  migh vehrk-yahr hyehr   Mig verkjar hér.

I have ...
  yehgh ehr mehð ...   Ég er með ...

Ailments

a cold	*kvehf*	kvef
constipation	*haarð-lee-vi*	harðlífi
diarrhoea	*nið-ür-gowng*	niðurgang
fever	*hi-tah*	hita
a headache	*her-vüð-vehrk*	höfuðverk
indigestion	*mehlt-ing-ahr-trüb-lün*	meltingartruflun
influenza	*flehn-sü*	flensu
low/high blood pressure	*low-ahn/how-ahn blohð-threest-ing*	lágan/háan blóðþrýsting
sore throat	*howls-bohl-gü*	hálsbólgu
sprain	*togh-nün*	tognun
a stomachache	*maagh-ah-vehrk*	magaverk
sunburn/I am sunburnt.	*sohl-brü-ni/yehgh ehr sohl-brün-in*	sólbruni/Ég er sólbrunninn.

Some Useful Words & Phrases

I'm ...
   yehgh ehr ... Ég er ...

diabetic	*sik-ür-syu-kür*	sykursjúkur
epileptic	*flogh-ah-vay-kür*	flogaveikur
asthmatic	*mehð ahs-mah*	með asma

I'm allergic to antibiotics/
penicillin.
   yehgh ehr mehð ov-nai-mi   Ég er með ofnæmi fyrir
   fir-ir fu-kah-liv-yüm/pehn-   fúkalyfjum/pensilíni.
   si-lee-ni
I'm pregnant.
   yehgh ehr thun-güð   Ég er þunguð

I have been vaccinated.
   yehgh fyehk oh-nai-mis-   Ég fékk ónæmissprautu.
   sprell-tü
I have my own syringe.
   yehgh ehr með mee-nah   Ég er með mína eigin
   ay-in sprell-tü   sprautu.
I feel better/worse.
   meehr leeð-ür beh-tür/vehr   Mér líður betur/verr.

antibiotics	*fu-kah-lif*	fúkalyf
antiseptic	*soht-hrayns-aandi*	sótthreinsandi
blood pressure	*blohð-threest-ing-ür*	blóðþrýstingur
blood test	*blohð-prüvah*	blóðprufa
contraceptive	*gyeht-naað-ahr-verdn*	getnaðarvörn
injection	*sprell-tah*	sprauta
medicine	*lif*	lyf
menstruation	*blaið-ing-ahr*	blæðingar
nausea	*oh-ghleh-ði*	ógleði
toothache	*tahn-pee-nah*	tannpína

At the Chemist

I need medication for ...
   yehgh thaarf lif við ...   Ég þarf lyf við ...
I have a prescription.
   yehgh ehr með lif-sehð-il   Ég er með lyfseðil.

Time & Dates

What date is it today?
   kvaað-ah daagh-ür ehr ee   Hvaða dagur er í dag?
   daagh?

What time is it?
kvaað er klük-ahn?   Hvað er klukkan?

It is ... am/pm.
hoon ehr ... fir-ir how-day-i/   Hún er ... fyrir hádegi/eftir
ehf-dir how-day-i   hádegi.

in the morning	*aað mo-dni*	að morgni
in the afternoon	*ehft-ir how-day-i*	eftir hádegi
in the evening	*aað kverl-di*	að kvöldi

Days of the Week

Monday	*mow-nü-daagh-ür*	mánudagur
Tuesday	*thrið-yü-daagh-ür*	þriðjudagur
Wednesday	*mið-vik-ü-daagh-ür*	miðvikudagur
Thursday	*fim-tü-daagh-ür*	fimmtudagur
Friday	*fers-dü-daagh-ür*	föstudagur
Saturday	*leügh-ah-daagh-ür*	laugardagur
Sunday	*sün-ü-daagh-ür*	sunnudagur

Months

January	*yaa-nu-ahr*	janúar
February	*fehb-ru-ahr*	febrúar
March	*mahrs*	mars
April	*aa-preel*	apríl
May	*mahee*	maí
June	*yu-nee*	júní
July	*yu-lee*	júlí
August	*ow-gust*	ágúst
September	*sehft-ehm-behr*	september
October	*okt-oh-behr*	október
November	*noh-vehm-behr*	nóvember
December	*dehs-ehm-behr*	desember

ICELANDIC

Seasons

summer	*sü-maar*	sumar
autumn	*heüst*	haust
winter	*veh-tür*	vetur
spring	*vor*	vor

Present

today	*ee daagh*	í dag
this morning	*ee mor-gün*	í morgun
tonight	*ee kverld*	í kvöld
this week	*thes-ah vi-kü*	þessa viku
this year	*theht-ah owr*	þetta ár
now	*nu-nah*	núna

Past

yesterday	*ee gair*	í gær
(two) days ago	*fir-ir tvay-mür*	fyrir tveimur
	dergh-üm	dögum

Future

tomorrow	*ow mor-gün*	á morgun
in (two) days	*ehf-dir tvo daag-ah*	eftir tvo daga

During the Day

afternoon	*ehf-dir how-day-i*	eftir hádegi
day	*daagh-ür*	dagur
midnight	*miðnait-i*	miðnætti
morning	*mor-gün*	morgun
night	*noht*	nótt
noon	*how-day-i*	hádaegi
sundown	*sohl-ahr-laagh*	sólarlag
sunrise	*sohl-ahr-üp-rows*	sólarupprás

ICELANDIC

Numbers & Amounts

0	*nul*	núll
1	*aydn*	einn
2	*tvayr*	tveir
3	*threer*	þrír
4	*fyoh-rir*	fjórir
5	*fimm*	fimm
6	*sehks*	sex
7	*syer*	sjö
8	*owt-dah*	átta
9	*nee-ü*	níu
10	*tee-ü*	tíu
20	*tü-tülgh-ü*	tuttugu
100	*ayt hün-drahð*	eitt hundrað
1000	*ayt thus-ünd*	eitt þúsund
one million	*ayn mil-yohn*	ein milljón
a little (amount)	*lee-tið*	lítið
few	*fow-ir*	fáir
more	*may-rah*	meira
some	*nok-rir*	nokkrir
too much	*ov mi-kið*	of mikið

Abbreviations

fyrsti	1st
annar	2nd
þriðji	3rd
eftir/fyrir Krist	AD/BC
áunnin ónæmisbæklun	AIDS
fyrir hádegi/eftir hádegi	am/pm
doktor	Dr

ICELANDIC

aðalpósthús	GPO
nafnskírteini	ID
Hr/Frú/Frk	Mr/Mrs/Ms
norður/suður	Nth/Sth
gata/vegur	St/Rd

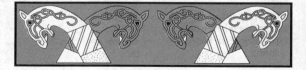

NORWEGIAN

Norwegian

Introduction

Norway has two official written language forms. They are quite alike, and every Norwegian learns both at school. Bokmål, literally 'book-language', hereafter referred to as BM, is the urban-Norwegian variety of Danish, the language of the former rulers of Norway. BM, also called Dano-Norwegian, has high prestige in some circles. It is written by more than 80% of the population, but not widely spoken. Nonetheless, many business people, officials and others do speak it.

The other written langage is Nynorsk, or 'New Norwegian' – as opposed to Old Norwegian, the language in Norway before 1500 AD, that is, before Danish rule. Nynorsk, hereafter referred to as NN, is a kind of common denominator of everyday speech in all its widely spoken dialects. It is therefore very appropriate for the traveller who wants to communicate with Norwegians all over the country, although it must be noted that NN is disliked by some members of society, especially class-conscious people. You may even come across those who claim that NN doesn't really exist!

In speech the distinction between BM and NN is no problem, since Norwegians understand either. Both are used in the media, although BM is predominant in the daily papers and is used exclusively in the gutter press. The towns and villages in the tourist areas, fjords and mountains have NN as their working written language, the cities often use BM. However, the Norwegian language situation is far more complicated than it looks from the sketch given above.

A striking feature of both written languages is that many words have two or more officially authorised forms of spelling in either language. One can choose according to one's speech or social aspirations. In many cases it is possible to choose spellings which are common to either language. Although many speak their Norwegian more or less as if it were a mingling of NN and BM, they generally frown upon a written rendering of this cocktail.

In the rural (and therefore mostly NN) areas you may come across people who hardly speak a word of English, and if you show an effort to speak their tongue, it will help a great deal to establish contact. Many Norwegians will answer you in English, as they are only too eager to show off their knowledge. It seems as if they generally feel ill at ease with the fact that they belong to a small language community.

Quite a few Norwegians, especially those engaged in commerce, like to make you believe that you are travelling in an English-speaking country. They give their shops, restaurants, companies and products English names, and use signs and billboards expressed in English. The fact that this English, let alone its spelling, sometimes makes little sense to the English speaker, doesn't appear to bother these people in the least.

Pronunciation
Vowels

Length, as a distinctive feature of vowels, is very important in the pronunciation of Norwegian. Almost every vowel has a (very) long and a (very) short counterpart, when appearing in a stressed syllable. Generally, it is long when followed by one consonant, and short when followed by two or more consonants.

A few words, mainly function words like pronouns and auxiliaries, are 'misspelt': the vowel is short in spite of the fact that it is followed by only one consonant.

Norwegian	Pronunciation Guide	Sound
a	*ah*	as in 'cut'
a long	*aa*	as in 'father'
å	*o*	as in British English 'pot'
å long	*or*	as in British English 'lord'
æ		has the same pronunciation as the first four varieties of **e**
e	*a*	before **r**, as in British English 'bat'
e long	*ā*	before **r**, as in British English 'bad'
e	*eh*	as in 'bet'
e long	*ē*	as in posh British 'day'; close to German *sehen*
e	*uh*	as the 'u' in 'lettuce', always unstressed
i	*ee*	like 'beat', but very short, as the French *si, il*
i long	*ēē*	as in 'seethe'
o	*u*	as in British 'pot'
o long	*oo*	like the American 'zoo', but more like the German *u* in *suchen*
o	*u*	as the 'u' in 'put'
o long	*or*	as in 'lord'
ø	*er*	as in German *zwölf* , or French *boeuf*
ø long	*ør*	as in British 'fern'
u	*ü*	as in French *sud*
u long	*üü*	like British 'soon', but more like German *süss*
y	*ȳ*	between French *sud* and *si*
y long	*ȳȳ*	between 'seethe' and German *süss*

Diphthongs

ai	*ai*	as in 'dive'
ei	*ay*	similar to Australian English 'day'
au	*ohw*	similar to Australian English 'shown'
øy	*öy*	as the French *eui* in *fauteuil*

Consonants & Semivowels

d   at the end of a word, or between two vowels, it is often silent

g   as in 'get', but before the letters or combinations **ei, i, j, øy**, and **y** it is, in most cases, pronounced like the 'y' in 'yard'. The combination **gn** is pronounced as the 'ng' of 'sing', followed by an 'n'.

h   like the 'h' in 'her', but before **v** and **j** it is silent

j   always like the 'y' in 'yard'

k   a hard sound as in 'kin', but before the letters or combinations **ei, i, j, øy**, and **y**, it is, in most words, pronounced as the 'ch' in 'chin'. In many areas though, these combinations are pronounced like the 'h' in 'huge', or like the German *ch* in the word *ich*.

l   pronounced thinly, as in 'list', except after the phonetic *ah, aa, o* and *or* sounds, when it becomes the 'l' sound of 'all'.

ng   in most areas, like the 'ng' sound in 'sing'

r   trilled, as in Spanish (rendered as *rr* in our pronunciation guide). In south-west Norway, however, the **r** is pronounced gutturally, as in French.

The combinations **rd, rl, rn, rt** sound a bit like American 'weird', 'earl', 'earn' and 'start', but with a much weaker 'r'. The resulting consonants are made with the tip of the tongue curled well behind the teeth, and the preceding vowel is lengthened. These consonants occur even when the **r** is the last letter of one word and the **d, l, n,** or **t** is the first letter of the next word. In some words, however, where the **d** in the combination **rd** is silent, the preceding vowel is often lengthened but the **r** trilled: for example, the word gard, meaning farm, is pronounced *gaarr*, not *gahrd*.

The combination **rs** is pronounced 'sh' as in 'fish'.

s always voiceless, like the 's' in 'us'. The combination **sk** followed by **ei, i, j, øy** and **y** is pronounced as 'sh': so the Norwegian word ski sounds like the English 'she'.

t like the English 't', except in two cases where it is silent: in the Norwegian word det (meaning 'it, that'), roughly pronounced like British English 'dare'; and in the definite singular ending -et of Norwegian neutral nouns

v is nearly always pronounced like the English 'w' but without rounding the lips – rather like a German speaker would pronounce a 'w'

Greetings & Civilities
Top Useful Phrases

Hello.
   gud-daag   Goddag.

Goodbye.
   mo-rnah   Morna.

Yes.
   yaa.   Ja.

No.
   nay   Nei.

Excuse me.
  ün-shȳl
    Unnskyld.

May I? Do you mind?
  *for-rr eh **lorv**? haa rdü*
  *nor-ko i-**moot** deh?*
    Får eg lov? Har du noko
    imot det? (NN)
  *for-rr yeh **lorv**? haa rdü*
  *noo-uh i-**moot** deh?*
    Får jeg lov? Har du noe
    imot det? (BM)

Sorry. (excuse me, forgive me)
  *ün-shȳl (ēg ä **rlay** fo rdē)*
    Unnskyld. (eg er lei for det)
    (NN)
  *om fo-**rlaa**-dl-suh*
    Om forlatelse. (BM)

Please.
  *vä sho **sneel***
    Ver så snill. (NN)
  *vä sho **sneel***
    Vær så snill. (BM)

Thank you.
  tahk
    Takk.

Many thanks.
  tüüsn tahk
    Tusen takk.

That's fine. You're welcome.
  eeng-ah or-shaak
    Inga årsak. (NN)
  eeng-uhn or-shaak
    Ingen årsak. (BM)

Greetings

Good morning.
  *gu **mo-rr**-gon*
    God morgon. (NN)
  *gu **mor**-rn*
    God morgen. (BM)

Good afternoon.
  *gud-**daag***
    Goddag.

Good evening/night.
  *gu **kveh-l**/gu **nah-t***
    God kveld./God natt.

NORWEGIAN

How are you?
   *ku-rleys **haa** rdü deh?*   Korleis har du det? (NN)
   *vu-rdahn **haa** rdü deh?*   Hvordan har du det? (BM)
Well, thanks.
   brraa tahk   Bra, takk.

Forms of Address

madam/Mrs	*gud **daag**/frrüü ...*	goddag/fru ...
sir/Mr	*gud **daag**/harr ...*	goddag/herr ...
Miss	*gud **daag**/düü/**frrēr-kuhn***	goddag/du/frøken
companion, friend (m)	*kah-mah-**rraat**, vehn*	kamerat, venn
companion, friend (f)	*vehn-**neen**-nuh*	venninne

Small Talk
Meeting People

What is your name?
   *kaa **hey**-tuh rdü?*   Kva heiter du? (NN)
   *vaa **hē**-tuh rdü?*   Hva heter du? (BM)
My name is ...
   *eh **hey**-tuhrr ...*   Eg heiter ... (NN)
   *ya **hē**-tuhrr ...*   Jeg heter ... (BM)
I'd like to introduce you to ...
   deh-tuh ārr ...   Dette er ...
I'm pleased to meet you.
   *hȳg-guh-leh o **trreh**-fuh dēg* hyggeleg å treffe deg. (NN)
   *hȳguh-lee o **trreh**-fuh day*   hyggelig å treffe deg (BM)

Nationalities

Where are you from?

kvaar ā rdü frror?		Kvar er du frå? (NN)
vurr ā rdü frraa?		Hvor er du fra? (BM)

I am from ...

ēg ārr frror ...		Eg er frå ... (NN)
ya ārr frrah ...		Jeg er fra ... (BM)

Australia	*ohw-**strraa**-lee-ah*	Australia
Canada	*kah-nah-dah*	Kanada
England	*ehng-lahn*	England
Ireland	*ēē-rlahn*	Irland
New Zealand	*nŷŷ sē-lahn*	Ny Zealand
Norway	*nor-rrehg/**norr**-guh*	Noreg/Norge (NN)
	norr-guh	Norge (BM)
Scotland	*skot-lahn*	Skottland
the USA	*sahm-bahn-staa-tah-nuh, üü-wehs-saa*	Sambandsstatane, USA (NN)
	dee forr-ēn-tuh staa-tuhrr, üü-wehs-saa	De Forente Stater, USA (BM)
Wales	*vehls*	Wales

Age

How old are you?

*kurr **gahm**-mahl ā rdüü?*		Kor gammal er du? (NN)
*vurr **gahm**-mahl ā rdüü?*		Hvor gammel er du? (BM)

I am ... years old.

ēg ārr ...		Eg er ... (NN)
ya ārr ...		Jeg er ... (BM)

Occupations

What (work) do you do?

kaa drrēēv dü mē? — Kva driv du med? (NN)

vaa drrēē-vuh rdü mē? — Hva driver du med? (BM)

I am a/an …

ēg ārr … — Eg er … (NN)

ya ārr … — Jeg er … (BM)

artist	*künst-nahrr*	kunstnar (NN)
	künst-nuhrr	kunstner (BM)
business man/woman	*fo-rreht-neengs-mahn/fo-rreht-neengs-kveen-nuh*	forretningsmann/ forettningskvinne
doctor	*lē-guh*	lege
engineer	*eensh-uhn-yēr-rr*	ingeniør
farmer	*gaarr-brrüü-kahrr*	gardbrukar (NN)
	gaarr-brrüü-kuhrr	gardbruker (BM)
journalist	*shü-rnah-leest*	journalist
lawyer	*yü-rreest*	jurist
manual worker	*ahrr-bay-ahrr*	arbeidar (NN)
	ahrr-bay-duhrr	arbeider (BM)
mechanic	*meh-kaa-nee-kahrr*	mekanikar (NN)
	meh-kaa-nee-kuhrr	mekaniker (BM)
nurse	*shüü-kuh-play-ahrr*	sjukepleiar (NN)
	shüü-kuh-play-uhrr	sjukepleier (BM)
office worker	*kun-too-rr-ahrr-bay-ahrr*	kontorarbeidar (NN)
	kun-too-rr-ahrr-bay-duhrr	kontorarbeider (BM)
scientist	*vēēt-skaaps-mahn*	vitskapsmann (NN)
	vēē-tuhn-skaaps-mahn	vitenskapsmann (BM)

student	*stü-deh-nt*	student
teacher	*lā-rrahrr*	lærar (NN)
	lā-rruhrr	lærer (BM)
waiter	*kehl-nuhrr/sehrr-vē-rreengs-daa-muh*	kelner/serveringsdame
writer	*fo-rr-faht-tahrr*	forfattar (NN)
	fo-rr-faht-tuhrr	forfatter (BM)

Religion

What is your religion?
| *kvaa ā deen reh-lee-gyoon?* | Kva er din religion? (NN) |
| *vaa ā deen reh-lee-gyoon?* | Hva er din religion? (BM) |

I am not religious.
| *ēg ārr eech-uh trüü-ahn-duh* | Eg er ikkje truande. (NN) |
| *ya ārr eek-kuh troo-uhn-nuh* | Jeg er ikke truende. (BM) |

I am ...
ēg ārr ...	Eg er ... (NN)
ya ārr ...	Jeg er ... (BM)
Buddhist	*büd-deest*	buddhist
Catholic	*kah-tolsk*	katolsk
Hindu	*heen-dü*	hindu
Jewish	*yēr-duh*	jøde
Muslim	*müs-leem*	muslim
Protestant	*prro-teh-stahnt*	protestant

Family

Are you married?
| *ā dü yeeft?* | Er du gift? |

I am single. I am married.
| *ēg ārr ayns-leh. ēg ārr yeeft* | Eg er einsleg. Eg er gift. (NN) |
| *ya ārr ēns-lee.ya ārr yeeft* | Jeg er enslig. Jeg er gift. (BM) |

NORWEGIAN

How many children do you have?

kurr mahng-uh bon haa rdü?
Kor mange born har du? (NN)

vurr mahng-uh baa-rn haa rdü?
Hvor mange barn har du? (BM)

I don't have any children.

eh hahch-uh nor-kon bon
Eg har ikkje nokon born. (NN)

ya hahk-kuh noon baa-rn
Jeg har ikke noen barn. (BM)

I have a daughter/a son.

eh haarr ay dot-tuhrr/ayn sorn
Eg har ei dotter/ein son. (NN)

ya haarr ay daht-tuhrr/ehn sern
Jeg har ei datter/en sønn. (BM)

How many brothers/sisters do you have?

kurr mahng-uh sȳsh-uhn haa rdü?
Kor mange sysken har du? (NN)

vurr mahng-uh sers-kuhn haa rdü?
Hvor mange søsken har du? (BM)

Is your husband/wife here?

ärr mahn-n deen härr/ärr kor-nah dee härr?
Er mannen din her?/Er kona di her? (NN)

ärr mahn-n deen härr/ärr koo-nah dee härr?
Er mannen din her?/Er kona di her? (BM)

Do you have a boyfriend/girlfriend?

haa rdü fahst fer-l-yuh?
Har du fast fylgje? (NN)

haa dü fahst fer-l-luh?
Har du fast følge? (BM)

brother	*brroorr*	bror
children	*baa-rn*	barn
daughter	*dot-tuhrr*	dotter (NN)
	daht-tuhrr	datter (BM)
family	*fah-mēē-lee-uh*	familie
father	*faarr*	far
grandfather	*behs-tuh-faarr*	bestefar
grandmother	*behs-tuh-moorr*	bestemor
husband	*mahn*	mann
mother	*moorr*	mor
sister	*sȳs-tuhrr*	syster (NN)
	ser-s-tuhrr	søster (BM)
son	*sor-n*	son (NN)
	ser-n	sønn (BM)
wife	*kor-nuh*	kone (NN)
	koo-nuh	kone (BM)

Feelings

I (don't) like …
eh lēē-kuhrr (eech-uh) …   Eg liker (ikkje) … (NN)
ya lēē-kuhrr (eek-uh) …   Jeg liker (ikke) … (BM)

I feel cold/hot.   *eh frrȳȳs/eh haa*   Eg frys./Eg har
   rdeh vahrrnt   det varmt. (NN)
   ya frrȳȳs-uhrr/ya   Jeg fryser./Jeg har
   haa rdeh vah-rnt   det varmt. (BM)

I am hungry/   *ēg ā svol-tuhn/*   Eg er svolten/
    thirsty.   *ter-sht*   tørst. (NN)
   ya ā shül-tuhn/   Jeg har sulten/
   ter-sht   tørst. (BM)

NORWEGIAN

I am in a hurry.	*eh haarr hahst-varrk*	Eg har hastverk. (NN)
	ya haarr hahst-varrk	Jeg har hastverk. (BM)
You are right.	*dü haa rreht*	Du har rett.
I am sleepy.	*ēg ā sher-v-nee*	Eg er søvnig. (NN)
	ya ā sher-v-nee	Jeg er søvnig. (BM)

I am ...		
ēg ārr ...		Eg er ... (NN)
ya ārr ...		Jeg er ... (BM)
angry	*seen-nah*	sinna
happy/sad	*lÿk-kuh-lee/nē-forr*	lykkelig/nedfor
tired	*trrer-t*	trøtt
well	*brraa*	bra
worried	*ü-rroo-leh*	uroleg (NN)
	ü-rroo-lee	urolig (BM)

I am sorry. (condolence)		
kon-du-lē-rruhrr		Kondolerer.
I am grateful.		
ēg ā tahk-sahm		Eg er takksam. (NN)
ya ā tahk-nehm-lee		Jeg er takknemlig. (BM)

Language Difficulties

Do you speak English?

| *snah-kah rdü ehng-uhlsk?* | Snakkar du engelsk? (NN) |
| *snah-kuh rdü ehng-uhlsk?* | Snakker du engelsk? (BM) |

Does anyone speak English?
  ā deh nor-kon som snah-kahrr **ehng**-*uhlsk harr?*
  ā deh noon som snah-kuhrr **ehng**-*uhlsk harr?*

Er det nokon som snakkar engelsk her? (NN)
Er det noen som snakker engelsk her? (BM)

I speak a little …
  eh snah-kahrr **leet** …
  ya snah-kuh **leet** …

Eg snakkar litt … (NN)
Jeg snakker litt … (BM)

I don't speak …
  eh snah-kahrr ee-chuh …
  ya snah-kuhrr eek-kuh …

Eg snakkar ikkje … (NN)
Jeg snakker ikke … (BM)

I (don't) understand.
  eh fosh-tor-rr (eechuh)
  ya fosh-tor-rr (eekuh)

Eg forstår (ikkje). (NN)
Jeg forstår (ikke). (BM)

Could you speak more slowly please?
  kahn dü snah-kuh **lahng**-*sah-mah-rruh?*
  kahn dü snah-kuh **lahng**-*som-muh-rruh?*

Kan du snakke langsamare? (NN)
Kan du snakke langsommere? (BM)

Could you repeat that?
  kahn dü **yehn**-*tah dē?*

Kan du gjenta det?

How do you say …?
  kvaa hay-tuhrr … por noshk?
  vaa hē-tuhrr … por noshk?

Kva heiter … på norsk? (NN)
Hva heter … på norsk? (BM)

What does … mean?
  kvaa buh-tȳȳrr …?
  vaa buh-tȳȳrr …?

Kva betyr …? (NN)
Hva betyr …? (BM)

I speak …
   eh snah-kahrr …   Eg snakkar … (NN)
   ya snah-kuhrr …   Jeg snakker … (BM)

English	*ehng-ehlsk*	engelsk
French	*frrahnsk*	fransk
German	*tÿsk*	tysk
Norwegian	*noshk*	norsk
Spanish	*spahnsk*	spansk

Some Useful Phrases

Sure.
   veest   Visst.
Just a minute.
   vehnt leet   Vent litt.
It's (not) important.
   deh ärr (eech-uh) veek-tee   Det er (ikkje) viktig. (NN)
   deh är (eek-uh) veek-tee   Det er (ikke) viktig. (BM)
It's (not) possible.
   deh är (eech-uh) mor-gleh   Det er (ikkje) mogleg. (NN)
   deh är (eek-uh) müü-lee   Det er (ikke) mulig. (BM)
Wait!
   vehnt!   Vent!
Good luck!
   lÿk-kuh teel!   Lykke til! (BM)

Signs

BAGGAGE COUNTER	REISEGODS
CHECK-IN COUNTER	BAGASJEINNLEVERING
CUSTOMS	TOLL
EMERGENCY EXIT	NØDUTGANG

ENTRANCE	INNGANG
EXIT	UTGANG
FREE ADMISSION	GRATIS TILGJENGE (NN)
	GRATIS ADGANG (BM)
HOT/COLD	VARM/KALD
INFORMATION	OPPLYSNINGAR (NN)
	OPPLYSNINGER (BM)
NO ENTRY	IKKJE TILGJENGE (NN)
	INGEN ADGANG (BM)
NO SMOKING	IKKJE RØYK (NN)
	RØYKING FORBUDT (BM)
OPEN/CLOSED	OPEN/STENGD (NN)
	ÅPEN/STENGT (BM)
PROHIBITED	FORBODE (NN)
	FORBUDT (BM)
RESERVED	RESERVERT
TELEPHONE	TELEFON
TOILETS	TOALETTAR (NN)
	TOALETTER (BM)

Emergencies

POLICE	POLITI
POLICE STATION	POLITISTASJON/ LENSMANNSKONTOR

Help!
  yehlp!   Hjelp!

NORWEGIAN

It's an emergency!
deht-tuh ārr eht ah-küt-teel-fehl-luh! — Dette er eit akutt-tilfelle! (NN)
deht-tuh ārr eht ah-küt-teel-fehl-luh! — Dette er et akutt-tilfelle! (BM)

There's been an accident!
deh haa shehd ay üü-lȳk-kuh! — Det har skjedd ei ulykke!

Call a doctor!
rreeng ehn lē-guh! — Ring ein lege!

Call an ambulance!
rreeng eht-tuhr ehn shüü-kuh-bēēl! — Ring etter ein sjukebil!

I've been raped.
ēg ārr vahl-tē-kuhn — Eg er valdteken. (NN)
ya ārr vol-taht — Jeg er voldtatt. (BM)

I've been robbed.
ēg ārr rraa-nah — Eg er rana. (NN)
ya ārr rraa-nah — Jeg er rana. (BM)

Call the police!
rreeng pu-lee-tēē-uh! — Ring politiet!

Where is the police station?
kvaarr ārr pu-lee-tēē-stah-shoon-n? — Kvar er politistasjonen? (NN)
vurr ārr pu-lee-tēē-stah-shoon-n? — Hvor er politistasjonen? (BM)

Go away!/Buzz off!
fo-shveen!/peeg-aav! — Forsvinn!/Pigg av!

I'll call the police!

eh *teel-kahl-lahr* pu-lee-*tēē*-uh!	Eg tilkallar politiet! (NN)
ya *teel-kahl-luhr* pu-lee-*tēē*-uh!	Jeg tilkaller politiet! (BM)

Thief!

chüüv!	Tjuv! (NN)
tÿÿv!	Tyv! (BM)

I am ill.

ēg ārr **shüük**	Eg er sjuk. (NN)
yay ā **shüük**	Jeg er sjuk. (BM)

I am lost.

ēg haarr got meh veel	Eg har gått meg vill. (NN)
ya haarr got meh veel	Jeg har gått meg vill. (BM)

Where are the toilets?

kvaarr ārr tuah-leht-tah-nuh?	Kvar er toalettane? (NN)
vurr ārr tuah-leht-tuh-nuh?	Hvor er toalettene? (BM)

Could you help me please?

kahn dü yehl-puh meh **kahn-shuh?**	Kan du hjelpe meg kanskje?

Could I please use the telephone?

kahn eh for lor-nuh t eh-leh-foon-n?	Kan eg få låne telefonen? (NN)
kahn ya for lor-nuh teh-leh-foon-n?	Kan jeg få låne telefonen? (BM)

I'm sorry.

ēg ā lay fo rdē	Eg er lei for det. (NN)
yay ā lay fo rdē	Jeg er lei for det. (BM)

I didn't realise I was doing anything wrong.

eh vaarr eech-uh klaarr or-vuhrr aht eh yoo-rruh nor-ko gaa-luh

Eg var ikkje klar over at eg gjorde noko gale. (NN)

ya vaarr eek-kuh klaarr or-vuhrr aht ya yoo-rruh noo-uh gaalt

Jeg var ikke klar over at jeg gjorde noe galt. (BM)

I didn't do it.

ēg haarr eech-uh yu-rt dē

Eg har ikkje gjort det. (NN)

ya haarr eek-kuh yu-rt dē

Jeg har ikke gjort det. (BM)

I wish to contact my embassy/consulate.

va-sho-sneel o laa meh for kon-tahk-tuh ahm-bah-saa-dn meen/kon-sü-laa-tuh meet

Ver så snill og la meg få kontakte ambassaden min/konsulatet mitt. (NN)

va-sho-sneel o laa meh for kon-tahk-tuh meen ahm-bah-saa-duh/meet kon-sü-laat

Vær så snill og la meg få kontakte min ambass-ade/mitt konsulat. (BM)

I speak English.

eh snah-kahrr ehng-uhlsk

Eg snakkar engelsk. (NN)

ya snah-kuhrr ehng-uhlsk

Jeg snakker engelsk. (BM)

I have medical insurance.

ēg haa shüü-kuh-fo-sheek-rreeng

Eg har sjukeforsikring. (NN)

ya haa shüü-kuh-fo-sheek-rreeng

Jeg har sjukeforsikring. (BM)

My possessions are insured.

ayg-nuh-lüüt-nuh mēē-nuh ārr ʃo-sheek-rra	Eignelutene mine er forsikra. (NN)
ay-uhn-dē-luh-nuh mēē-nuh ārr fo-sheek-rruht	Eiendelene mine er forsikret. (BM)

My ... was stolen.

... *meen ārr stor-luhn*	... min er stolen. (NN)
... *meen ārr styor-luht*	... min er stjålet. (BM)

I've lost ...

eh haarr mees-tah ...	Eg har mista ... (NN)
ya haarr mees-tah ...	Jeg har mista ... (BM)
my bags	*bah-gaa-shuhn meen*	bagasjen min
my handbag	*vehs-kah mēē*	veska mi
my money	*pehng-ah-nuh mēē-nuh*	pengane mine
my travellers' cheques	*rray-suh-shehk-kah-nuh mēē-nuh*	reisesjekkane mine
my passport	*pahs-suh meet*	passet mitt

Paperwork

name	*nahmn*	namn (NN)
	nahvn	navn (BM)
address	*ah-drreh-suh*	adresse
date of birth	*fer-t-suhls-daa-tu*	fødselsdato
place of birth	*fēr-duh-staa*	fødestad (NN)
	fēr-duh-stē	fødested (BM)
age	*ahl-duhrr*	alder
sex	*cher-n*	kjønn
nationality	*nah-shu-nah-lee-tēt*	nasjonalitet
religion	*rreh-lee-gyoon*	religion

reason for travel	*seek-tuh-mor-luh*	siktemålet med
	meh rray-sah	reisa (NN)
	hehn-seekt meh	hensikt med
	rray-sn	reisen (BM)
profession	*ȳrr-kuh*	yrke
marital status	*see-vēēl-stahn*	sivilstand
passport	*pahs*	pass
passport number	*pahs-num-muhrr*	passnummer
visa	*vēē-süm*	visum
tourist card	*tü-rreest-ku-rt*	turistkort
identification	*lē-gē-tee-mē-rreeng*	legetimering
birth certificate	*fer-ts-ls-aht-tehst*	fødselsattest
driver's licence	*fēr-rrahrr-kurrt*	førarkort (NN)
	fēr-rruhrr-ko-rt	førerkort (BM)
car owner's title	*vong-n-ko-rt*	vognkort
car registration	*chehn-nuh-taykn*	kjenneteikn (NN)
	chehn-nuh-tayn	kjennetegn (BM)
customs	*tol*	toll
immigration	*een-vahn-drreeng*	innvandring
border	*grrehn-suh*	grense

Getting Around

ARRIVALS	INNKOMST (NN)
	ANKOMST (BM)
BUS STOP	BUSSTOPP
DEPARTURES	AVGANG
STATION	STASJON
SUBWAY	T-BANE
TICKET OFFICE	BILETTKONTOR
TIMETABLE	RUTEPLAN
TRAIN STATION	JERNBANESTASJON

What time does ... leave/arrive?

kaa tēē gor-rr/cheh-m ...?	Kva tid går/kjem ...? (NN)	
norr gor-rr/kom-muhrr ...?	Når går/kommer ...? (BM)	
the (air)plane	*flȳȳ-yuh*	flyet
the boat	*bor-tn*	båten
the bus (citybus)	*büsn (bȳȳ-büsn)*	bussen (bybussen)
the bus (intercity)	*büsn (leen-yuh-büsn)*	bussen (linje-bussen)
the train	*tor-guh*	toget
the tram	*trreek-kuh-n*	trikken

Directions

Where is ...?

kurr ārr ...?	Kor er ...? (NN)
vurr ārr ...?	Hvor er ...? (BM)

How do I get to ...?

kurr-lays chehm ēg teel ...?	Korleis kjem eg til ...? (NN)
vu-rdahn kom-muhrr ya teel ...?	Hvordan kommer jeg til ...? (BM)

Is it far from/near here?

ā deh lahngt hārr-ee-frror?	Er det langt herifrå? (NN)
ā rdeh lahngt hārr-frrah?	Er det langt herfra? (BM)

Can I walk there?

kahn eh gor dēēt?	Kan eg gå dit? (NN)
kahn ya gor dēēt?	Kan jeg gå dit? (BM)

Can you show me (on the map)?

kahn dü vēē-suh mā (po kah-rtuh)?	Kan du vise meg (på kartet)?

NORWEGIAN

Are there other means of
getting there?

   ā rdeh ehn **ahn**-*nahn mor-*   Er det ein annan måte å
   tuh o kor-muh **dēēt** *po?*   kome dit på? (NN)
   ā rdeh ehn **aa**-*uhn mor-tuh*   Er det en annen måte å
   or kom-muh **dēēt** *po?*   komme dit på? (BM)

I want to go to …

   eh skahl teel …   Eg skal til … (NN)
   ya skahl teel …   Jeg skal til … (BM)

Go straight ahead.

   deh **ā** **rreht** *frrahm*   Det er rett fram.

It's two blocks down.

   deh **ā** *too kvah-rtaal*   Det er to kvartal vidare.
   vēē-ah-rruh   (NN)
   deh **ā** *too kvah-rtaal*   Det er to kvartal videre.
   vēē-duh-rruh   (BM)

Turn right …

   taa teel **hēr**-*grruh …*   Ta til høgre. (NN)
   taa teel **höy**-*rruh …*   Ta til høyre. (BM)

Turn left …

   taa teel vehns-trruh …   Ta til venstre …

at the next corner

   veh **nehs**-*tuh yēr-nuh*   ved neste hjørnet

at the traffic lights.

   veh **lȳȳs**-*krrȳs-suh*   ved lyskrysset

behind	*bak*	bak
in front of	*frrahm-fo-rr*	framfor
far	*lahngt*	langt
near	*närr*	nær
opposite	*or-vuhrr-fo-rr*	overfor

Buying Tickets

Excuse me, where is the ticket office?

*ün-shȳl **kurr** ärr bee-**leht**-lüü-kah?*	Unnskyld, kor er billettluka? (NN)
*ün-shȳl **vurr** ärr bee-**leht**-lüü-kah?*	Unnskyld, hvor er billettluka? (BM)

Where can I buy a ticket?

***kurr** kahn eh löysuh bee-**leht**?*	Kor kan eg løyse bilett? (NN)
***vurr** kahn ya lēr-suh bee-**leht**?*	Hvor kan jeg løse bilett? (BM)

I want to go to …

eh skahl teel …	Eg skal til … (NN)
ya skahl teel …	Jeg skal til … (BM)

Do I need to book?

*ä deh ner-d-**vehn**-dee o buh-**steel**-luh plahs?*	Er det nødvendig å bestille plass?

You need to book.

*dü **mor** buhsteel-luh plahs*	Du må bestille plass.

I would like to book a seat to …

*eh veel yā-rnuh buh-**steel**-luh see-chuh-plahs teel …*	Eg vil gjerne bestille sitje-plass til … (NN)
*ya veel yā-rnuh buh-**steel**-luh see-tuh-plahs teel …*	Jeg vil gjerne bestille sitte-plass til … (BM)

I would like …

eh veel yā-rnuh haa …	Eg vil gjerne ha … (NN)
ya veel yā-rnuh haa …	Jeg vil gjerne ha … (BM)

| a one-way ticket | *ehn-**kehlt**-bee-**leht*** | enkcltbillett |
| a return ticket | *tüü-rruh-**tüürr*** | tur-retur |

NORWEGIAN

two tickets	*too bee-leht-tahrr*	to billettar
tickets for all of us	*beeleh-tahrr teel os*	billettar til oss
a student's fare	*ahl-luh sah-mahn*	alle saman
	stü-dehnt-rah-baht	studentrabatt
a child's/pensioner's fare	*baa-rnuh-bee-leht/* *ho-nēr-rr-bee-leht*	barnebillett/honnør-billett
1st class	*fer-sh-tuh klahs-suh*	første klasse
2nd class	*ahn-drruh klahs-suh*	andre klasse
	aa-uhn klahs-suh	annen klasse (BM)

It is full.
  deh ärr fült   Det er fullt.
Is it completely full?
  ā deh haylt fült?   Er det heilt fullt?
Can I get a stand-by ticket?
  kahn eh for ehn shahn-suh-bee-leht?   Kan eg få ein sjansebillett? (NN)
  kahn ya for uhn shahn-suh-bee-leht?   Kan jeg få en sjansebilett? (BM)

Air

| CHECK-IN | INNSJEKKING |
| LUGGAGE PICKUP | BAGASJE |

Is there a flight to …?
  ā deh eht flÿÿ teel …?   Er det eit fly til …?
When is the next flight to …?
  no-rr ā nehs-tuh flÿÿ-yuh til …?   Når er neste flyet til …?

How long does the flight take?
  *kurr **lehng**-uh tēk*   Kor lenge tek flyginga?
  flȳȳ-yeeng-ah?   (NN)
  *vurr **lehng**-uh taarr*   Hvor lenge tar flyginga?
  flȳȳ-geeng-ah?   (BM)
What is the flight number?
  *kaa **ärr flait**-nu-muh-rruh?*   Kva er flightnummeret? (NN)
  *vaa **ärr flait**-nu-muh-rruh?*   Hva er flightnummeret? (BM)
You must check in at ...
  dü mor shehk-kuh een   Du må sjekke inn ved ...
  veh ...

airport tax	*lüft-hahmn-aa-yeeft*	lufthamnavgift (NN)
	lüft-hahvn-aav-yeeft	lufthavnavgift (BM)
boarding pass	*um-boo-rr-stēēg(n)eeng-sko-rt*	ombordstig(n)ings-kort
customs	*tol*	toll

Bus

BUS/TRAM STOP	BUSS/TRIKKHALDEPLASS (NN)
	BUSS/TRIKKHOLDEPLASS (BM)

NORWEGIAN

Where is the bus/tram stop?
  *kvaarr **ärr büs**/**trreek**-hahl-duh-plahsn?*   Kvar er buss/
                         trikkhaldeplassen? (NN)
  *vurr **ärr büs**/**trreek**-hol-luh-plahsn?*   Hvor er buss/
                         trikkholdeplassen? (BM)

Which bus goes to …?
   kvaa büs gor rteel …?   Kva buss går til …? (NN)
   veel-kuhn büs gor rteel …?   Hvilken buss går til …? (BM)
Does this bus go to …?
   gor rdehn-nuh büsn teel …?   Går denne bussen til …?
How often do buses pass by?
   kurr mahng-uh büs-sahrr   Kor mange bussar går det?
   gor-rdeh?   (NN)
   vurr mahng-uh büs-suhrr   Hvor mange busser går det?
   gor-rdeh?   (BM)

What time is the … bus?
   kaa tēē chehm … büsn?   Kva tid kjem …-bussen? (NN)
   no-rr kom-muhr … büsn?   Når kommer …-bussen? (BM)

next	*nehs-tuh*	neste
first	*fer-shtuh*	første
last	*sees-tuh*	siste

Train

DINING CAR	SPISEVOGN
EXPRESS	EKSPRESSTOG
PLATFORM NO	SPOR
SLEEPING CAR	SOVEVOGN

Is this the right platform
for …?
   ā rdeht-tuh rreht-tuh plaht-   Er dette rette plattforma for
   fo-rr-mah fo-rr tor-guh   toget til …?
   teel …?

The train leaves from
platform ...
   tor-guh gor-rr frror   Toget går frå spor ...
   spoorr ...

Passengers must ...
   rray-sahn-duh mor ...   Reisande må ... (NN)
   rray-suhn-duh mor ...   Reisende må ... (BM)

change trains	*bȳt-tuh **tor-g***	byte tog
change platforms	*gor teel spoorr* ...	gå til spor ...
dining car	*spēē-suh-vong-n*	spisevogn
express	*ehks-**prrehs**-tor-g*	ekspresstog
local	*lu-**kaal**-tor-g*	lokaltog
sleeping car/ couchette car	*sor-vuh-**vong-n**/ leeg-guh-**vong-n***	sovevogn/ligge-vogn

Metro

METRO/UNDERGROUND	T-BANE
CHANGE (for coins)	VEKSLING
THIS WAY TO	(DENNE VEGEN) TIL
WAY OUT	UTGANG

Which line takes me to ...?
   *kvaa **leen**-yuh/**baa**-nuh mor*
   eh taa teel ...?   Kva linje/bane må eg ta til
   *veel-kuhn **leen**-yuh/**baa**-* ...? (NN)
   nuh mor eh taa teel ...?   hvilken linje/bane må eg ta
                        til ...? (BM)Taxi
What is the next station?
   *kvaa ä **rnehs**-tuh*
   stah-shoon?   Kva er neste stasjon? (NN)
   *vaa ä **rnehs**-tuh*
   stah-shoon?   Hva er neste stasjon? (BM)

Taxi

Where can I get hold of a
taxi? (NN)
   *korr kahn eh for **taak** ee ay*   Kor kan eg få tak i ei
   drro-shuh?   drosje? (NN)
   ***vorr** kahn ya for **taak** ee ay*   Hvor kan jeg få tak i ei
   drro-shuh?   drosje? (BM)

Can you take me to …?
   *kahn dü **chēr-rruh** mā*   Kan du kjøre meg til …?
   teel …?

Please take me to …
   *veel dü **chēr-rruh** mā*   Vil du kjøre meg til …?
   teel …?

How much does it cost to go
to …?
   *korr **mȳch-uh** kos-tarr deh*   Kor mykje kostar det å
   o chy-rruh teel …?   køyre til …? (NN)
   *vorr **mȳȳ-yuh** kos-tuhrr deh*   Hvor mye koster det å kjøre
   *o **chēr-rruh** teel …?*   til …? (BM)

Instructions

Here is fine, thank you.
   *dü kahn **stop-puh** **hārr**, tahk*   Du kan stoppe her, takk.

The next corner, please.
   *kahn dü **stop-puh** veh*   Kan du stoppe ved neste
   ***nehs-tuh** yēr-rnuh*   hjørnet?

Continue!
   ***furt**-sheht bah-rruh!*   Fortsett bare!

The next street to the left/right.
   ***nehs**-tuh gaa-tah teel **vehn**-*   Neste gata til venstre/høgre.
   *strruh/**hēr**-grruh (höy-rruh)*   (BM: høyre)

Stop here!
  stop hãrr!   Stopp her!
Please slow down.
  *vã sho **sneel** o chöyrr leet*   Ver så snill og køyr litt
  ***lahng**-sah-mah-rruh*   langsamare. (NN)
  *vã sho **sneel** o chør-rr leet*   Vær så snill og kjør litt
  ***lahng**-som-muh-rruh*   langsommere. (BM)
Please wait here.
  *vãrr sor sneel o **vehn**-tuh*   Ver så snill å vente her. (NN)
  hãrr
  *vãrr sor sneel o **vehn**-tuh*   Vær så snill å vente her.
  hãrr   (BM)

Car

DETOUR	OMKJØRING
FREEWAY	MOTORVEG
GARAGE	GARASJE
GIVE WAY	VIKEPLIKT
MECHANIC	MEKANIKAR (NN)
	MEKANIKER (BM)
NO ENTRY	INNKJØRING FORBODE (NN)
	INNKJØRING FORBUDT (BM)
NO PARKING	PARKERING FORBODE (NN)
	PARKERING FORBUDT (BM)
NORMAL	NORMAL

ONE WAY	EINVEGSKØYRING (NN)
	ENVEISKJØRING (BM)
REPAIRS	BILVERSTAD (NN)
	BILVERKSTED (BM)
SELF SERVICE	SJØLVBETJENING (NN)
	SELVBETJENING (BM)
STOP	STOPP
SUPER	SUPER
UNLEADED	BLYFRI

Where can I rent a car?
   kurr kahn eh **lay**-guh ehn
   bēēl?
   vurr kahn ya **lay**-uh uhn
   bēēl?

Kor kan eg leige ein bil?
(NN)
Hvor kan jeg leie en bil?
(BM)

How much is it …?
   korr **mȳchuh** **kos**-tarr
   deh …?
   vorr **mȳȳȳuh** **kos**-tuhrr
   deh …?

Kor mykje kostar det …?
(NN)
Hvor mye koster det …?
(BM)

daily/weekly
   parr **daag**/**vē**-kuh
   parr **daag**/**üü**-kuh

pr. dag/veke (NN)
pr. dag/uke (BM)

Does that include insurance/
mileage?
   ärr deh **mē**-rehk-nah
   fo-**sheek**-reengofrrēē **chēry**-
   rruh-aa-stahn?
   ärrdeh **mē**-rehng-nah fo-
   sheek-reeng/frrēē **chēr**-
   rruh-aa-stahn?

Er det medrekna forsikring
og fri køyreavstand? (NN)

Er det medrekna forsikring
og fri kjøreavstand? (BM)

NORWEGIAN

Where's the next petrol
station?

   kurr ā narr-mahs-tuh behn-   Kor er nærmaste
   sēēn-stah-shoon-n?   bensinstasjonen? (NN)
   vurr ā rnarr-muhs-tuh   Hvor er nærmeste
   behn-sēēn-stah-shoon-n?   bensinstasjonen? (BM)

Please fill the tank.

   fül tahngk tahk   Full tank, takk.

I want … litres of petrol (gas).

   eh veel haa … lēē-tuhrr   Eg vil ha … liter bensin.
   ben-sēēn   (NN)
   ya veel haa … lēē-tuhrr   Jeg vil ha … liter bensin.
   ben-sēēn   (BM)

Please check the oil and water.

   kahn dü shehk-kuh ul-yuh   Kan du sjekke olje og vatn
   og vahtn/vahn?   (BM: vann)?

How long can I park here?

   kurr lehng-uh kan bēēl-n   Kor lenge kan bilen min stå
   meen stor hārr?   her? (NN)
   vurr lehng-uh kan bēēl-n   Hvor lenge kan bilen min
   meen stor hārr?   stå her? (BM)

Does this road lead to …?

   ā dehtuh vē-yuhn teel …?   Er dette vegen til …?

air (for tyres)	*lüft*	luft
battery	*baht-tuh-rrēē*	batteri
brakes	*brrehm-suhrr*	bremser
clutch	*kler-ch*	kløtsj
driver's licence	*fēr-rrahrr-ko-rt*	førarkort (NN)
	fēr-rruhrr-ko-rt	førerkort (BM)
engine	*moo-turr*	motor

NORWEGIAN

lights	*lȳk-tuhrr*	lykter
oil	*ul-yuh*	olje
puncture	*pung-tē-rreeng*	punktering
radiator	*rrahdee-yaa-turr*	radiator
road map	*kah-rt*	kart
tyres	*dehk*	dekk
windscreen	*frront-rrüü-tuh*	frontrute

Some Useful Phrases

The train is delayed/cancelled.

tor-guh ǟrr fo-sheeng-kah/een-steelt — Toget er forsinka/innstilt.

How long will it be delayed?

kurr mȳch-uh ä deh fo-sheeng-kah? — Kor mykje er det forseinka? (NN)

vurr mȳȳ-yuh ä deh fo-sheeng-kah? — Hvor mye er det forsinka? (BM)

There is a delay of ... hours.

tor-guh ǟrr ... tēē-mahrr ehtuhrr rüü-tuh — Toget er ... timar etter rute. (NN)

tor-guh ǟrr ... tēē-muhrr ehtuhrr rüü-tuh — Toget er ... timer etter rute. (BM)

Can I reserve a seat?

kahn eh buh-steel-luh plass? — Kan eg bestille plass? (NN)

kahn ya buh-steel-luh plass? — Kan jeg bestille plass? (BM)

How long does the trip take?

kurr lehng-uh tēk rray-sah? — Kor lenge tek reisa? (NN)

vurr lehng-uh taarr rray-sah? — Hvor lenge tar reisa? (BM)

Is it a direct route?

*ā deh eht dee-**rrehk**-tuh tor-g?* Er det eit direkte tog? (NN)

*ā deh eht dee-**rrehk**-tuh tor-g?* Er det et direkte tog? (BM)

Is that seat taken?

*ā **dehn**-nuh stoo-ln up-taht?* Er denne stolen opptatt?

I want to get off at ...

eh veel gor aav ee ... Eg vil gå av i ... (NN)

ya veel gor aav ee ... Jeg vil gå av i ... (BM)

Excuse me.

ün-shȳl Unnskyld.

Where can I hire a bicycle?

*kvaarr kahn eh for **lay**-guh ehn sȳk-kuhl?* Kvar kan eg få leige ein sykkel? (NN)

*vurr kahn ya **lay**-uh uhn sȳk-kuhl?* Hvor kan jeg leie en sykkel? (BM)

Car Problems

I need a mechanic.

*eh haarr **brrüük** fo-rr ayn beel-meh-kaa-nee-kahrr* Eg har bruk for ein bilmekanikar. (NN)

*ya haarr **brrüük** fo-rr uhn beel-meh-kaa-nee-kuhrr* Jeg har bruk for en bilmekaniker. (BM)

What make is it?

*kvaa fo-rr **marr**-kuh ā rdeh deh yehld?* Kva for merke er det det gjeld? (NN)

*veel-kuht **marr**-kuh ā rdeh?* Hvilket merke er det? (BM)

The battery is flat.

*baht-tuh-**rrēē**-uh ārr **flaht** Batteriet er flatt.

The radiator is leaking.

*rrah-dee-**aa**-too-rn ā rlehk* Radiatoren er lekk.

NORWEGIAN

I have a flat tyre.
   yüü-luh ärr pung-tē-rt   Hjulet er punktert.
It's overheating.
   moo-tu-rn koo-kahrr   Motoren kokar. (NN)
   mootu-rn koo-kuhrr   Motoren koker. (BM)
It's not working.
   deh füng-gē-rruhrr eech-uh   Det fungerer ikkje. (NN)
   deh füng-gē-rruhrr eek-kuh   Det fungerer ikke. (BM)

Accommodation

CAMPING GROUND	KAMPING/LEIRPLASS
GUESTHOUSE	GJESTGIVERI/
	PENSIONAT
HOTEL	HOTELL
YOUTH HOSTEL	VANDRERHJEM

I am looking for ...
   eh ärr por layt ehturr ...   Eg er på leit etter ... (NN)
   ya lay-tuhrr ehturr ...   Jeg leiter etter ... (BM)

Where is ...?
   kvaarr ärr ...?   Kvar er ...? (NN)
   vurr ärr ...?   Hvor er ...? (BM)

a cheap hotel	*eht beel-lee hu-tehl*	eit (BM et) billig hotell
a good hotel	*eht got hu-tehl*	eit godt hotell (NN)
	eht got hu-tehl	et godt hotell (BM)
a nearby hotel	*eht hu-tehl ee närr-laykuhn*	eit hotell i nærleiken (NN)
	eht hu-tehl ee närr-hētah	et hotell i nærheten (BM)

| a nice/quaint hotel | *eht koo-shleh/**gahm**-mahl-dahks hu-**tehl*** | eit koseleg/gam-maldags hotell (NN) |
| | *eht koo-shlee/**gahm**-mahl-dahks hu-**tehl*** | et koselig/gam-meldags hotell (BM) |

What is the address?
   *kvaa ārr ah-**drrehs**-ah?*   Kva er adressa? (NN)
   *vaa ārr ah-**drrehs**-ah?*   Hva er adressa? (BM)
Could you write the address, please?
   kahn dü vā-rruh so sneel o   Kan du vere (BM være) så
   *skrrēē-vuh up ah-**drrehs**-*   snill å skrive opp adressa?
   ah?

At the Hotel

Do you have any rooms available?
   *haa rdü lē-dee-uh **rrum**?*   Har du ledige rom?

I would like ...
   eh veel yā-nuh ...   Eg vil gjerne ... (NN)
   ya veel yā-rnuh ...   Jeg vil gjerne ... (BM)

a single room	*haa eht **ehng**-kuhlt-rrum*	ha eit enkeltrom
a double room	*haa eht **dob**-uhlt-rrum*	ha eit dobbeltrom
a room with a bathroom	*haa eht rrum meh **baad***	ha eit rom med bad
to share a dorm	*leeg-guh por sor-vuh-saa-luhn*	ligge på sovesalen

Do you have identification?
haa rdü lē-gee-tee-mah-shoon?   Har du legitimasjon?

Your membership card, please.
*mē-lehms-ko-rtuh deet **tahk***   Medlemskortet ditt, takk.

Sorry, we're full.
eh ā lay fo dē men deh ārr füll   Eg er lei for det men det er fullt. (NN)

buh-klaa-guhrr deh ārr fült   Beklager, det er fullt. (BM)

How long will you be staying?
*kurr **lehng**-yuh blēē-rr dü hārr?*   Kor lengje blir du her? (NN)

*vurr **lehng**-uh blēē-rr dü hārr?*   Hvor lenge blir du her? (BM)

How many nights?
*kurr mahng-uh **neht**-tuhr?*   Kor mange netter? (NN)

*vurr mahng-uh **neht**-tuhr?*   Hvor mange netter? (BM)

It's ... per day/per person.
deh ārr ... pa rdaag/parr pa-shoon   Det er ... pr. dag/pr. person.

There are four of us.
*vee ārr fēē-rruh **stÿk**-kuh (stÿk-kuhrr)*   Vi er fire stykke (BM: stykker).

I want a room with a ...
eh veel yā-nuh haa eht rrum meh ...   Eg vil gjerne ha eit rom med ... (NN)

ya veel yā-nuh haa uht rrum meh ...   Jeg vil gjerne ha et rom med ... (BM)

| bathroom | *baad* | bad |
| shower | *düsh* | dusj |

television	*fyā-rn-sȳȳn*	fjernsyn
window	*veen-dü*	vindauge (NN)
	veen-dü	vindu (BM)

I'm going to stay for ...

*eh haa **tehnkt** o blēē hārr ee ...*	Eg har tenkt å bli her i ... (NN)
*ya haa **tehnkt** o blēē hārr ee ...*	Jeg har tenkt å bli her i ... (BM)
one day	*ayn daag*	ein dag
two days	*too daa-gahrr*	to dagar
one week	*ay vē-kuh*	ei veke

How much is it per night/per person?

| *kurr **mȳch-uh** ā deh pa **rdaag**/parr pa-**shoon**?* | Kor mykje er det pr. dag/pr. person? (NN) |
| *vurr **mȳȳ-yuh** ā deh pa **rdaag**/parr pa-**shoon**?* | Vor mye er det pr. dag/pr. person? (BM) |

Can I see it?

| *kahn eh for **shor** deh?* | Kan eg få sjå det? (NN) |
| *kahn ya for se deh?* | Kan jeg få se det? (BM) |

Are there any others?

| *haa rdü **ahn**-drruh?* | Har du andre? |

Are there any cheaper rooms?

| *haa rdü **beel**-leh-gah-rruh rrum?* | Har du billegare rom? (NN) |
| *haa rdü **beel**-lee-uh-rruh rrum?* | Har du billigere rom? (BM) |

Can I see the bathroom?

| *kahn eh fo **shor** baa-duh?* | Kan eg få sjå badet? (NN) |
| *kahn eh fo se baa-duh?* | Kan eg få se badet? (BM) |

NORWEGIAN

Is there a reduction for
students/children?
   *yēē rdü stü-**dehnt**-rrah-*
   ***baht**/**baa**-rnuh-rrah-**baht**?*

Gir du studentrabatt/
barnerabatt?

Does it include breakfast?
   frrüü-kostn mē-rrehk-nah?
   *eenklÿ-sēēv-uh **frroo**-kostn?*

Frukosten medrekna? (NN)
Inklusive frokosten? (BM)

It's fine, I'll take it.
   brraa *eh tēk deh*
   brraa *ya taa rdeh*

Bra, eg tek det. (NN)
Bra, jeg tar det. (BM)

I'm not sure how long I'm
staying.
   eh vayt ēēch-uh kurr
   lehng-uh eh skah blēē
   vā-rrahn-duh hārr

Eg veit ikkje kor lenge eg
skal bli verande her. (NN)

   ya vayt ēēk-kuh vurr
   leh-ng-uh ya skah blēē
   vā-rruh-nuh hārr

Jeg veit ikke hvor lenge jeg
skal bli værende her. (BM)

Is there a lift?
   feens deh uhn hays hārr?
   feens deh uhn hays hārr?

Finst det ein heis her? (NN)
Fins det en heis her? (BM)

Where is the bathroom?
   *kurr ārr **baa**-duh?*
   *vurr ārr **baa**-duh?*

Kor er badet? (NN)
Hvor er badet? (BM)

Is there hot water all day?
   *ā deh **vahrrmt** vahtn*
   *der-ng-nuh **rrunt**?*
   *ā deh **vah-rnt** vahn*
   *döy-nuh **rrünt**?*

Er det varmt vatn døgnet
rundt? (NN)
Er det varmt vann døgnet
rundt? (BM)

Do you have a safe where I
can leave my valuables?

*haa rdü ehn **sayf** dārr eh
kan **lehg**-guh va-**rdēē**-saa-
kuh-nuh **mēē**-nuh?*

*haa rdü ehn **sayf** dārr ya
kan **lehg**-guh va-**rdēē**-saa-
kuh-nuh **mēē**-nuh?*

Har du ein safe der eg kan
leggje verdisakene mine?
(NN)

Har du en safe der jeg kan
legge verdisakene mine?
(BM)

Is there somewhere to wash
clothes?

*kahn eh vahs-kuh **klē**-ah
mēē-nuh **ehng**-kahn staan?*

*kahn ya vahs-kuh **klā**-rnuh
mēē-nuh noon-**stēts**?*

Kan eg vaske kleda mine
einkvan staden? (NN)

Kan jeg vaske klærne mine
noensteds? (BM)

Can I use the kitchen?

*ā rdeh **lor**-v o **brrüü**-kuh
cher-k-kuh-nuh?*

Er det lov å bruke
kjøkkenet?

Can I use the telephone?

*kahn eh for **lor**-nuh
tē-**lē**-**foon**-n?*

*kahn ya for **lor**-nuh
tē-**lē**-**foon**-n?*

Kan eg få låne telefonen?
(NN)

Kan jeg få låne telefonen?
(BM)

Requests & Complaints

Please wake me up at ...

*vā sho **sneel** o **vehch**-uh
meh ...*

*vā sho **sneel** o **vehk**-kuh
mā ...*

Ver så snill å vekkje meg ...
(NN)

Vær så snill å vekke meg ...
(BM)

NORWEGIAN

The room needs to be cleaned.
   *deht-tuh **rrum**-muh bĕrr-rr*
   *yă-rrahst **rraynt***
   *deht-tuh **rrum**-muh bĕrr-rr*
   *yĕr-rruhs **rraynt***

Dette rommet bør gjerast reint. (NN)

Dette rommet bør gjøres reint. (BM)

Please change the sheets.
   *vă sho sneel o **sheeft**-uh*
   ***sehng**-uh-töy*
   *vă sho sneel o **sheeft**-uh*
   ***sehng**-uh-töy*

Ver så snill å skifte sengetøy. (NN)

Vær så snill å skifte sengetøy. (BM)

I can't open/close the window.
   *eh **grray**-uhrr eech-uh or-p-nuh/**luk**-kuh veen-dü-uh*
   *ya **grray**-uhrr eek-kuh or-p-nuh/**luk**-kuh veen-dü-uh*

Eg greier ikkje opne/lukke vindauget. (NN)

Jeg greier ikke åpne/lukke vinduet. (BM)

I've locked myself out of my room.
   *eh haa **lor-st** meh üü-tuh aa **rrum**-muh meet*
   *ya haa **lor-st** mă üü-tuh aa **rrum**-muh meet*

Eg har låst meg ute av rommet mitt. (NN)

Jeg har låst meg ute av rommet mitt. (BM)

The toilet won't flush.
   *eh for-rr eech-uh spÿÿlt nĕ po tua-**leht**-tuh*
   *ya for-rr eek-kuh spÿÿlt nĕ po tua-**leht**-tuh*

Eg får ikkje spylt ned på toalettet. (NN)

Jeg får ikke spylt ned på toalettet. (BM)

I don't like this room.
   *eh **lēē**-kuhrr eechuh **deht**-tuh rrum-uh*
   *ya **lēē**-kuhrr eek-kuh **deht**-tuh rrum-uh*

Eg liker ikkje dette rommet. (NN)

Jeg liker ikke dette rommet. (BM)

It's too small.	*deh ărr fo lee-tuh*	Det er for lite.
It's noisy.	*deh ărr fo-rr mȳȳ-yuh brror-k*	Det er for mye bråk.
It's too dark.	*deh ărr fo-rr mer-rrt*	Det er for mørkt.
It's expensive.	*deh ă rdȳȳ-rt*	Det er dyrt.

Some Useful Phrases

I am leaving now/tomorrow.

| *eh rray-suhrr nor/ee-mo-rro* | Eg reiser ... nå/i morgon (NN) |
| *ya rray-suhrr nor/ee-mo-rro* | Jeg reiser ... nå/i morgon (BM) |

I would like to pay the bill.

| *kahn eh for rrehk-neeng-ah tahk?* | Kan eg få rekninga, takk? (NN) |
| *kahn ya for rrehng-neeng-ah tahk?* | Kan jeg få rekninga, takk? (BM) |

name	*nahmn*	namn (NN)
	nahvn	navn (BM)
surname	*eht-tuh-nahmn*	etternamn (NN)
	eht-tuh-nahvn	etternavn (BM)
room number	*rrum-num-muhrr*	romnummer

Some Useful Words

address	*ah-drrehs-suh*	adresse
air-conditioning	*klēē-mah-ahn-lehg*	klimaanlegg
balcony	*bahl-kong*	balkong
bathroom	*baad*	bad
bed	*sehng*	seng
bill	*rrehk-neeng*	rekning (NN)
	rrehng-neeng/rray-neeng	rekning/regning (BM)
blanket	*tehp-puh*	teppe

candle	*steh-ah-**rrēēn**-lȳȳs*	stearinlys
chair	*stool*	stol
clean	*rrayn*	rein
cupboard	*skaap*	skap
dark	*mer-rrk*	mørk
dirty	***sheet**-n*	skitten
double bed	***dob**-buhlt-sehng*	dobbeltseng
electricity	*strrohw-m*	straum (NN)
	strrer-m	strøm (BM)
excluded	*ehks-klü-**sēēv***	eksklusiv
fan	*veef-tuh*	vifte
included	*eeng-klü-**dē-rt***	inkludert
key	***ner-k**-kuhl*	nøkkel
lift (elevator)	*hays*	heis
light bulb	*lȳȳs-pā-rruh*	lyspære
lock (n)	*lor-s*	lås
mattress	*mah-**drrahs***	madrass
mirror	*spē-guhl*	spegel (NN)
	spayl	speil (BM)
padlock	***hehng**-uh-lor-s*	hengelås
pillow	***püü**-tuh*	pute
quiet	***steel**-luh*	stille
room (in hotel)	*rrum*	rom
	*vā-**rruhl**-suh*	værelse (BM)
sheet	*laa-kuhn*	laken
shower	*düsh*	dusj
soap	*sor-puh*	såpe
suitcase	*kuf-fuh-rt*	koffert
swimming pool	*sȳm-yuh-hahl*	symjehall (NN)
(indoor)	*sver-m-muh-hahl*	svømmehall (BM)
table	*boo-rr*	bord

NORWEGIAN

toilet	*toa-**leht***	toalett
toilet paper	*doo-pah-**pēē**-rr*	dopapir
towel	*hahng-kluh*	handkle (NN)
	hong-kluh	håndkle (BM)
water	*vaht-n*	vatn
	vahn	vann (BM)
cold water	*kahlt vahtn*	kaldt vatn
	kahlt vahn	kaldt vann (BM)
hot water	*vah-rnt vahtn*	varmt vatn (NN)
	vah-rnt vahn	varmt vann (BM)
window	*veen-dohw-uh*	vindauge (NN)
	veen-dü	vindu (BM)

Around Town

I'm looking for ...

| *eh **lay**-tuhrr eht-tuhrr ...* | Eg leiter etter ... (NN) |
| *ya **lay**-tuhrr eht-tuhrr ...* | Jeg leiter etter ... (BM) |

the art gallery	*künst-gahl-luh-**rēē**-uh*	kunstgalleriet
a bank	*bahng-kuhn*	banken
the church	*chÿrr-chah*	kyrkja (NN)
	cheerr-kah	kirka (BM)
the city centre	*sehn-**trrüm***	sentrum
the ... embassy	*den ... ahm-bahs-saa-duh*	den ... ambassade
my hotel	*hutehl-luh meet*	hotellet mitt
the market	*to-**rr**-guh*	torget
the museum	*mü-**sē**-uh*	museet
the police	*pu-lee-**tee**-uh*	politiet
the post office	*post-kun-**too**-rruh*	postkontoret

a public toilet	*eht of-fuhntleh*	eit offentleg
	toa-leht	toalett (NN)
	eht of-fuhntlee	et offentlig toalett
	toa-leht	(BM)
the telephone centre	*tē-luh-varr-kuh*	televerket
the tourist information office	*tü-rreest-een-fo-rr-mah-shoon*	turistinformasjon

What time does it open?
   kaa tēē ärr ahn up-puh?   Kva tid er han oppe? (NN)
   no-rr ä rdehn up-puh?   Når er den oppe? (BM)
What time does it close?
   kaa tēē stehng-uhrr ahn?   Kva tid stenger han? (NN)
   no-rr stehng-uh rdehn?   Når stenger den? (BM)

What ... is this?
   kvaa fo-rr ... ä dē?   Kva for ... er det? (NN)
   veelkuhn ... ä rdē?   Hvilken ... er det? (BM)

| street | *gaa-tuh* | gate |
| suburb | *fo-rr-staad* | forstad |

For directions, see the Getting Around section, page 211.

At the Bank

I want to exchange some
money/traveller's cheques.

*eh veel **yā**-rnuh **vehks**-luh
pehng-ahrr/**hē**-vuh nok-
rruh **rra**-ysuh-shehk-kahrr*

Eg vil gjerne veksle pengar/
heve nokre reisesjekkar.
(NN)

*ya veel **yā**-rnuh **vehks**-luh
pehng-uhrr/**hē**-vuh noon
rray-suh-shehk-kuhrr*

Jeg vil gjerne veksle
penger/heve noen reisesjek-
ker. (BM)

What is the exchange rate?

*kvaa **ārr** vah-**lüü**-tah-kü-
shuhn?*

Kva er valutakursen? (NN)

*vaa **ārr** vah-**lüü**-tah-kü-
shuhn?*

Hva er valutakursen? (BM)

How many Norwegian kroner
per dollar?

*kurr **mahng**-uh krroo-
nuhrr fo-rr **ayn** dol-**lahrr**?*

Kor mange kroner for ein
dollar? (NN)

*vurr **mahng**-uh krroo-
nuhrr fo-rr **ēn** dol-lahrr?*

Hvor mange kroner for en
dollar? (BM)

Can I have money transferred
here from my bank?

*kahn eh for or-vuhrr-**fēr**-rt
pehng-ahrr **hēēt** frror
bahng-kuhn meen?*

Kan eg få overført pengar
hit frå banken min? (NN)

*kahn ya for or-vuhrr-**fēr**-rt
pehng-uhrr **hēēt** frraa
bahng-kuhn meen?*

Kan jeg få overført penger
hit fra banken min? (BM)

How long will it take to
arrive?

*kurr **lehng**-yuh veel deh **taa**?*	Kor lenge vil det ta? (NN)	
*vurr **lehng**-uh veel deh **taa**?*	Hvor lenge vil det ta? (BM)	

Has my money arrived yet?

*haarr **pehng**-ah-nuh mēē-nu kor-muh noo?*	Har pengane mine kome no? (NN)
*haarr **pehng**-uh-nuh mēē-nuh **kom**-muht nor?*	Har pengene mine kommet nå? (BM)

bank draft	***vehk**-sl/rreh-**mees**-suh*	veksel/remisse
bank notes	***pehng**-uh-seht-lahrr*	pengesetlar (NN)
	***pehng**-uh-sehd-luhrr*	pengesedler (BM)
cashier	*kah-**sē**-rrahrr*	kasserar (NN)
	*kah-**sē**-rruhrr*	kasserer (BM)
coins	*m**ȳn**-tahrr*	myntar (NN)
	*m**ȳn**-tuhrr*	mynter (BM)
credit card	*krreh-**deet**-ko-rt*	kredittkort
exchange	***vehk**-sleeng*	veksling
loose change	***vehk**-sluh-pehng-ahrr*	vekslepengar (NN)
	***vehk**-sluh-pehng-uhrr*	vekslepenger (BM)
signature	*ün-nuhrr-skrree^et*	underskrift

At the Post Office

I would like to send

*eh veel **sehn**-duh …*	Eg vil sende … (NN)	
*ya skah **sehn**-nuh …*	Jeg skal sende … (BM)	
a letter	*eht **brrēv***	eit brev (NN)
	*eht **brrēv***	et brev (BM)
a postcard	*eht **post**-ku-rt*	eit postkort (NN)
	*eht **post**-ku-rt*	et postkort (BM)

a parcel	*ay **pahk**-kuh*	ei pakke
a telegram	*eht tē-luh-**grrahm***	eit telegram (NN)
	*eht tē-luh-**grrahm***	et telegram (BM)

I would like some stamps.
*eh veel yā-rnuh **haa** nok-*
*rruh **frrēē**-marr-kuh*
Eg vil gjerne ha nokre
frimerke. (NN)
*ya veel yā-rnuh **haa** noon*
***frrēē**-marr-kuh*
Jeg vil gjerne ha noen
frimerker. (BM)

How much does is it to send
this to …?
*kurr **mӯch**-uh kos-tahrr deh*
*o **sehn**-duh dēh-tuh til …?*
Kor mykje kostar det å
sende dette til …? (NN)
*vurr **mӯӯ**-yuh kos-tuhrr deh*
*o **sehn**-nuh dēh-tuh til …?*
Hvor mye koster det å
sende dette til …? (BM)

an aerogram	*eht aa-ē-rru-**grrahm***	eit aerogram (NN)
	*eht aa-ē-rru-**grrahm***	et aerogram (BM)
air mail	*lüft-post*	luftpost
envelope	*kon-vu-**lüt***	konvolutt
mail box	*post-kahs-suh*	postkasse
parcel	*pahk-kuh*	pakke
registered mail	*rreh-kom-mahn-**dē-rt** post*	rekommandert post
surface mail	*or-vuhrr-flaa-tuh-post*	overflatepost

Telephone

I want to ring …
*eh veel **rreeng**-yuh teel …*
Eg vil ringje til … (NN)
*ya veel **rreeng**-uh teel …*
Jeg vil ringe til … (BM)

The number is ...
> *num-muh-rruh ärr ...*   Nummeret er ...

I want to speak for three minutes.
> *eh veel **snahk**-kuh ee **trrē** mee-nüt*   Eg vil snakke i tre minutt. (NN)
>
> *ya veel **snahk**-kuh ee **trrē** mee-nüt-tuhrr*   Jeg vil snakke i tre minutter. (BM)

How much does a three-minute call cost?
> *kurr **mӯch**-uh kos-tahrr ehn **trrē** mee-**nüts sahm**-taa-luh?*   Kor mykje kostar ein tre minutts samtale? (NN)
>
> *vurr **mӯӯ**-yuh kos-tuhrr ehn **trē** mee-nüt-tuhsh **sahm**-taaluh?*   Hvor mye koster et tre minutters samtale? (BM)

How much does each extra minute cost?
> *kurr **mӯch**-uh kos-tahrr **kvah-rt** ehks-trrah mee-nüt?*   Kor mykje kostar kvart ekstra minutt? (NN)
>
> *vurr **mӯӯ**-yuh kos-tuhrr va-**rt** ehks-trrah mee-nüt?*   Hvor mye koster hvert ekstra minutt? (BM)

I would like to speak to Mr Sælen.
> *eh skül-luh **yā**-rnuh for **snahk**-kuh mē harr **sē**-luhn*   Eg skulle gjerne få snakke med herr Sælen. (NN)
>
> *ya skül-luh **yā**-rnuh for **snahk**-kuh mē harr **sē**-luhn*   Jeg skulle gjerne få snakke med herr Sælen. (BM)

I want to make a reverse-
charges phone call.

*eh veel **teeng-**uh ehn **sahm**-
taa-luh meh noo-tē-rreengs-
or-vuhrr-fēr-rreeng*
Eg vil tinge ein samtale
med noteringsoverføring.
(NN)

*ya veel buh-**steel**-luh ehn
sahm-taa-luh meh noo-tē-
rreengs-or-vuhrr-fēr-rreeng*
Jeg vil bestille en samtale
med noteringsoverøfring.
(BM)

It's engaged.

*deh ārr **upp**-taht*
Det er opptatt.

I've been cut off.

*sahm-taa-luhn blay
brror-tuhn*
Samtalen blei broten. (NN)

*sahm-taa-luhn blay **brrüt***
Samtalen ble brutt. (BM)

Sightseeing

Do you have a guidebook/
local map?

*haa rdü ehn **gaid**/eht om-
rror-duh-kah-rt?*
Har du ein guide/eit
områdekart? (NN)

*haa rdü ehn **gaid**/eht om-
rror-duh-kah-rt?*
Har du en guide/et
områdekart? (BM)

What are the main attractions?

*kvaa ā rday veek-tee-ahs-
tuh aht-trrahk-shoo-nah-
nuh?*
Kva er dei viktigaste
attraksjonane? (NN)

*vaa ā rdee veek-tee-stuh sē-
varr-dee-hē-tuhr?*
Hva er de viktigste
severdigheter? (BM)

What is that?

kvaa ā rdē?
Kva er det? (NN)

vaa ā rdē?
Hva er det? (BM)

NORWEGIAN

How old is it?
  kurr gahm-mahlt ā rdeh?   Kor gammalt er det? (NN)
  vurr gahm-muhlt ā rdeh?   Hvor gammelt er det? (BM)
Can I take photographs?
  for-rr eh taa bēē-lētuh?   Får eg ta bilete? (NN)
  for-rr ya taa beel-duhrr?   Får jeg ta bilder? (BM)
What time does it open/close?
  kaa tēē or-p-nahrr deh?   Kva tid opnar det? (NN)
  no-rr or-p-nuhrr deh?   Når åpner det? (BM)

ancient	*gahm-mahl*	gammal
beach	*strrahn*	strand
castle	*shlot*	slott
cathedral	*kah-teh-drraal*	katedral
church	*chȳrr-chuh*	kyrkje (NN)
	cheerr-kuh	kirke (BM)
concert hall	*kon-sa-rt-hüüs*	konserthus
library	*bee-blee-yu-tēk*	bibliotek
main square	*(stoo-rr)-to-rrguh*	(stor)torget
market	*to-rr-guh*	torget
monastery	*klos-turr*	kloster
monument	*hees-too-rreesk bȳg-neeng*	historisk bygning
mosque	*mos-kē*	moskē
old town	*gahm-mahl bȳȳ*	gammal by
	gahm-muhl bȳȳ	gammel by (BM)
the old city	*gahm-luh-bȳȳ-yuhn*	gamlebyen
opera house	*oo-puh-rrah-hüüs*	operahus
palace	*shlot*	slott
ruins	*rrü-ēē-nahrr*	ruinar (NN)
	rrü-ēē-nuhrr	ruiner (BM)

NORWEGIAN

stadium	*staa-dee-on*	stadion
statues	*bee-lēt-ster-tuh*	biletstøtte (NN)
	beel-luhd-ster-tuhrr	billedstøtter (BM)
synagogue	*sȳ-nah-goo-guh*	synagoge
temple	*hor-v/tehm-puhl*	hov/tempel
university	*ü-nee-va-shee-tēt*	universitet

Entertainment

What's there to do in the evenings?

> *kvaa kahn ayn yā-rruh um kvehl-n?*

Kva kan ein gjere om kvelden? (NN)

> *vaa kahn mahn yēr-rruh om kvehl-n?*

Hva kan man gjøre om kvelden? (BM)

Are there any discos?

> *ā rdeh nor-kon dees-ku-tēk?*

Er det nokon diskotek? (NN)

> *ā rdeh noon dees-ku-tēk-uhrr?*

Er det noen diskoteker? (BM)

Are there places where you can hear local folk music?

> *ā rdeh nor-kon staarr dārr ayn kahn höy-rruh po noshk fol-kuh-mü-seek?*

Er det nokon stader der ein kan høyre på norsk folkemusikk? (NN)

> *ā rdeh noo-uhn stē-duhrr dārr ehn kahn her-rruh po noshk fol-kuh-mü-seek?*

Er det noen steder der en kan høre på norsk folkemusikk? (BM)

How much does it cost to get in?

> *kurr mȳch-uh kostahrr deh fo-rr o kor-muh een?*

Kor mykje kostar det for å kome inn? (NN)

> *vurr mȳȳ-yuh kostuhrr deh fo-rr o ko-muh een?*

Hvor mye koster det for å komme inn? (BM)

NORWEGIAN

cinema	**chēē-nu**	kino
concert	**kon-sa-rt**	konsert
discotheque	**dees-ku-tēk**	diskotek
theatre	**tē-aa-tuhrr**	teater

In the Country
Weather

What's the weather like?
   kaa ārr **vārr**-mehl-leeng-ah? — Kva er vermeldinga? (NN)
   vaa ārr **vārr**-mehl-leeng-ah? — Hva er værmeldinga? (BM)

The weather is today.
   vā-rruh ārr ... ee-**daag** — Veret er ... i dag. (NN)
   vā-rruh ārr ... ee-**daag** — Været er ... i dag. (BM)
Will it be ... tomorrow?
   va-rt deh ... ee-**mo-rr**-go? — Vert det ... i morgon? (NN)
   blēē rdeh ... ee-**mo-rn**? — Blir det ... i morgen? (BM)

cloudy	**or**-vuh-shȳȳ-yah	overskya
cold	**kahlt**	kaldt
foggy	**tor**-kuh	tåke
frosty	**frrost**-vā-rr	frostvêr (NN)
	frrost-vā-rr	frostvær (BM)
hot	**vah**-rrmt	varmt (NN)
	vah-rnt	varmt (BM)
raining	**rrehng**-n	regn
	rrayn	regn (BM)
snowing	**snør**	snø

sunny	*mỹ-chuh **sool***	mykje sol (NN)
	*mỹỹ-yuh **sool***	mye sol (BM)
windy	*mỹ-chuh **veen***	mykje vind (NN)
	*mỹỹ-yuh **veen***	mye vind (BM)

Camping

Am I allowed to camp here?
(tent)

> *for-rr eh **lorv** teel o **shlor**
> up **tehl**-tuh meet härr?*
> Får eg lov til å slå opp teltet
> mitt her? (NN)
> *for-rr ya **lorv** teel o **shlor**
> op **tehl**-tuh meet härr?*
> Får jeg lov til å slå opp
> teltet mitt her? (BM)

Is there a campsite nearby?

> *feenst deh ehn **kam**-peeng
> ee **närr**-lay-kuhn?*
> Finst det ein camping i
> nærleiken? (NN)
> *feens deh ehn **kam**-peeng
> ee **närr**-ē-tuhn?*
> Finst det ein camping i
> nærheten? (BM)

backpack	*rrỹg-sehk*	ryggsekk
can opener	*boks-or-**pnahrr***	boksopnar (NN)
	*boks-or-**pnuhrr***	boksåpner (BM)
compass	*kom-**pahs***	kompass
crampons	*brrod-dahr*	broddar (NN)
	brrod-duhr	brodder (BM)
firewood	*vē*	ved
gas cartridge	*prru-paan-buh-**hahl**-dahrr*	propanbehaldar (NN)
	*prru-paan-buh-**hol**-luhrr*	propanbeholder (BM)
ice axe	*ēēs-er-ks*	isøks
mattress	*mah-**drrahs***	madrass

penknife	*lum-muh-knēēv*	lommekniv
rope	*tohw*	tau
tent	*tehlt*	telt
tent pegs	*tehlt-plüg-gahrr*	teltpluggar (NN)
	tehlt-plüg-guhrr	teltplugger (BM)
torch (flashlight)	*lum-muh-lȳkt*	lommelykt
sleeping bag	*sor-vuh-poo-suh*	sovepose
stove	*koo-kuh-ahp-pah-rraat*	kokeapparat
water bottle	*vahss-flahs-kuh*	vassflaske (NN)
	vahn-flahs-kuh	vannflaske (BM)

Food

breakfast	*frrüü-kost*	frukost (NN)
	frroo-kost	frokost (BM)
lunch	*ler-nsh*	lunsj
dinner	*meed-daag*	middag

Table for ..., please.
   eht boo-rr teel ..., tahk   Eit bord til ..., takk.

Can I see the menu please?
   kahn eh for meh-nȳȳ-yuhn, tahk   Kan eg få menyen, takk. (NN)
   kahn ya for meh-nȳȳ-yuhn, tahk   Kan jeg få menyen, takk. (BM)

I would like today's special, please.
   eh veel yá-rnuh haa daa-guhns rreht, takk   Eg vil gjerne ha dagens rett, takk. (NN)
   ya veel yá-rnuh haa daa-guhns rreht, takk   Jeg vil gjerne ha dagens rett, takk. (BM)

What does it include?

*kvaa um-**faht**-tah rdē?*	Kva omfattar det? (NN)
*vaa om-**faht**-tuh rdē?*	Hva omfatter det? (BM)

Is service included in the bill?

*árr buh-**va**-**rt**-neeng-ah*	Er bevertninga medrekna?
mē-rrek-nah?	(NN)
*árr buh-**va**-**rt**-neeng-ah*	Er bevertninga iberegnet?
ēē-buh-rray-nuht?	(BM)

Not too spicy please.

*eech-uh fo **shtarrt***	Ikkje for sterkt krydra, takk.
krrüd-drrah tahk	(NN)
*eek-kuh fo **shtarrt***	Ikke for sterkt krydra, takk.
krrüd-drrah tahk	(BM)

ashtray	*os-kuh-bē-guhrr*	oskebeger (NN)
	ahs-kuh-bē-guhrr	askebeger (BM)
the bill	*rrehk-neeng-ah*	rekninga (NN)
	rray-neeng-uhn	regningen (BM)
a cup	*ehn kop*	ein kopp (NN)
	uhn kop	en kopp (BM)
dessert	*deh-sárr*	dessert
a drink	*ehn drreengk*	ein drink (NN)
	uhn drreengk	en drink (BM)
a fork	*ehn gahf-fuhl*	ein gaffel (NN)
	uhn gahf-fuhl	en gaffel (BM)
fresh	*fashk*	fersk
a glass	*eht glaas*	eit glas (NN)
	uht glahs	et glass (BM)
a knife	*ehn knēēv*	ein kniv (NN)
	uhn knēēv	en kniv (BM)

NORWEGIAN

a plate	*ehn **tahl**-larrk*	ein tallerk (NN)
	*uhn **tahl**-larr-kuhn*	en tallerken (BM)
spicy	*starrkt (**krrȳd**-rrah)*	sterkt (krydra)
a spoon	*ay **shay***	ei skei
	*ay **shē***	ei skje (BM)
stale	*dor-vuhnt*	dovent
starter	*fo-rr-reht*	forrett
sweet	*sēr-t*	søt
teaspoon	*tē-shay*	teskei
	tē-shē	teskje (BM)
toothpick	***tahn**-peerr-kahrr*	tannpirkar (NN)
	***tahn**-peerr-kuhrr*	tannpirker (BM)

Vegetarian Meals

I am a vegetarian.

ēg árr veh-geh-tah-rree-aa-nahrr Eg er vegetarianar. (NN)

ya árr veh-geh-tah-rree-aa-nuhrr Jeg er vegetarianer. (BM)

I don't eat meat.

*ēg **ēt** eech-uh **cher-t*** Eg et ikkje kjøt. (NN)

*ya **spee**-suhrr eek-kuh **cher-t*** Jeg spiser ikke kjøtt. (BM)

I don't eat chicken, fish, or ham.

*ēg **ēt korr**-chuh **chȳl**-leeng, ehl-luhrr **feesk** ,ehl-luh **sheeng**-kuh* Eg et korkje kylling, eller fisk, eller skinke. (NN)

*ya **spēē**-suhrr **varr**-kuhn **chül**-leeng ehl-luhrr **feesk** ehl-luh **sheeng**-kuh* Jeg spiser verken kylling eller fisk eller skinke. (BM)

Breakfasts & Breads

koldtbord	buffet of cold dishes (fish, meat, cheese, salad and a sweet)
rømmegraut	boiled sour cream porridge with cinnamon and sugar
sildesalat	salad with slices of herring, cucumber, onions, etc
brød	bread, loaf
flatbrød	thin wafer of rye/barley
fleskepølse	pork sandwich spread
frokost, frukost	breakfast

biscuit	*kjeks*
brown bread	*grovbrød*
crisp-bread	*knekkebrød*
cured ham	*spekeskinke*
food on top of a sandwich, like cold cuts	*pålegg*
honey	*honning*
jam	*syltetøy*
oatmeal biscuits	*havrekjeks*
oatmeal porridge	*havregraut*
open sandwich	*smørbrød*
peanut butter	*peanøttsmør*
porridge, cereal	*graut, grøt*
roll	*rundstykke*
rusk	*kavring*
slice	*skive*
thin pancake	*lefse*
white bread	*loff*
wholemeal bread	*heilkornbrød*

Potatoes & Staples

mashed potatoes	*potetmos*
potato chips	*pommes frites*
potato dumplings	*raspeballar, kumle*
potato pancake	*lompe, lumpe*
rice	*ris*

Dairy Products

gammalost	semi-hard brown cheese with strong flavour
geitost	sweet brown goat cheese
gudbrands dalsost	cheese similar to *geitost*
mysost	brown whey cheese
normannaost	Danish Blue
pultost	soft fermented cheese, often with caraway seeds
riddarost	Munster cheese
remuladesaus	cream mayonnaise with chopped gherkins and parsley

butter	*smør*
cheese	*ost*
cream	*fløyte, fløte*
cream cheese	*fløyteost*
sour cream	*rømme*
whipped cream	*krem, piska krem*

Eggs

fried egg (sunny side up)	*speilegg*
hard-boiled	*hardkokt*
scrambled eggs	*eggerøre forlorent*
soft-boiled	*blautkokt, bløtkokt*

NORWEGIAN

Soups & Mixed Dishes

dagens rett	today's special
fårikål	lamb in cabbage stew
gryte(rett)	casserole
italiensk salat	salad of diced cold meat, potatoes, apples and vegetables in mayonnaise
lapskaus	thick stew of diced meat, potatoes, onions and other vegetables
koldtbord	buffet of cold dishes (fish, meat, cheese, salad and a sweet)
pyttipanne	chunks of meat and potatoes, fried with onions, etc
suppe	soup
surkål	boiled cabbage flavoured with caraway seeds, sugar and vinegar

Meat

bankebiff	slices/chunks of beef simmered in gravy
beinlause fuglar, benløse fugler	rolled slices of veal stuffed with minced meat
blodpudding	black pudding
bris, brissel	sweetbread
dyresteik	roast venison
elgsteik	roast elk
fena(d)lår	cured leg of lamb
fleskepannekake	thick pancake with bacon, baked in the oven
fyll	stuffing, forcemeat
fårikål	lamb in cabbage stew
kålrulettar	minced meat in cabbage leaves
kalvetunge	calf's tongue

NORWEGIAN

kjøttdeig	minced meat
kjøttkake	small hamburger steak
kjøttpålegg	cold cuts
kjøttpudding	meat loaf
lam(mebog)	(shoulder of) lamb
lever(postei)	liver (pâté)
lungemos	hash of pork lungs and onions
medaljong	small round fillet
medisterkake	pork hamburger steak
okserull	rolled stuffed beef, cold
pai	pie
pinnekjøtt	salted and fried lamb ribs
postei	meat pie
sauesteik	leg of lamb
skive	slice
smalehovud	roast head of lamb
spekemat, spike-mat	cured meat (lamb, beef, pork, reindeer, often served with scrambled eggs)
spekepølse	air-dried sausage
syltelabb	boiled, salt-cured pig's trotter

beef	*oksekjøtt*
fillet of beef	*oksefilet*
game	*vilt*
ham	*skinke*
kid	*geitekilling*
kidney	*nyre*
lamb/mutton	*sauekjøtt*
meat	*kjøtt*
meatball	*kjøttbolle*
pork	*svinekjøtt*

pork chop	*svinekotelett*
roast beef	*oksesteik*
roast pork	*svinesteik*
roast reindeer	*reinsdyrsteik*
rump steak	*mørbrad*
sausage	*pølse*
spare rib	*svineribbe*
veal	*kalvekjøtt*

Seafood

fiskebolle	fish ball
fiskegrateng	fish casserole
fiskekabaret	fish, shellfish and vegetables in aspic
fiskekake	fried fishball
gaffelbitar	salt- and sugar-cured sprat/herring fillets
gravlaks	salt- and sugar-cured salmon with dill and a creamy sauce
kaviar	smoked cod-roe spread
klippfisk	salted and dried cod
lutefisk	stockfish treated in lye solution, boiled
postei	fish pie
plukkfisk	poached fish in white sauce
rakefisk	cured and fermented fish (often trout)
sildesalat	salad with slices of herring, cucumber, onions, etc
spekesild	salted herring, often served with pickled beetroot, potatoes and cabbage
torsketunger	codtongues, often in sour cream sauce

NORWEGIAN

anchovy	*ansjos*
catfish	*steinbit*
coalfish	*sei*
cod	*torsk*
crab	*krabbe*
crayfish	*kreps*
eel	*ål*
flounder	*flyndre*
frog fish/angler fish	*breiflabb*
haddock	*hyse, kolje*
halibut	*hellefisk, kveite*
herring	*sild*
lobster	*hummer*
mackerel	*makrell*
mussel	*blåskjel(l)*
plaice	*raudspette, rødspette*
rainbow trout	*regnbogeaure/regnbueørret*
roe	*rogn*
salmon	*laks*
sea trout	*sjøaure, sjøørret*
shellfish	*skaldyr, skalldyr*
shrimps	*reker*
small mackerel	*pir*
smoked salmon	*røykelaks*
sole	*sjøtunge*
soused herring	*kryddersild, sursild*
sprat/sardine	*brisling*
trout	*aure, ørret*
tuna	*tunfisk*
whale steak	*hvalbiff, kvalbiff*
young coalfish	*pale*

Poultry & Wildfowl

black grouse	*årfugl, orrfugl*
chicken	*kylling*
chicken fricassee	*hønsefrikasse*
duck	*and*
fowl	*fugl*
goose (liver)	*gås(elever)*
partridge	*rapphøne*
ptarmigan	*rype*
quail	*vaktel*
turkey	*kalkun*

Vegetables

beans	*bønner*
beetroot	*raudbete, rødbete*
Brussels sprouts	*rosenkål*
butter beans	*voksbønner*
button mushroom	*sjampinjong*
cabbage	*kål*
carrots	*gulrøter*
cauliflower	*blomkål*
chives	*grasløk/gressløk*
cucumber	*agurk, slangeagurk*
French beans	*brekkbønner*
horseradish	*peparrot/pepperrot*
leek	*langeløk, purre*
lentils	*linser*
marrow/squash	*graskar/gresskar*
mushroom	*sopp*
onion	*løk/lauk*
peas	*erter*
pickled gherkin	*sylteagurk*

NORWEGIAN

radish	*reddik*
red cabbage	*raudkål, rødkål*
sliced French beans	*snittebønner*
spinach	*spinat*
sugar peas	*sukkererter*
tomato	*tomat*
vegetables	*grøn(n)saker*

Spices, Herbs & Condiments

caraway seeds	*karve*
cardamom	*kardemomme*
chives	*grasløk/gressløk*
cinnamon	*kanel*
curry	*karri*
garlic	*hvitløk/kvitløk*
mustard	*sennep*
parsley	*persille*
pepper	*pepar, pepper*
spices, herbs	*krydder*
stuffing/forcemeat	*fyll*
sugar	*sukker*
tarragon	*estragon*
thyme	*timian*
vinegar	*eddik*

Methods of Cooking

baked	*bakt*
boiled/cooked	*kokt*
crumbed	*panert*
fried/roasted	*steikt, stekt*
grilled	*grilla, grillet*
grilled/toasted	*rista, ristet*

home-made	*heimelaga, hjemmelaget*
rare	*råsteikt*
raw	*rå*
sautéed	*lettsteikt*
smoked	*røykt, røk(e)t*
stewed (fruit); creamed (vegetables)	*stua; stuet*

Fruit

apple	*eple*
apricot	*aprikos*
banana	*banan*
bilberries	*blåbær*
blackberries	*bjørnebær*
blackcurrants	*solbær*
cherry, morello	*kirsebær*
cranberries	*tyttebær*
currant	*korint*
fruit	*frukt*
fruit salad	*fruktsalat*
gooseberries	*stikkelsbær*
grapes	*druer*
lemon	*sitron*
orange	*appelsin*
peach	*fersken*
pear	*pære*
pineapple	*ananas*
plum	*plomme*
raisin	*rosin*
raspberries	*bringebær*
redcurrants	*rips*

NORWEGIAN

rhubarb	*rabarbra*
stewed plums	*plommegraut*
stewed prunes	*sviskegraut*
strawberries	*jordbær*

Desserts, Cakes & Cookies

arme riddarar, riddere	slices of bread dipped in batter, fried and served with jam
bløtkake	rich sponge layer cake with whipped cream
fløyteis, fløteis	ice cream made of cream
fløytevaffel	cream-enriched waffle with jam
fromasj	mousse, blancmange
fruktis	sherbet, water ice
havrekjeks	oatmeal biscuit
hasselnøtt	hazelnut
julekake	rich fruit cake
kveitebolle	bun, sweet roll
kransekake	pile of almond-macaroon rings
kringle	ring-twisted bread with raisins
lefse	thin pancake (without eggs)
napoleonskake	custard slice
ris(gryns)graut	rice pudding with cinnamon and sugar, warm
riskrem	boiled rice with whipped cream, with raspberry jam
rislapp	small sweet rice cake
rødgrød	fruit pudding with vanilla cream
rømmegraut	boiled sour cream porridge with cinnamon and sugar
rørte tyttebær	mashed uncooked cranberries
sirupsnipp	ginger cookie

NORWEGIAN

tilslørte bonde- piker	layers of apple sauce and breadcrumbs, topped with whipped cream
vannbakkels, vassbakkels	cream puff
vørterkake	spiced malt bread
wienerbrød	Danish pastry

almonds	*mandlar/mandler*
apple cake	*eplekake*
biscuit, cookie	*småkake*
bun, sweet roll	*hvetebolle*
cake	*kake*
chocolate	*sjokolade*
jam	*syltetøy*
ice cream	*is*
meringue	*marengs*
nut	*nøtt*
pancake	*pannekake*
sponge cake	*sukkerbrød*
tart	*terte*
wafer	*vaffel*
walnut	*valnøtt*

Drinks – Nonalcoholic

brus	fizzy fruit drink
kefir	fermented milk, kefir
kulturmjølk	cultured thick milk
vørterøl	nonalcoholic beer

apple juice	*eplemost*
cocoa	*kakao*
coffee	*kaffi/kaffe*

fruit juice	*fruktsaft*
ice	*is*
milk	*mjølk/melk*
mineral water	*farris*
nonalcoholic	*alkoholfri*
orangeade	*appelsinbrus*
squash	*saft*
tea	*te*
water	*vatn, vann*

Drinks – Alcoholic

akevitt	kind of gin flavoured with spices
dram	drink/tot/shot
exportøl	strong, light-coloured beer
gløgg	kind of mulled wine, with brandy and spices
heimebrent	home-made brandy
lett-	with little/less alcohol or sugar
pils	lager
pjolter	long drink of whisky and soda water
toddi	mulled wine

beer	*øl*
bock	*bokkøl*
brandy	*brennevin*
cognac	*konjakk*
dark beer	*bayer*
double	*dobbel*
dry	*tørr*
light lager	*lager*
liqueur	*likør*

neat	*bar, berr*	
port	*portvin*	
red wine	*rødvin/raudvin*	
rum	*rom*	
sparkling	*musserande*	
white wine	*hvitvin/kvitvin*	
wine	*vin*	

Shopping

How much is it …?

| *korr mȳchuh kos-tarr deh …?* | Kor mykje kostar det …? (NN) |
| *vorr mȳȳyuh kos-tuhrr deh …?* | Hvor mye koster det …? (BM) |

bookshop	*book-hahn-dl*	bokhandel
camera shop	*foo-tu-fo-**rreht**-neeng*	fotoforretning
clothing store	*klēs-bü-teek*	klesbutikk
delicatessen	*deh-lee-kah-tehs-suh-fo-**rreht**-neeng*	delikatesseforretning
general store, shop	*daa-leh-vaa-rruh-fo-**rreht**-neeng*	daglegvareforretning (NN)
	*daa-lee-vaa-rruh-fo-**rreht**-neeng*	dagligvareforretning (BM)
laundry	*rrayn-suh-**rrēē***	reinseri (NN)
	*rrehnsuh-**rrēē***	renseri (BM)
market	*mahrrk-nah*	marknad (NN)
	mahrr-kuhd	marked (BM)
newsagency/ stationers	*chyosk*	kiosk

NORWEGIAN

pharmacy	*ah-pu-tēk*	apotek
shoeshop	*skoo-töy-fo-rreht-neeng*	skotøyforretning
souvenir shop	*süü-vuh-nēē-rr-shahp*	suvenirsjapp
supermarket	*snaarr-cherp(s-bü-teek)*	snarkjøp(sbutikk)
vegetable shop	*grer-n-saaks-hahn-dlahrr*	grønsakshandlar (NN)
	grer-n-saaks-hahn-dluhrr	grønnsakshandler (BM)

I would like to buy …
   eh kahn for … — Eg kan få … (NN)
   ya kahn for … — Jeg kan få … (BM)
Do you have others?
   *haa rdü **ahn**-drruh?* — Har du andre? (NN)
I don't like it.
   deh lēē-kuhrr ehg eech-uh — Det liker eg ikkje. (NN)
   deh lēē-kuhrr ya eek-kuh — Det liker jeg ikke. (BM)
Can I look at it?
   *kahn eh for **shor** po dē?* — Kan eg få sjå på det? (NN)
   kahn ya for sē po dē? — Kan jeg få se på det? (BM)
I'm just looking.
   eh ba-rruh sē-rr meh rrünt — Eg berre ser meg rundt. (NN)
   ya baa-rruh sē-rr ma rrünt — Jeg bare ser meg rundt. (BM)
Can you write down the price?
   kahn du skrrēē-vuh up prrēē-sn? — Kan du skrive opp prisen?

Do you accept credit cards?
*taa rdü ee-moot krrē-**deet**-ko-rt?*

Tar du imot kredittkort?

Could you lower the price?
*kän-nuh dü seht-tuh **ned** prrēē-sn?*

Kunne du sette ned prisen?

I don't have much money.
*eh **haarr** eech-uh mȳch-uh **pehng**-ahrr ēg*

Eg har ikkje mykje pengar, eg. (NN)

*ya **haarr** eek-kuh mȳȳ-yuh **pehng**-uhrr yay*

Jeg har ikke mye penger, jeg. (BM)

Can I help you?
kahn eh yehl-puh dēg?

Kan eg hjelpe deg? (NN)

kahn ya yehl-puh day?

Kan jeg hjelpe deg? (BM)

Will that be all?
*vaa rdeh sor nor-ko **ahn**-nah?*

Var det så noko anna? (NN)

*vaa rdeh sor noo **aant**?*

Var det så noe annet? (BM)

Would you like it wrapped?
*skahl eh **pahk**-kuh deh **een** fo rdēg?*

Skal eg pakke det inn for deg? (NN)

*skahl ya **pahk**-kuh deh **een** fo rday?*

Skal eg pakke det inn for deg? (BM)

Sorry, this is the only one.
*eh ā **rlay** fo rdē mehn deht-tuh ā rduhn ay-nahs-tuh*

Eg er lei for det, men dette er den einaste. (NN)

*buh-**klaa**-guhrr deht-tuh ā rduhn ē-nuhs-tuh*

Beklager, dette er den eneste. (BM)

NORWEGIAN

How much/many do you want?

*kurr **mȳch**-uh/**mahng**-uh veel dü **haa**?*	Kor mykje/mange vil du ha? (NN)	
*vurr **mȳȳ**-yuh/**mahng**-uh veel dü **haa**?*	Hvor mye/mange vil du ha? (BM)	

Souvenirs

earrings	**öy**-rruh-**dob**-bahrr	øyredobbar (NN)
	ēr-rruh-**dob**-buhrr	øredobber (BM)
glasswork	**glahs**-töy	glastøy, glasstøy
handicraft	**künst**-hahn-varrk	kunsthandverk
necklace	**hahls**-chē-duh	halskjede
Norwegian vest	**kuf**-tuh	kufte, kofte
pottery	**stayn**-töy	steintøy
ring	**rreeng**	ring
rug	**rrȳȳ**-yuh	rye

Clothing

clothing	**klē**-yuh	klede (NN)
	klārr	klær (BM)
coat	**frrahk**	frakk
dress	**choo**-luh	kjole
jacket	**yahk**-kuh	jakke
jumper (sweater, jersey)	**gehn**-suhrr	genser
shirt	**shu**-rtuh	skjorte
shoes	**skoo**	sko
skirt	**sher**-rt	skjørt
trousers	**buk**-suhrr	bukser

It doesn't fit.
   *deh **pahs**-sahrr eech-uh*   Det passar ikkje. (NN)
   *deh **pahs**-suhrr eek-kuh*   Det passer ikke. (BM)

It is …
   *deh **ärr** …*   Det er …

too big	*fo **shtoo**-rt*	for stort
too small	*fo **lēē**-tuh*	for lite
too short	*fo-rr **ko**-rt*	for kort
too long	*fo-rr **lahngt***	for langt
too tight	*fo **teht**-seet-tahn-nuh*	for tettsittande
too loose	*fo **lohw**-st*	for laust

Materials

cotton	*bum-**ül***	bomull
handmade	*hahn-**laa**-gah*	handlaga (NN)
	*hon-**laa**-guht*	håndlaget (BM)
leather	*lärr*	lêr (NN)
	lärr	lær (BM)
of brass	*mehs-**seeng***	messing-
of gold	*gül*	gull-
of silver	*ser-lv*	sølv-
silk	*seelk*	silk
wool	*ül*	ull

Toiletries

comb	*kahm*	kam
condoms	*kun-**doom***	kondom
deodorant	*dē-yu-du-**rrahnt***	deodorant
hairbrush	*hor-rr-**ber**-shte*	hårbørste
moisturising cream	*fuk-tee-**hēts**-krrēm*	fuktighetskrem

razor	*bahrr-bē-rr-hør-vuhl*	barberhøvel
sanitary napkins	*daa-muh-been*	damebind
shampoo	*shahm-poo*	sjampo
shaving cream	*bahrr-bē-rr-krrēm*	barberkrem
soap	*sor-puh*	såpe
sunblock cream	*ser-n-blok-ul-yuh*	sunblock-olje
tampons	*tahm-pong-ahrr*	tampongar (NN)
	tahm-pong-uhrr	tamponger (BM)
tissues	*pah-pēē-rr-lum-muh-ter-rr-kluh*	papirlommetørkle
toilet paper	*doo-pah-pēē-rr*	dopapir
toothbrush	*tahn-ber-shtuh*	tannbørste
toothpaste	*tahn-krrēm*	tannkrem

Stationery & Publications

map	*kah-rt*	kart
newspaper	*ah-vēēs*	avis
newspaper in English	*ehng-uhlsk-sprror-kleh ah-vēēs*	engelskspråkleg avis (NN)
	ehng-uhlsk-sprror-klee ah-vēēs	engelskspråklig avis (BM)
novels in English	*ehng-uhl-skuh rru-maa-nahrr*	engelske romanar (NN)
	ehng-uhl-skuh rru-maa-nuhrr	engelske romaner (BM)
paper	*pah-pēē-rr*	papir
pen (ballpoint)	*pehn (küü-luh-pehn)*	penn (kulepenn)
scissors	*sahks*	saks

Photography

How much is it to process this film?

kurr mȳch-uh kos-tahrr deh o frrahm-kahl-luh dehn-nuh feel-muhn?	Kor mykje kostar det å framkalle denne filmen? (NN)
vurr mȳȳ-yuh kos-tuhrr deh o frrahm-kahl-luh dehn-nuh feel-muhn?	Hvor mye koster det å framkalle denne filmen? (BM)

When will it be ready?

no-rr ā rduhn fa-rdee?	Når er den ferdig?

I'd like a film for this camera.

eh veel yā-rnuh haa ehn feelm teel dehn-nuh kaa-muh-rrahn	Eg vil gjerne ha ein film til denne kameraen. (NN)
ya veel yā-rnuh haa uhn feelm teel dehn-nuh kaa-muh-rrahn	Jeg vil gjerne ha en film til denne kameraen. (BM)

B&W (film)	*svahrrt-kveet svah-rt-veet*	svart-kvitt (NN) svart-hvitt (BM)
camera	*kaa-muh-rrah*	kamera
colour (film)	*fahrr-guh(-feelm)*	farge(film)
film	*feelm*	film
flash	*bleets*	blitz
lens	*leen-suh*	linse
light meter	*lȳȳs-mor-lahrr lȳȳs-mor-luhrr*	lysmålar (NN) lysmåler (BM)

Smoking

A packet of cigarettes, please.

*ay pahk-kuh see-gah-**rreht**-tahrr, tahk*	Ei pakke sigarettar, takk. (NN)
*ay pahk-kuh see-gah-**rreht**-tuhrr, tahk*	Ei pakke sigaretter, takk. (BM)

Are these cigarettes strong/mild?

*ā rdehs-suh see-gah-**rreht**-tah-ne **krrahf**-tee-yuh/**meel**-luh?*	Er desse sigarettane kraftige/milde? (NN)
*ā rdees-suh see-gah-**rreht**-tuh-ne **krrahf**-tee-yuh/**meel**-luh?*	Er disse sigarettene kraftige/milde? (BM)

Do you have a light?

haa rdü fÿÿrr?	Har du fyr?

cigarette papers	*rrül-luh-pah-pēē-rr*	rullepapir
cigarettes	*see-gah-**rreht**-tahrr*	sigarettar (NN)
	*see-gah-**rreht**-tuhrr*	sigaretter (BM)
filtered	*feel-tuhrr*	filter
lighter	*lai-tuhrr*	lighter
matches	*fÿÿ-shteek-kuhrr*	fyrstikker
menthol	*mehn-tol*	mentol
pipe	*pēē-puh*	pipe
tobacco (pipe)	*(pēē-puh)-tu-bahk*	(pipe)tobakk

Colours

black	*svah-rt*	svart
blue	*blor*	blå
brown	*brrüün*	brun

green	*grrēr-n*	grøn (NN)
	grrer-n	grønn (BM)
pink	*rroo-sah*	rosa
red	*rohw*	raud (NN)
	rør	rød (BM)
white	*kvēēt*	kvit (NN)
	vēēt	hvit (BM)
yellow	*güül*	gul

Sizes & Comparisons

small	*lēē-tn*	liten
big	*stoo-rr*	stor
heavy	*tung*	tung
light	*leht*	lett
more	*mayrr*	meir (NN)
	mehrr	mer (BM)
less	*meen-drruh*	mindre
too much/many	*fo-rr mÿch-uh/ mahng-uh*	for mykje/mange (NN)
	fo-rr mÿÿ-yuh/ mahng-uh	for mye/mange (BM)
many	*mahng-uh*	mange
enough	*nok*	nok
also	*ok-so*	også (NN)
	os-so	også (BM)
a little bit	*leet*	litt

NORWEGIAN

Health

Where is ...?
kurr/kvaarr ärr ...?		Kor/kvar er ...? (NN)
vurr ärr ...?		Hvor er ...? (BM)
the doctor	**lē-guhn**	legen
the hospital	**shüü-kuh-hüü-suh**	sjukehuset
the chemist	**ah-pu-tē-kuh**	apoteket
the dentist	**tahn-lē-guhn**	tannlegen

I am sick.
ehg ä shüük	Eg er sjuk. (NN)
ya ä shüük	Jeg er syk. (BM)

My friend is sick.
vehn-n meen ä shüük	Vennen min er sjuk.

Could I see a female doctor?
kahn eh for snahk-kuh mēn	Kan eg få snakke med ein
kveen-nuh-leh lē-guh?	kvinneleg lege? (NN)
kahn ya for snahk-kuh mēn	Kan jeg få snakke med en
kveen-nuh-lee lē-guh?	kvinnelig lege? (BM)

What's the matter?
kvaa ärr ee vē-guhn?	Kva er i vegen? (NN)
vaa ärr ee vay-uhn?	Hva er i vegen? (BM)

Where does it hurt?
kurr yä rdeh vunt?	Kor gjer det vondt? (NN)
vurr yør rdeh vunt?	Hvor gør det vondt? (BM)

It hurts here.
deh yärr vunt härr	Det gjer vondt her. (NN)
deh yør-rr vunt härr	Dette gjør vondt. (BM)

My ... hurts.
deh yärr vunt ee ...	Det gjer vondt i ... (NN)
deh yør-rr vunt ee ...	Det gjør vondt i ... (BM)

Parts of the Body

(my/your)

ankle	*uk-lah*	okla (NN)
	ahng-kuh-luhn	ankelen (BM)
arm	*ahrr-muhn*	armen
back	*rrÿg-guhn*	ryggen
chest	*brrÿst-kahs-sah*	brystkassa
ear	*öy-rruh*	øyret (NN)
	ēr-rruh	øret
eye	*ohw-guh*	auget (NN)
	öy-uh	øyet (BM)
finger	*feeng-uh-rruhn*	fingeren
foot	*foo-tn*	foten
hand	*hahn-nah*	handa (NN)
	hon-nah	hånda (BM)
head	*hor-wuh*	hovudet (NN)
	hoo-duh	hodet (BM)
heart	*yahrr-tuh*	hjartet (NN)
	ya-rtuh	hjertet (BM)
leg	*bay-nuh*	beinet
mouth	*mün-n*	munnen
nose	*naa-suhn*	nasen (NN)
	nē-sah	nesa (BM)
skin	*hüü-dah*	huda (NN)
	hüü-dn	huden (BM)
teeth	*tehn-n-nuh*	tennene
throat	*strrüü-puhn*	strupen

NORWEGIAN

Ailments

I have …

eh haarr …		Eg har … (NN)
ya haarr …		Jeg har … (BM)
an allergy	*ehn ahl-lehrr-gēē*	ein allergi (NN)
	uhn ahl-lehrr-gēē	en allergi (BM)
anaemia	*bloo-mahng-uhl*	blodmangel
a burn	*eht brrehn-sor-rr*	eit brennsår (NN)
	uht brrehn-sor-rr	et brennsår (BM)
a cold	*snüü-uh*	snue
constipation	*fo-shtop-peeng*	forstopping (NN)
	fo-shtop-puhlsuh	forstoppelse (BM)
a cough	*hus-tuh*	hoste
diarrhoea	*maa-guh-shohw*	magesjau
fever	*fē-buhrr*	feber
a headache	*vunt ee hor-wuh*	vondt i hovudet (NN)
	vunt ee hoo-duh	vondt i hodet (BM)
hepatitis	*güül-sot*	gulsott
indigestion	*dor-rleh fo-rdöy-e eng*	dårleg fordøying (NN)
	dor-rlee fo-rdöy-uhl-suh	dårlig fordøyelse (BM)
an infection	*ehn buh-tehn-uhl-suh*	ein (BM en) betennelse
influenza	*een-flü-ehn-sah*	influensa
low/high blood pressure	*lor-kt/her-kt bloo-trrÿk*	lågt/høgt blodtrykk (NN)
	laaft/höyt bloo-trrÿk	lavt/høyt blodtrykk (BM)
a pain	*sma-rtuh*	smerte
sore throat	*vunt ee hahl-sn*	vondt i halsen

sprain	*ay foshtüü-eeng*	ei forstuing
sunburn	*sool-brrehnt-hayt*	solbrentheit (NN)
	sool-brrehnt-hēt	solbrenthet (BM)
a venereal	*ehn cher-n-*	ein (BM en)
disease	*shüükdom*	kjønnssjukdom
worms	*een-vor-ls-mahk*	innvolsmakk (NN)
	een-vols-mahrrk	innvollsmark (BM)

Some Useful Words & Phrases

I'm …

eh haarr …	Eg har … (NN)
ya haarr …	Jeg har … (BM)
diabetic	*suk-kuh-shüü-kuh*	sukkersjuke
epileptic	*fahl-luh-shüü-kuh*	fallesjuke
asthmatic	*ahst-mah*	astma

I'm allergic to …

ēg ārr ah-lehrr-geesk moot …	Eg er allergisk mot … (NN)
ya ārr ah-lehrr-geesk moot …	Jeg er allergisk mot … (BM)
antibiotics	*ahn-tee-bee-yoo-tee-kah*	antibiotika
penicillin	*pehn-nee-see-lēēn*	penicillin

I'm pregnant.

| *ēg ārr grrah-vēēd* | Eg er gravid. (NN) |
| *ya ārr grrah-vēēd* | Jeg er gravid. (BM) |

I'm on the pill.

| *eh tēk pē-peel-lah* | Eg tek P-pilla. (NN) |
| *ya taarr pē-peel-luhn* | Jeg tar P-pillen. (BM) |

NORWEGIAN

I haven't had my period for ... months.

eh haarr eech-uh haht vē-kah por ... mornaarr
Eg har ikkje hatt veka på ... månader. (NN)

ya haarr eek-kuh haht vē-kah por ... mor-ntuhrr
Jeg har ikke hatt veka på ... måneder. (BM)

I have been vaccinated.

ēg ärr vahk-see-nē-rt
Eg er vaksinert. (NN)

ya ärr vahk-see-nē-rt
Jeg er vaksinert. (BM)

I have my own syringe.

eh haarr meen ay-guhn sprröy-tuh-spees
Eg har min eigen sprøytespiss. (NN)

ya haarr meen ē-guhn sprröy-tuh-spees
Jeg har min egen sprøytespiss. (BM)

I feel better/worse.

eh chehn-nuhrr meh bē-rruh/varr-uh
Eg kjenner meg betre/verre. (NN)

ya fēr-luhrr meh bē-druh/varr-uh
Jeg føler meg bedre/verre. (BM)

accident	*üü-lỹk-kuh*	ulykke
addiction	*aav-hehng-ee-hayt*	avhengigheit (NN)
	aav-hehng-ee-hēt	avhengighet (BM)
aspirin	*dees-prreel*	dispril
bandage	*bahn-daa-shuh*	bandasje
blood test	*bloo-prrør-vuh*	blodprøve
contraceptive	*prrē-vehn-shoons-meedl*	prevensjonsmiddel
injection	*sprröy-tuh*	sprøyte
menstruation	*mehns-trrü-ah-shoon*	menstruasjon

At the Chemist

I need medication for ...
eh trrehng eht meedl moot ...   Eg treng eit middel mot ... (NN)
ya trrehng-uhrr eht meedl moot ...   Jeg trenger et middel mot ... (BM)

I have a prescription.
eh haarr ehn rruh-sehpt   Eg har ein resept. (NN)
ya haarr uhn rruh-sehpt   Jeg har en resept. (BM)

Time & Dates

What time is it?
kvaa ärr klok-kah?   Kva er klokka? (NN)
vaa ärr klok-kah?   Hva er klokka? (BM)

It is ... (am/pm)
klok-kah ärr ...   Klokka er ...

in the morning	*um fo-rr-meed-daa-guhn*	om formiddagen
in the afternoon	*um eht-tuhrr-meed-daa-guhn*	om ettermiddagen
in the evening	*um kvehl-n*	om kvelden

What date is it today?
kvaa daa-tu ärr deh ee-daag?   Kva dato er det i dag? (NN)
vaa daatu ärr deh ee-daag?   Hva dato er det i dag? (BM)

Days of the Week

Monday	*mon-daa(g)*	måndag (NN)
	mahn-daa(g)	mandag (BM)
Tuesday	*tȳȳs-daa(g)*	tysdag (BM)
	tēēsh-daa(g)	tirsdag (BM)
Wednesday	*uns-daa(g)*	onsdag

Thursday	*toosh-daa(g)*	torsdag
Friday	*frrē-daa(g)*	fredag
Saturday	*lohw-rdaa(g)*	laurdag (NN)
	ler-rdaa(g)	lørdag (BM)
Sunday	*ser-n-daa(g)*	søndag
	sun-daa(g)	sundag (NN)

Months

January	*yah-nü-waarr*	januar
February	*feh-brrü-waarr*	februar
March	*maash*	mars
April	*ah-prreel*	april
May	*maa-ee*	mai
June	*yüü-nee*	juni
July	*yüü-lee*	juli
August	*ohw-güst*	august
September	*sehp-tehm-buhrr*	september
October	*uk-too-buhrr*	oktober
November	*no-vehm-buhrr*	november
December	*dē-sehm-buhrr*	desember

Seasons

summer	*soo-mahrr*	sommar (NN)
	som-muhrr	sommer (BM)
autumn	*hohw-st*	haust (NN)
	her-st	høst (BM)
winter	*veen-tuhrr*	vinter
spring	*vor-rr*	vår

Present

today	*ee-daag*	i dag
this morning	*ee-daag mo-rr-gon*	i dag morgon (NN)
	ee-mo-rr-uhs	i morges (BM)

NORWEGIAN

tonight (evening)	*ee-kvehl*	i kveld
this week	*dehn-nuh vē-kah*	denne veka (NN)
	dehn-nuh üü-kah	denne uka (BM)
this year	*ee-yor-rr*	i år
now	*nor*	nå
	noo	no (NN)

Past

yesterday	*ee-gor-rr*	i går
day before yesterday	*ee fēr-rr-dahks*	i førdags (NN)
	ee fo-rr-gor-sh	i forgårs (BM)
yesterday morning	*ee-gor-rr fo-rr-meed-daag*	i går formiddag
last night	*ee-naht*	i natt
last week/month	*sees-tuh vē-kuh/ mor-nah*	siste veke/månad (NN)
	sees-tuh üü-kuh/ mor-nt	siste uke/måned (BM)
last year	*ee-fyoo-rr*	i fjor

Future

tomorrow	*ee-mo-rr-gon*	i morgon (NN)
	ee-mor-rn	i morgen (BM)
day after tomorrow	*ee-or-vuhrr-mo-rr-gon*	i overmorgon (NN)
	ee-or-vuhrr-mor-rn	i overmorgen (BM)
tomorrow morning	*ee-mo-rr-gon fo-rr-meed-daag*	i morgon formiddag (NN)
next week	*nehs-tuh vē-kah*	neste veka (NN)
	nehs-tuh üü-kah	neste uke (BM)
next year	*nehs-tuh or-rr*	neste år

NORWEGIAN

During the Day

afternoon	***eht*-tuhrr-meed-daag**	ettermiddag
dawn, very early morning	***daa*-grrȳȳ**	daggry
day	*daag*	dag
early	***tēē*-lehg**	tidleg (NN)
	***tēē*-lee**	tidlig (BM)
midnight	***meet*-naht**	midtnatt
morning	***fo-rr*-meed-daag**	formiddag
night	*naht*	natt
noon	**klok-kah *tol***	klokka tolv
sundown	***sool*-nē-gahng**	solnedgang
sunrise	***sool*-up-gahng**	soloppgang

Numbers & Amounts

0	*nül*	null
1	*ayn*	ein (NN)
	ēn	en (BM)
2	*too*	to
3	*trrē*	tre
4	***fēē*-rruh**	fire
5	*fehm*	fem
6	*sehks*	seks
7	*shüü*	sju
8	***ot*-tuh**	åtte
9	*nēē*	ni
10	*tēē*	ti
11	***el*-vuh**	elleve
12	*tol*	tolv
20	*chü-uh*	tjue
30	***trreht*-tee**	tretti
	***trrehd*-vuh**	tredve

40	*fer-rtee*	førti
50	*fem-tee*	femti
60	*sehks-tee*	seksti
70	*sȳt-tee*	sytti (NN)
	ser-tee	sytti (BM)
80	*ot-tee*	åtti
90	*neet-tee*	nitti
100	*hün-drruh*	hundre (BM)
1000	*tüüs-uhn*	tusen
one million	*ayn mee-lee-yoon*	ein million (NN)
	ēn mee-lee-yoon	en million (BM)

¼	*ehn kvah-rt*	ein (BM en) kvart
⅓	*ehn trrē-dēl*	ein (BM en) tredel
½	*ehn hahl*	ein (BM en) halv
¾	*trrē-kvah-rt*	trekvart

1st	*fer-sh-tuh*	første
2nd	*aa-uhn*	annen, (NN) annan
	ahn-drruh	andre
3rd	*trreh-dyuh*	tredje

Some Useful Words

a little (amount)	*leet*	litt
double	*dob-buhlt*	dobbelt
a dozen	*tol*	tolv
Enough!	*nok!*	nok!
few	*for*	få
less	*meen-drruh*	mindre
many	*mahng-uh*	mange

NORWEGIAN

more	*mayrr/**flay**-rruh*	meir/fleire (NN)
	*mē-rr/**flē**-rruh*	mer/flere (BM)
once	*ayn gong*	ein gong (NN)
	ēn gahng	en gang (BM)
a pair	*eht paarr*	eit par (NN)
	eht pahrr	et par (BM)
percent	*prru-**sehnt***	prosent
some	***noo**-n*	noen
	***nok**-rruh*	nokre (NN)
too much	*fo-rr **mȳȳ**-yuh*	for mye
	*fo-rr **mȳch**-uh*	for mykje (NN)
twice	***too** gong-uhrr*	to gonger
	***too** gahng-uhrr*	to ganger (BM)

Abbreviations

AS	company
EF	EC
e.Kr./f.Kr.	AD/BC
FN	UN
f.o.m.	from (eg. today)
gt./vn.	St/Rd
hovudpostkontor	GPO
Herr/Fru	Mr/Mrs/MS
m.o.h.	meter above sealevel
NAF	AA (Automobile Association)
nord/sør	Nth/Sth
NSB	Norwegian Railway Company
postnummer	ZIP-code
Storbritannia	UK

NORWEGIAN

SWEDISH

Swedish

Introduction

Swedish belongs to the Nordic branch of the Germanic languages. It is spoken by the Swedes, who number close to nine million, and by the Finnish-Swedish minority in southern Finland, including the island of Åland. The language is closely related to Danish and Norwegian, in fact, Scandinavians can usually make themselves understood in these neighbouring countries. Outside of this northern outpost, however, it is a different matter, so most Swedes speak at least some English, which is a compulsory subject on school curriculums, and many actually enjoy practising their English on tourists.

Since English and Swedish have common roots in ancient Germanic, there are many similarities between the languages. Many words were also borrowed from Old Norse into the English language during the Viking period (which ended about a thousand years ago), making the language connection even stronger. In modern times the borrowing is going the opposite direction with Swedish borrowing from mainly American English.

There are also quite a few differences between the two languages. For a start, you will notice that there are three extra letters in the Swedish alphabet: **å**, **ä** and **ö**. These are the last three letters of the alphabet, so if you want to look up Åkesson in the telephone directory, you will have to look near the end.

Verbs are relatively easy to handle as they are the same regardless of person: 'I am, you are, etc' is, in Swedish, *Jag är, du är*, and so on. Furthermore, Swedish does not distinguish

280

between simple and continuous forms. There are three regular conjugations (verb groups), and the language has its share of irregular verbs as well.

Nouns are abit more complicated. Swedish has two genders, both neutral. The indefinite articles are *en* and *et* in the singular with no article in the plural. The definite article is attached to th end of the noun, which will then end either with an *-n* or a *-t* in the singular, and *-na* or *-en* in the plural. To determine if a noun belongs to the *-n* or the *-t* category can be difficult, so it should be learnt with each new word.

Even though you won't have much difficulty getting around in Sweden with English, making the effort to learn a few common phrases will definitely enhance your travel experience. Apart from feeling a little more a part of the local scene, you'll find your attempts will be greatly appreciated by the Swedes, who are not used to visitors speaking their language.

Pronunciation

Sweden is a large country but with a relatively small population. Since people in the past lived scattered and isolated, there is a great variety of dialects. The pronunciation guide here reflects a neutral Swedish, rikssvenska, but don't be surprised if you are given a slightly different pronunciation from a Swede. It all depends on where they are from.

Stress

It's important to get the stress right in words. Swedish can have a single or a double accent on a word, giving it its sing-song quality, and sometimes the difference of meaning between two identical-looking words can be quite vast depending on which accent is used. A good example is anden, ***ahn-dehn,*** meaning 'the duck' and anden, ***ahn-dehn***, 'the spirit/ghost'.

Vowels

There are nine vowels and each vowel has a long and short variant. In a stressed syllable a vowel is short if it is followed by two consonants; when followed by just one consonant the vowel is generally long. Unstressed syllables have only short vowel sounds.

The letter *e* is always pronounced in Swedish, even at the end of words, and the letter *y* is always a vowel. The vowels are divided into two groups: hard vowels *a, o, u,* and *å,* and the soft vowels *e, i, y, ä* and *ö.*

Swedish Letter	Our Guide	Long	Our Guide	Short
a	aa	as in 'father'	ah	as in 'cut'
o	oo	as in 'zoo'	u	as in 'pot'
	or	as in 'thaw'	o	as in 'pot' (cf)
u	uu	between 'zoo' and the German *ü* in *über*	uh	between u in 'pull' and er in 'fern', but very short
å	or	as in 'thaw'	o	as in 'pot'
e	ea	as in British English 'fear'	eh	as in 'bet'
i	ee	as in 'see'	i	as in 'in'
y	üü	as in German *über*	ü	as in German süss
ä	air	as in British English 'fair'	eh	as in 'bet'
	ae	as in 'act' but longer	a	as in 'act'
ö	eu	as in German *schvn*	er	as in 'fern' but shorter

Consonants

Swedish Letter	Our Guide	Pronunciation
c	s	as in 'cell' in front of soft vowels
	k	as in 'cap' in front of hard letters
ck	k	as in 'pick'
d	k	similar to d in 'duck' but with a flattened tongue that touches your front teeth
dj	y	see the letter j
g	g	as in 'get' in front of hard letters
	y	as in 'yet' in front of soft vowels (cf. j)
gn	ngn	as in the meeting of sounds in 'hang-nail'
j	y	as in 'yet'. This sound can be spelt dj, g, gj, hj or lj at the beginning of words.
k	k	as the c in 'cup' in fromt of hard letters
	ch	as tj in front of soft vowels
l	l	similar to the l in 'language' but with a flattened tongue that touches your front teeth
ng	ng	as in 'ring'
q	k	only used in names
r	r	slightly trilled in most Swedish dialects
rd	D	as in ford
rs	sh	similar to the sh in 'cash' but slightly closer to a whistle
rt	T	as in 'short'
s	s	as in 'sun'. S is always soundless in Swedish.
sj	fh	not unlike sh in 'ship' but try touching your lower lip with your front teeth while saying it. Can be spelt ch, sch, skj or stj.
sk	fh	as sj in front of soft vowels. In other positions each letter is pronounced separately.

t	t	similar to the t in 'turn' but with a flattened tongue that touches your front teeth.
tj	ch	as in 'cheap' but without the slight initial t-sound. Can be spelt *ch* and *kj*.
w	v	as in 'valley'. Only used in names. Mixed with *v* in the telephone directory.
z	s	as in 'sun'

Greetings & Civilities
Top Useful Phrases

Hello.	*hay*	Hej.
Goodbye.	*ah-yeu/hay dor!*	Adjö/Hej då!
Yes./No.	*yaa/nay*	Ja./Nej.
Excuse me.	*uu-shehk-taa may*	Ursäkta mig.
Thank you.	*tahk*	Tack.
Many thanks.	***stoot tahk***	Stort tack.

May I? Do you mind?
    ***forr** yah?* ***yerr** deh **nor**-got* Får jag? Gör det något?
Sorry. (excuse me, forgive me)
    *fer-**lort*** Förlåt.
That's fine. You're welcome.
    *dea air **braa**. **vahsh**-o-good* Det är bra. Varsågod.

Greetings

Good morning.	*gu-**morr**-on*	Godmorgon.
Good afternoon.	*gu-**mid**-dah*	God middag.
Good evening/night.	*gu-**kvehl**/naht.*	Godkväll/natt.
How are you?	*huur **morr** duh?*	Hur mår du?
Well, thanks.	***braa**, tahk*	Bra, tack.

SWEDISH

Forms of Address

Mrs	*fruu*	Fru
Mr	*hehr*	Herr
Miss	*frer-kehn*	Fröken
companion, friend	*kahm-raat, vehn*	kamrat, vän

Small Talk
Meeting People

What is your name?
   *vah **hea**-tehr duh?*   Vad heter du?

My name is ...
   *yah **hea**-tehr ...*   Jag heter ...

I'd like to introduce you to ...
   *forr yah preh-sehn-**tea**-ra*   Får jag presentera dig för ...
   day ferr ...

I'm pleased to meet you.
   ahn**-yeh-**nairmt   Angenämt.

Nationalities

Where are you from?
   ***vaa**-ri-frorn **kom**-mehr **duu**?*   Var ifrån kommer du?

I'm from ...	*yah air frorn ...*	Jag är från ...
Australia	*ah-uh-**straa**-li-ehn*	Australien
Canada	***kah**-nah-dah*	Kanada
England	***ehng**-lahnd*	England
Ireland	***eer**-lahnd*	Irland
New Zealand	*nüü-ah **sea**-lahnd*	Nya Zealand
Scotland	***skot**-lahnd*	Skottland
Sweden	***svar**-yeh*	Sverige
the USA	*uu-ehs-**aa***	USA
Wales	*wayls*	Wales

Age

How old are you?
*huur **gahm**-ahl air du?* Hur gammal är du?
I am ... years old.
*yah air ... orr **gahm**-ahl* Jag är ... år gammal.

Occupations

What (work) do you do?
*vah **yerr** duh?* Vad gör du?
*vah haar duh ferr **ür-keh**?* Vad har du för yrke?

I am (a/an) ...	*yah air ...*	Jag är ...
artist	***konst-naer***	konstnär
businessperson	***ah-faesh-mahn***	affärsman
doctor	***lair**-kah-**reh***	läkare
engineer	*in-fhehn-**yerr***	ingenjör
farmer	***bun-deh***	bonde
journalist	*fhur-nah-**list***	journalist
lawyer	*ahd-vu-**kaat***	advokat
manual worker	***hahnt-vehrk**-ahr-eh*	hantverkare
mechanic	*meh-**kaan**-i-kehr*	mekaniker
nurse	***fhuuk-fheu**-tehsh-kah*	sjuksköterska
office worker	*kon-tur-**ist***	kontorist
scientist	*veat-ehn-skaaps-**mahn***	vetenskapsman
student	*stu-**dehnt***	student
teacher	***laer**-ahr-eh*	lärare
waiter	*sehr-vi-**trees***	servitris (f)
	*sehr-vi-**terr***	servitör (m)
writer	*ferr-**faht**-ahr-eh*	författare

Religion

What is your religion?
vah haar duh ferr reh-li-yoon? Vad har du för religion?

I am not religious.
yah air in-teh reh-li-fheus Jag är inte religiös.

I am ...	*yah air ...*	Jag är ...
Buddhist	*buhd-dist*	buddist
Catholic	*kah-tu-leek*	katolik
Christian	*kris-tehn*	kristen
Hindu	*hin-duu*	hindu
Jewish	*yuu-deh*	jude
Muslim	*muhs-leem*	muslim

Family

Are you married?
air duh yift? Är du gift?

I am single.
yah air oo-yift Jag är ogift.

I am married.
yah air yift Jag är gift.

How many children do you have?
huhr mong-ah baarn haar duh? Hur många barn har du?

I don't have any children.
yah haar ing-ah baarn Jag har inga barn.

I have a daughter/a son.
yah har ehn dot-tehr/sorn Jag har en dotter/son.

How many brothers/sisters do you have?

*huhr mong-ah **breu**-dehr/*
***süs**-trahr **haar** duh?*

Hur många bröder/systrar har du?

Is your husband/wife here?

*air din **mahn/fruu haer**?*

Är din man/fru här?

Do you have a boyfriend/girlfriend?

*haar duh ehn **poyk-vehn/flik-vehn**?*

Har du en pojkvän/flickvän?

brother	*broor*	bror
children	*baarn*	barn
daughter	***dot**-tehr*	dotter
family	*fah-**mily***	familj
father	*faar*	far
husband	*mahn*	man
mother	*moor*	mor
sister	***süs**-tehr*	syster
son	*soorn*	son
wife	*fruu*	fru

Feelings

I like ...	*yah **tük**-kehr om ...*	Jag tycker om ...
I don't like ...	*yah **tük**-kehr **in**-teh om ...*	Jag tycker inte om ...
I am in a hurry.	*yah haar **brot**-tom*	Jag har bråttom.
I am right.	*yah haar **reht***	Jag har rätt.
I am sorry. (condolence)	*yah beh-**klaa**-gahr*	Jag beklagar.
I am grateful.	*yah air **tahk**-sahm*	Jag är tacksam.

I am ...	*yah air ...*	Jag är ...
hot	*vahrm*	varm
hungry/thirsty	***huhng-ri/ter-shti***	hungrig/törstig
sleepy	***serm-ni***	sömnig
angry	*ahry*	arg
happy/sad	*glaad/**lehs-ehn***	glad/ledsen
tired	*trert*	trött
worried	***oo-ru**-li*	orolig

| I am cold. | *yah **früü**-sehr* | Jag fryser. |
| I am well. | *yah morr **braa*** | Jag mår bra. |

⚓ Language Difficulties

Do you speak English?
*****taal**-ahr duh **ehng-ehl**-skah?*** Talar du engelska?

Does anyone speak English?
*fins deh **nor**-gon **haer** som taa-lahr **ehng-ehl**-skah?* Finns det någon här som talar engelska?

I speak a little ...
*yah taal-ahr **lee**-teh ...* Jag talar lite ...

I don't speak ...
*yah taal-ahr **in**-teh ...* Jag talar inte ...

I (don't) understand.
*yah fer-**shtorr** (in-teh)* Jag förstår (inte).

Could you speak more slowly please?
*kahn duh vaa-rah **snehl** or taa-lah lee-teh **long-sahm**-ma-reh?* Kan du vara snäll och tala lite långsammare?

Could you repeat that?
*kahn duh **uhp-rea**-pah **dea**?* Kan du upprepa det?

How do you say ...?
huur say-ehr mahn ...?   Hur säger man ...?
What does ... mean?
vah beh-tüü-dehr ...?   Vad betyder ...?

I speak ...   *yah taal-ahr ...*   Jag talar ...
  Dutch   ***hol-lehn-skah***   holländska
  English   ***ehng-ehl-skah***   engelska
  French   ***frahn-skah***   franska
  German   ***tü-skah***   tyska
  Swedish   ***svehns-kah***   svenska

Some Useful Phrases

Sure.   *yaa-vist*   Javisst.
Just a minute.   *eht eu-gon-blik*   Ett ögonblick.
It's (not) important. *dea air (in-teh)*   Det är (inte)
                            vik-tit   viktigt.
It's (not) possible. *dea air (in-teh)*   Det är (inte)
                            may-lit   möjligt.
Good luck!   *lü-kah til!*   Lycka till!

Signs

BAGGAGE COUNTER	BAGAGEINLÄMNING
CHECK-IN COUNTER	INCHECKNING
CUSTOMS	TULL
EMERGENCY EXIT	NÖDUTGÅNG
ENTRANCE	INGÅNG
EXIT	UTGÅNG
FREE ADMISSION	GRATIS INTRÄDE
HOT/COLD	VARM/KALL
INFORMATION	INFORMATION
NO ENTRY	EJ INGÅNG

SWEDISH

NO SMOKING	RÖKNING FÖRBJUDEN
OPEN/CLOSED	ÖPPET/STÄNGT
PROHIBITED	FÖRBJUDET
RESERVED	RESERVERAD
TELEPHONE	TELEFON
TOILETS	TOALETTER

Emergencies

Help!	*yehlp!*	Hjälp!
Call the police!	***ring** pu-lees-ehn!*	Ring polisen!
Go away!	*fer-shvin!*	Försvinn!
	***gor** din **vairg**!*	Gå din väg!
I'll call the police!	*yah **kahl**-lahr po pu-lees!*	Jag kallar på polisen!

It's an emergency!
  *dea air ehn **neud**-sit-wah-**fhoon**!*
  Det är en nödsituation!

There's been an accident!
  *deh haar hent ehn **oo-lük**-ah!*
  Det har hänt en olycka!

Call a doctor!
  ***ring** ehf-tehr ehn **dok**-tor!*
  Ring efter en doktor!

Call an ambulance!
  ***ring** ehf-tehr ehn ahm-buh-**lahns**!*
  Ring efter en ambulans!

I've been raped.
  *yah haar blee-vit **vold-taa**-gehn*
  Jag har blivit våldtagen.

I've been robbed!
  *yah haar blee-vit **ror-nahd**!*
  Jag har blivit rånad!

SWEDISH

I'm lost.
*yah haar got **vil-seh*** — Jag har gätt vilse.

Where are the toilets?
*vaar air too-ah-**leht**-ehn?* — Var är toaletten?

Where is the police station?
*vaar air pu-**lees**-stah-**fhoon**-ehn?* — Var är polisstationen?

Could you help me please?
*kahn duh **yehl**-pah may?* — Kan du hjälpa mig?

I am/My friend is ill.
*yah air/min **vehn** air fhuuk* — Jag är/Min vän är sjuk.

May I use the telephone?
*kahn yah for **lor**-nah teh-leh-**for**-nehn?* — Kan jag få låna telefonen?

I'm sorry. I apologise.
*fer-**lort**. yah bear om **uu-shehkt*** — Förlåt. Jag ber om ursäkt.

I didn't realise I was doing anything wrong.
*yah fer-**stood** in-teh aht yah **yoor**-deh nor-got **feal*** — Jag förstod inte att jag gjorde något fel.

I didn't do it.
*yah **yoor**-deh deh **in-teh*** — Jag gjorde det inte.

I wish to contact my embassy/consulate.
*yah ern-skahr kon-**tahk**-tah min ahm-bah-**saad**/mit kon-suh-**laat*** — Jag önskar kontakta min ambassad/mitt konsulat.

I speak English.
*yah taal-ahr **ehng**-ehl-skah* — Jag talar engelska.

I have medical insurance.
*yah haar **fhuuk**-fer-**shairk**-ring*   Jag har sjukförsäkring.

My possessions are insured.
*mee-nah **air-gu-dea**-lahr air fer-**sehk**-rah-deh*   Mina ägodelar är försäkrade.

My ... was stolen.	*min ... haar blee-vit **stuu**-lehn*	Min ... har blivit stulen.
I've lost ...	*yah haar fer-**loor**-aht ...*	Jag har förlorat ...
my bags	*mee-nah **vehs**-kur*	mina väskor
my handbag	*min **hahnd-vehs**-kah*	min handväska
my money	*mee-nah **pehng**-ahr*	mina pengar
my travellers' cheques	*mee-nah **reas-eh-chehk**-ahr*	mina resecheckar
my passport	*mit **pahs***	mitt pass

Paperwork

name	*nahmn*	namn
address	*ah-**drehs***	adress
date of birth	*feu-dehl-seh-**daa**-tuhm*	födelsedatum
place of birth	*feu-dehl-seh-**ut***	födelseort
age	*ol-dehr*	ålder
sex	*cheun*	kön
nationality	*naht-fhu-nah-li-**teat***	nationalitet
religion	*reh-li-**yoon***	religon
reason for travel	*rea-sahns ehn-dah-morl*	resans ändamål
profession	*ürk-eh*	yrke

marital status	*yift/oo-yift*	gift/ogift
passport	*pahs*	pass
passport number	*pahs-nuh-mehr*	passnummer
visa	*vee-suhm*	visum
tourist card	*tuh-rist-kut*	turistkort
identification	*leh-gi-ti-mah-fhoon*	legitimation
birth certificate	*peh-shoon-beh-vees*	personbevis
driver's licence	*kerr-kut*	körkort
customs	*tuhl*	tull
immigration	*pahs-kont-rol*	passkontroll
border	*grehns*	gräns

Getting Around

ARRIVALS	ANKOMSTER
BUS STOP	BUSSHÅLLPLATS
DEPARTURES	AVGÅNGAR
SUBWAY	TUNNELBANA
TICKET OFFICE	BILJETTKONTOR
TIMETABLE	TIDTABELL
TRAIN STATION	JÄRNVÄGSSTATION

What time does the ... leave/arrive?	*huur dahks-gorr/kom-mehr ...?*	Hur dagsgår/kommer ...?
(air)plane	*flüüg-plaan-eht*	(flyg)planet
boat	*bor-tehn*	båten
bus	*buhs-sehn*	bussen
train	*tor-geht*	tåget
tram	*sporr-vahng-nehn*	spårvagnen

SWEDISH

Directions

Where is ...?
vaar air ...? — Var är ...?

How do I get to ...?
*huur **kom**-mehr yah til ...?* — Hur kommer jag till ...?

Is it near here?
*air deh **longt** hairr-ee-**frorn**?* — Är det långt härifrån?

Can I walk there?
*kahn yah **gor** deet?* — Kan jag gå dit?

Can you show me (on the map)?
*kahn duh **vees**-ah may (po **kaa**-Tahn)?* — Kan du visa mig (på kartan)?

I want to go to ...
*yah vil **or**-kah til ...* — Jag vill åka till ...

Go straight ahead.
*gor **raakt frahm*** — Gå rakt fram.

It's two blocks down.
*dea air **tvor** kvahr-**tear** ort* — Det är två kvarter åt det
*dea **hol**-leht* — hållet.

Turn left ...
*svehng til **vehn**-stehr ...* — Sväng till vänster ...

Turn right ...
*svehng til **heu**-gehr ...* — Sväng till öger...

at the next corner	veed **nehs**-tah hern	vid nästa hörn
at the traffic lights	veed trah-**feek-yuus**-eht	vid trafikljuset
behind	**baak**-om	bakom
in front of	**frahm**-ferr	framför
far	**longt**	långt
close	**nae**-rah	nära
opposite	**mit**-eh-**moot**	mitt emot

Booking Tickets

Excuse me, where is the ticket office?
*uu-**shehk**-tah may, vaar air bil-yet-kon-**toor**-eht?*
Ursäkta mig, var är biljettkontoret?

Where can I buy a ticket?
*vaar kahn yah **keu**-pah ehn bil-**yet**?*
Var kan jag köpa en biljett?

I want to go to ...
*yah vil **or**-kah til ...*
Jag vill åka till ...

Do I need to book?
***mos**-teh yah **boo**-kah?*
Måste jag boka?

You need to book.
*mahn **mos**-teh **boo**-kah*
Man måste boka.

I'd like to book a seat to ...
*yah **skuhl**-leh vil-yah **boo**-kah ehn **plahts** til ...*
Jag skulle vilja boka en plats till ...

I would like ...	yah **skuhl**-leh vil-yah **haa** ...	Jag skulle vilja ha ...
a one-way ticket	ehn **ehng**-kehl-bil-**yeht**	en enkelbiljett
a return ticket	ehn reh-**tur**-bil-yeht	en returbiljett
two tickets	**tvor** bil-**yeht**-ehr	två biljetter
tickets for all of us	bil-**yeht**-ehr fer os ahl-lah	biljetter för oss alla
a student's fare	ehn stuh-**dehnt**-bil-**yeht**	en studentbiljett
a child's fare	ehn **baarn**-bil-**yeht**	barnbiljett
1st class	fer-**shtah klahs**	första klass
2nd class	**ahn**-drah **klahs**	andra klass

It is full.
*dea air **fuhlt*** Det är fullt.
Is it completely full?
*air deh **healt fuhlt**?* Är det helt fullt?
Can I get a stand-by ticket?
*fins dea ehn **vehn**-teh-lis-tah?* Finns det en väntelista?

⮞ Air

CHECKING IN	INCHECKNING
LUGGAGE PICKUP	BAGAGEUTLÄMNING
REGISTRATION	INSKRIVNING

Is there a flight to ...?
*fins dea eht **flüüg** til ...?* Finns det ett flyg till ...?
When is the next flight to ...?
*naer gor **nehs**-tah **flüüg** til ...?* När går nästa flyg till ...?
How long does the flight take?
*hur **long** teed taar **flüüg-tuur**-rehn?* Hur lång tid tar flygturen?
What is the flight number?
*vah air **flüüg-nuhm**-reht?* Vad är flightnumret?
You must check in at ...
*duh **mos**-teh cheh-kah **in** klok-kahn...* Du måste checka in klockan ...

airport tax	*flüüg-plahts-**skaht***	flygplatsskatt
boarding pass	*ehm-bahr-**kear**-ings-kut*	embarkeringskort
customs	*tul*	tull

Bus

BUS/TRAM STOP	BUSS-/SPÅRVAGNS-HÅLLPLATS

Where is the bus stop?
*vaar air **buhs**-hoo-al-**plaht**-sehn?* Var är busshållplatsen?

Which bus goes to ...?
vil-kehn buhs gorr til ...? Vilken buss går till ...?

Does this bus go to ...?
*gorr dehn **haer buhs**-sehn til ...?* Går den här bussen till ...?

How often do buses pass by?
*huur **of**-tah **gorr** buhs-**ahr-nah**?* Hur ofta går bussarna?

Could you let me know when we get to ...?
*kahn duh sey-ah til naer vee **kom**-mehr til ...?* Kan du säga till när vi kommer till ...?

I want to get off!
*yah vil gor **aav**!* Jag vill gå av!

What time is ...?	*naer gorr ...?*	När går ...?
the next bus	*nehs-tah buhs*	nästa buss
the first bus	*fer-shtah buhs-sehn*	första bussen
the last bus	*sis-tah buhs-sehn*	sista bussen

SWEDISH

Metro

METRO/UNDERGROUND	TUNNELBANA
CHANGE (for coins)	VÄXEL
THIS WAY TO	TILL
WAY OUT	UTGÅNG

Which line takes me to ...?
*vil-kehn **leen**-yeh gorr til ...?*

Vilken linje går till ...?

What is the next station?
*vil-kehn air **nehs**-tah stah-**fhoon**?*

Vilken är nästa station?

Train

DINING CAR	RESTAURANGVAGN
EXPRESS	EXPRESSTÅG
PLATFORM NO	SPÅR
SLEEPING CAR	SOVVAGN

Is this the right platform for ...?
*air **deht**-tah **reht** pehr-**rong** ferr ...?*

Är detta rätt perrong för ...?

Passengers must change trains/platforms.
*pahs-sah-**fhea**-rah-reh til ... moo-as-teh **büü**-tah torg/pehr-**rong***

Passagerare till ... måste byta tåg/perrong.

The train leaves from
platform ...
tor-get aav-gorr
from sporr ...

Tåget avgår från spår ...

Taxi

Can you take me to ...?
*kahn du **ker**-rah may til ...?*

Kan du köra mig till ...?

Please take me to ...
til ..., tahk!

Till ..., tack!

How much is it to go to ...?
*vah **kost**-ahr deh til ...?*

Vad kostar det till ...?

Instructions

Here is fine, thank you.
***haer** bleer **braa**, tahk*

Här blir bra, tack.

The next corner, please.
***nehs**-tah **herrn**, tahk*

Nästa hörn, tack.

Continue!
***foort**-seht!*

Fortsätt!

The next street to the
left/right.
***nehs**-tah **gaa**-tah til*
***vehns**-tehr/**heu**-gehr*

Nästa gata till vänster/höger.

Stop here!
***stah**-nah **haer**!*

Stanna här!

Please slow down.
*vaar **snehl** or **sahk**-tah **near***

Var snäll och sakta ner.

Please wait here.
*vaar **snehl** or **vehn**-tah **haer***

Var snäll och vänta här.

Some Useful Phrases

The train is delayed/cancelled.
*tor-geht air ferr-sea-naht/
in-stehlt*

Tåget är försenat/inställt.

How long will it be delayed?
*huur **mük**-keht air deh
fer-shea-naht?*

Hur mycket är det försenat?

There is a delay of ...
hours/minutes.
*dea air ... **tim**-mahr/
mi-**nuu**-tehr fer-shea-naht*

Det är ... timmar/
minuter försenat.

Can I reserve a place?
*kahn yah rehs-ehr-**vear**-ah
ehn **plahts**?*

Kan jag reservera en plats?

How long does the trip take?
*huur long **teed** taar
reas-ahn?*

Hur lång tid tar resan?

Is it a direct route?
*air dea ehn dir-**ehkt**-ferr-
bind-ehl-seh?*

Är det en direktförbindelse?

Is that seat taken?
*air deh **haer** sae-teht **uhp-
taa**-geht?*

Är det här sätet upptaget?

I want to get off at ...
yah vil gor aav vee ...

Jag vill gå av vi ...

Excuse me.
*uu-**shehk**-tah **may**

Ursäkta mig.

Where can I hire a bicycle?
*vaar kahn yah **hüü**-rah ehn
sük-ehl?*

Var kan jag hyra en cykel?

SWEDISH

Car

FREEWAY	MOTORVÄG
GIVE WAY	VÄJNINGSPLIKT
GARAGE	GARAGE/VERKSTAD
MECHANIC	BILMEKANIKER
NO ENTRY	EJ INFART
NO PARKING	PARKERING FÖRBJUDEN
ONE WAY	ENKELRIKTAT
REPAIRS	REPARATIONER
SELF SERVICE	SJÄLVBETJÄNING
STOP	STOPP
SUPER	HÖGOKTANIG BENSIN
UNLEADED	BLYFRI

Where can I rent a car?
*vaar kahn yah **hüür**-rah ehn **beel**?*

Var kan jag hyra en bil?

How much is it daily/weekly?
*huur **mük**-eh **kos**-tahr deh paer **daag**/paer **veh**-kah?*

Hur mycket kostar det per dag/pervecka?

Does that include insurance/mileage?
*in-kluh-**dear**-ahr dea fer-**shaek**-ring/**free**-ah **meel**?*

Inkluderar det försäkring/fria mil?

Where's the next petrol station?
*vaar air **nehs**-tah behn-**seen**-stah-**fhoon**?*

Var är nästa bensinstation?

Please fill the tank.
***fuhl** tahngk, tahk!*

Full tank, tack!

I want ... litres of petrol (gas).
   *yah vil haa ... **leet**-ehr*   Jag vill ha ... liter bensin.
   *behn-**seen***
Please check the oil and water.
   *kahn duh **kol**-ah **ol**-ya or*   Kan du kolla olja och vatten.
   ***vaht**-ehn*
How long can I park here?
   *huur **lehng**-eh kahn yah*   Hur länge kan jag parkera
   *pahr-**kear**-ah **haer**?*   här?
Does this road lead to ...?
   *gorr dehn **haer** vae-gehn*   Går den här vägen till ...?
   til ...?

air (for tyres)	*luhft*	luft
battery	*baht-ehr-ee*	batteri
brakes	***broms**-ahr*	bromsar
clutch	*kop-ling*	koppling
driver's licence	***kerr**-kut*	körkort
engine	***moo**-tor*	motor
lights	***lüü**-seh*	lyse
oil	***ol**-yah*	olja
puncture	*puhngk-**tear**-ing*	punktering
radiator	*chüül-**ahr**-eh*	kylare
road map	***vairg-kaar**-tah*	vägkarta
tyres	*dehk*	däck
windscreen	*vind-**ruu**-tah*	vindruta

Car Problems

I need a mechanic.
   *yah beh-**heu**-vehr ehn*   Jag behöver en mekaniker.
   *meh-**kaan**-ik-ehr*
What make is it?
   *vil-keht **mar**-keh **air** deh?*   Vilket märke är det?

The battery is flat.
  *baht-eh-**ree**-eht air **sluut*** Batteriet är slut.
The radiator is leaking.
  ***chüül**-ahr-ehn **lehk**-kehr* Kylaren läcker.
I have a flat tyre.
  *yah haar puhngk-**tear**-ing* Jag har punktering.
It's overheating.
  *dehn **kook-ahr*** Den kokar.
It's not working.
  *dehn **gorr** in-teh* Den går inte.

Accommodation

CAMPING GROUND	CAMPINGPLATS
FULL	FULLT
NO VACANCIES	INGA LEDIGA RUM
GUESTHOUSE	PENSIONAT/
	GÄSTGIVERI
HOTEL	HOTELL
MOTEL	MOTELL
ROOMS AVAILABLE	LEDIGA RUM

I am looking for ...
  *yah **leat**-ahr ehf-tehr* Jag letar efter ...
Where is a ...?
  *vaar **finns** deh ...?* Var finns det ...?
cheap hotel   *eht **bil**-lit hu-**tehl***   ett billigt hotell
good hotel   *eht **braa** hu-**tehl***   ett bra hotell
nearby hotel   *eht **naer-lig**-ahn-*   ett närliggande
           *deh hu-**tehl***   hotell

What is the address?
*vilk-ehn ah-**drehs** air deh?*   Vilken adress är det?

Could you write the address, please?
*kahn duh skreev-ah **near** ah-**drehs**-ehn?*   Kan du skriva ner adressen?

At the Hotel

Do you have any rooms available?
*fins deh nor-grah **lead**-ig-ah **ruhm**?*   Finns det några lediga rum?

I would like ...
*yah **skuhl**-leh vil-ya haa ...*   Jag skulle vilja ha ...

a single room	*eht **ehnk-ehl-ruhm***	ett enkelrum
a double room	*eht **dub-ehl-ruhm***	ett dubbelrum
a room with a bathroom	*eht **ruhm** meh **baad***	ett rum med bad
to share a dorm	*deal-ah **sorv-saal***	dela sovsal
a bed	*ehn **sehng***	en säng

I want a room with a ...
*yaagh vil haa eht **rum** meh ...*   Jag vill ha ett rum med ...

balcony	*bahl-**kong***	balkong
bathroom	***baad-ruhm***	badrum
shower	***duhfh***	dusch
TV	***tea-vea***	teve
window	***fern-stehr***	fönster

I'm going to stay for ...
   *yah teng-kehr **stahn**-nah* ...   Jag tänker stanna ...
one day   ***ehn daag***   en dag
two days   ***tvor daar***   två dagar
one week   ***ehn vehk-ah***   en vecka

Do you have identification?
   haar duh leh-gi-ti-mah-   Har du legitimation?
   fhoon?
Your membership card, please.
   *dit **mead-lehms-kut**, tahk*   Ditt medlemskort, tack.
Sorry, we're full.
   *tü-**var**, dea air **fuhlt***   Tyvärr, det är fullt.
How long will you be staying?
   *huur **lehng**-eh kom-ehr nee* Hur länge kommer ni att
   *aht **stahn**-ah?*   stanna?
How many nights?
   *huur mong-ah **neht-tehr**?*   Hur många nätter?
It's ... per day/per person.
   *deh kos-tahr ... **paer***   Det kostar ... per dag/per
   ***daag/paer** peh-shoon*   person.

How much is it per night/per
person?
   *huur **mük**-eht **kost**-ahr deh* Hur mycket kostar det per
   *paer **naht/paer** peh-shoon?* natt/per person.
Can I see it?
   *kahn yah for **sea-deh**?*   Kan jag få se det?
Are there any others?
   fins deh nor-grah   Finns det några andra?
   ***ahnd**-rah?*

Are there any cheaper rooms?
*fins deh **bil**-ig-ahr-eh* **ruhm**?
Finns det billigare rum?

Can I see the bathroom?
*forr yah **sea** baad-ruhm-eht?*
Får jag se badrummet?

Is there a reduction for students/children?
*fins deh **stuh**-dehnt-rah-**baht**/**baarn**-rah-**baht**?*
Finns det studentrabatt/barnrabatt?

Does it include breakfast?
***in**-gorr fruh-kost?*
Ingår frukost?

It's fine, I'll take it.
*deh bleer **braa**, yah **taar** deh*
Det blir bra, jag tar det.

I'm not sure how long I'm staying.
*yah **veat** int-eh huur **lehng**-eh yah **stahn**-ahr*
Jag vet inte hur länge jag stannar.

Is there a lift?
*fins deh **his**?*
Finns det hiss?

Where is the bathroom?
vaar air baad-ruhm-eht?
Var är badrummet?

Is there hot water all day?
*fins deh **vahrm-vaht**-ehn **heal**-ah daag-ehn?*
Finns det varmvatten hela dagen?

Do you have a safe where I can leave my valuables?
*fins deh ferr-**vaar**-ings-box daer yah kahn **lehm**-nah mee-nah vaer-deh-**saak**-ehr?*
Finns det förvaringsbox där jag kan lämna mina värdesaker?

Is there somewhere to wash
clothes?
    *kahn yah tveht-ah **klaird-**
    ehr nor-gon-**stahns**?

Kan jag tvätta kläder
någonstans?

Can I use the kitchen?
    *kahn yah **ahn**-vehn-dah
    cheu-ket?*

Kan jag använda köket?

May I use the telephone?
    *forr yah **ahn**-vehn-dah teh-
    leh-**for**-nehn?*

Får jag använda telefonen?

Requests & Complaints

Please wake me up at ...
    *kahn nee **veh**-kah may
    klok-kahn ...*

Kan ni väcka mig
klockan ...?

The room needs to be cleaned.
    ***ruhm**-eht beh-heu-vehr
    stair-dahs*

Rummet behöver städas.

Please change the sheets.
    *kahn nee **büü**-tah laa-kahn?*

Kan ni byta lakan?

I can't open/close the
window.
    *yah kahn **int**-eh **erp**-nah/
    stehng-ah **fernst**-reht*

Jag kan inte öppna/stänga
fönstret.

I've locked myself out of my
room.
    *yah haar lorst may **uut**-eh*

Jag har låst mig ute.

I don't like this room.
    *yah yil-ahr int-eh
    deh haer ruhm-meht*

Jag gillar inte det här
rummet.

It's too ...	*dea air ferr ...*	Det är för ...
small	**leet-eht**	litet
noisy	**bul-rit**	bullrigt
dark	**merrkt**	mörkt
expensive	**düürt**	dyrt

Some Useful Phrases

I am/We are leaving now.
*yah/vee skah **or**-kah nuu*   Jag/Vi ska åka nu.
I would like to pay the bill.
yah skul-eh vil-ya   Jag skulle vilja betala
*beh-**taal**-ah **rairk**-ning-ehn*   räkningen.

name	*nahmn*	namn
surname	**ehft**-ehr-**nahmn**	efternamn
room number	**ruhms**-**nuhm**-mehr	rumsnummer

Some Useful Words

address	ah-**drehs**	adress
air-con	**luhft**-kon-di-fhu-nea-**ring**	luftkonditionering
balcony	bahl-**kong**	balkong
bathroom	**baad**-ruhm	badrum
bed	sehng	säng
bill	**rairk**-ning	räkning
blanket	filt	filt
candle	yuus	ljus
chair	stool	stol
clean	**stair**-dah	städa
cupboard	skorp	skåp
dark	merrkt	mörkt
dirty	**smuht**-sit	smutsigt

double bed	*duhb-behl-sehng*	dubbelsäng
electricity	*ehl-ehk-tri-si-teat*	elektricitet
excluded	*in-gorr ay*	ingår ej
fan	*flehkt*	fläkt
included	*in-beh-raek-naht/ in-gorr*	inberäknat/in går
key	*nük-ehl*	nyckel
lift (elevator)	*hiss*	hiss
light bulb	*gleud-lahm-pah*	glödlampa
lock (n)	*lors*	lås
mattress	*mah-drahs*	madrass
mirror	*spea-gehl*	spegel
padlock	*hehng-lorsh*	hänglås
pillow	*kuhd-deh*	kudde
quiet	*tüst*	tyst
room (in hotel)	*ruhm*	rum
sauna	*bahs-tuh*	bastu
sheet	*laak-ahn*	lakan
shower	*duhfh*	dusch
soap	*tvorl*	tvål
suitcase	*reas-vehs-kah*	resväska
swimming pool	*sim-bah-sehng*	simbassäng
table	*boord*	bord
toilet	*tu-ah-leht*	toalett
toilet paper	*tu-ah-leht-pahp-ehr*	toalettpapper
towel	*hahn-duuk*	handduk
water	*vaht-ehn*	vatten
cold water	*kahl-vaht-ehn*	kallvatten
hot water	*vahrm-vaht-ehn*	varmvatten
window	*ferns-tehr*	fönster

Around Town

I'm looking for ...
*yah **leat**-ahr ehft-ehr ...*   Jag letar efter ...

a bank	*ehn **bahnk***	en bank
the city centre	***sehnt**-rum*	centrum
the ... embassy	*... ahm-bah-**saad**-ehn*	... ambassaden
my hotel	*mit hu-**tehl***	mitt hotell
the market	***mahrk**-nahd-ehn*	marknaden
the police	*pu-**lees**-ehn*	polisen
the post office	***pos**-tehn*	posten
a public toilet	*ehn off-**ehnt**-li tu-ah-**leht***	en offentlig toalett
the telephone centre	*teh-leh-**forn**-sta-**fhoon**-ehn*	telefonstationen
the tourist information office	*tuh-**rist**-in-for-ma-**fhoon**-ehn*	turistinformationen

What time does it open?
*naer **erpn**-ahr dom?*   När öppnar de?

What time does it close?
*naer **stehng**-ehr dom?*   När stänger de?

What ... is this?
*vilk-ehn ... air **deht**-ah?*   Vilken ... är detta?

street	***gaat**-ah*	gata
suburb	***stahts**-deal/ferr-urt*	stadsdel/förort

For directions, see the Getting Around section, page 295.

At the Post Office

I'd like to send ...
yah skuhl-leh vil-yah
fhik-kah ...

Jag skulle vilja skicka ...

a letter	*eht **breav***	ett brev
a postcard	*eht **vüü**-kut*	ett vykort
a parcel	*eht pah-**keat***	ett paket
a telegram	*eht teh-leh-**grahm***	ett telegram

I would like some stamps.
yah skuhl-leh vil-ya haa
*nor-grah **free-mehrk**-ehn*

Jag skulle vilja ha några
frimärken.

How much is the postage?
*vah air **port**-ut?*

Vad är portot?

How much does it cost to
send this to ...?
*huur **mük**-eh **kost**-ahr dea*
*aht **fhik**-ah **deht**-ah til ...?*

Hur mycket kostar det att
skicka detta till ...?

an aerogram	*eht aer-u-**grahm***	ett aerogram
air mail	***flüüg**-post*	flygpost
envelope	*kuh-**vaer***	kuvert
mail box	***breav-lor**-dah*	brevlåda
parcel	*pah-**keat***	paket
registered mail	*reh-kom-ehn-**dear**-aht breav*	rekommenderat brev
surface mail	***üüt**-post*	ytpost

Telephone

I want to ring ...
*yah vil **ring**-ah til ...*   Jag vill ringa till ...
The number is ...
***nuhm**-reht air ...*   Numret är ...
I want to speak for three
minutes.
*yah vil **taal**-ah i **trea**   Jag vill tala i tre minuter.
min-**uu**-tehr*
How much does a three-
minute call cost?
*huur **mük**-eht **kost**-ahr eht   Hur mycket kostar ett tre
trea mi-**nuut**-ehrs **sahm**-   minuters samtal?
taal?*
How much does each extra
minute cost?
*huur **mük**-eht **kost**-ahr   Hur mycket kostar varje
vahr-yeh **ehx**-trah mi-nuut?*   extra minut?
I would like to speak to Göran
Persson.
*yah **skuhl**-leh vil-yah   Jag skulle vilja tala med
taa-lah meh **yer**-rahn   Göran Persson.
paer-shon*
I want to make a reverse-
charges phone call.
*yah **skuhl**-le vil-yah **yer**-rah   Jag skulle vilja göra ett ba-
eht **bea-aa**-sahm-**taal***   samtal.
It's engaged.
*dea air **uhp-taa**-geht*   Det är upptaget.
I've been cut off.
sahm**-taal-eht **breuts   Samtalet bröts.

At the Bank

I want to exchange some
money/traveller's cheques.
*yah skuhl-leh vil-yah vehx-lah lee-tah **pehng**-ahr/nor-grah **rea**-seh-**cheh**-kahr*

Jag skulle vilja växla lite pengar/några resecheckar.

What is the exchange rate?
*vah air **vehx**-ehl-**kuh**-shehn?*

Vad är växelkursen?

How many kronor per dollar?
*huur mong-ah **kroo**-nur paer **dol**-lahr?*

Hur många kronor per dollar?

Can I have money transferred
here from my bank?
*kaan yah flüt-tah **eu**-vehr **pehng**-ahr heet fron min **bahngk**?*

Kan jag flytta över pengar hit från min bank?

How long will it take to
arrive?
*huur long teed **taar** deht aht kom-ah **frahm**?*

Hur lång tid tar det att komma fram?

Has my money arrived yet?
*haar meen-ah **pehng**-ahr **kom**-it ehn?*

Har mina pengar kommit än?

bank notes	**sead**-lahr	sedlar
cashier	kahs-sah	kassa
coins	münt	mynt
credit card	kreh-**deet-kut**	kreditkort
exchange	vah-**luu-tah**	valuta
loose change	smor-**pehng**-ahr	småpengar
signature	**uhnd**-ehr-**skrift**	underskrift

Sightseeing

Do you have a guidebook/
local map?

>*haar nee ehn **reas-eh-***
>*hahnd-**book/kaar**-tah eu-*
>*vehr ...?*

Har ni en resehandbok/
karta över ...?

What are the main attractions?

>*vilk-ah air **huu**-vuhd-oht-*
>*rahk-**fhoon**-ehr-nah?*

Vilka är
huvudattraktionerna?

What is that?

>*vaad air dea?*

Vad är det?

How old is it?

>*huur **gahm**-ahl **air** dehn?*

Hur gammal är den?

May I take photographs?

>*forr yah fu-tu-grah-**fea**-rah?*

Får jag fotografera?

What time does it open/close?

>*vilk-ehn **teed** erp-nahr/*
>***stehng**-ehr dom?*

Vilken tid öppnar/stänger
de?

ancient	*foorn-teed-ah*	forntida
archaeological	*ahrk-eh-ol-or-gisk*	arkeologisk
beach	*strahnd*	strand
bridge	*broo*	bro
castle	*slot*	slott
cathedral	*dum-chür-kah*	domkyrka
church	*chür-kah*	kyrka
concert hall	*kon-saer-huus*	konserthus
island	*eu*	ö
lake	*fheu*	sjö
main square	*stoor-tor-yeht*	stortorge
market	*tory-hahn-dehl/*	torghandel/
	mahrk-nahd	marknad

monastery	*klost-ehr*	kloster
monument	*min-ehs-maerk-eh*	minnesmärke
old city	*gahm-lah staan*	gamla stan
palace	*pah-lahts/slot*	palats/slott
opera house	*oop-ehr-ah-huhs-eht*	operahuset
sea	*haav*	hav
square	*tory*	torg
stadium	*ee-drots-ah-rean-ah*	idrottsarena
statues	*stah-tüü-ehr*	statyer

Entertainment

What's there to do in the evenings?

> *vah fins deh aht ger-rah po kvehl-lahr-nah?*

Vad finns det att göra på kvällarna?

Are there places where you can hear Swedish music?

> *fins deh nor-gon-stahns daer mahn kahn heu-rah svehnsk muh-seek?*

Finns det någonstans där man kan höra svensk musik?

How much is it to get in?

> *huur mük-eht kost-ahr deh ee in-trair-deh?*

Hur mycket kostar det i inträde?

cinema	*bee-u*	bio
concert	*kon-saer*	konsert
discotheque	*disk-u-teak*	diskotek
theatre	*teh-aa-tehr*	teater

In the Country
Weather

What's the weather like?
*huur air **vaid**-reht?* | Hur är vädret?

It's ...

cloudy	*dea air **mol**-nit*	Det är molnigt.
cold	*dea air **kahlt***	Det är kallt.
foggy	*dea air **dim**-mit*	Det är dimmigt.
frosty	*dea air **frost** uu-teh*	Det är frost ute.
hot	*dea air **vahrmt***	Det är varmt.
raining	*deh **rehng**-nahr*	Det regnar.
snowing	*deh **sneu**-ahr*	Det snöar.
sunny	***sool**-ehn **fhee**-nehr*	Solen skiner.
windy	*deh **blor**-sehr*	Det blåser.

Camping

Am I allowed to camp here?
*forr yah **kahm**-pah **haer**?* | Får jag kampa här?

Is there a campsite nearby?
*fins deh ehn **kahmp**-ing-**plahts** i **naer-heat**-ehn?* | Finns det en kampingplats i närheten?

backpack	***rüg**-sehk*	ryggsäck
can opener	*kon-**sehrv**-erp-nahr-eh*	konservöppnare
compass	*kom-**pahs***	kompass
crampons	***ees-brod**-dahr*	isbroddar
firewood	*vead*	ved
gas cartridge	*gah-**sorl-flahs**-kah **ees-üx**-ah*	gasolflaska
ice axe	*ees-**üx**-ah*	isyxa
penknife	***fik-kneev***	fickkniv
rope	*reap*	rep

tent	*tehlt*	tält
tent pegs	*tehlt-pin-ahr*	tältpinnar
torch (flashlight)	*fik-lahmp-ah*	ficklampa
sleeping bag	*sorv-sehk*	sovsäck
stove (camping)	*gah-sorl-cheuk*	gasolkök
water bottle	*vaht-ehn-flahsk-ah*	vattenflaska

Activities

trekking (backpacking)	**vahn-drah**	vandra
canoeing	*pah-dlah kah-**noot***	paddla kanot
downhill skiing	*or-kah **slaa**-lom*	åka slalom
fishing	*fisk-ah*	fiska
running	**spring-ah**	springa
sailing	*seag-lah*	segla
skating	*or-kah **skri-skur***	åka skridskor
skiing	*or-kah **fhee-dur***	åka skidor
swimming	**baa-dah/sim-mah**	bada/simma

Food

Swedish *smörgårdbord* is famous throughout the world for its great variety of hot and cold dishes, but there is more to Swedish food than that. Many dishes are associated with different seasons and may be difficult to find at other times.

Spring

The first sign of spring is the *semla*, a sweet bun filledd with almond paste and whipped cream. It is traditionally served on Tuesdays during Lent. Some prefer it in a bowl with hot milk and it is then called hetvägg. Following Lent comes Easter with its tradition of brightly painted eggs which are eaten wtih ham or fish dishes like cured salmon, *gravad lax*.

Summer

During the summer, Swedes enjoy the warm weather and long daylight hours which produce an intensive growing season. The food is very light, with many cold meals, lots of fish and for dessert a variety of berries with cream, *grädde*, or ice cream, *glass*. During the midsummer celebrations pickled herring, *inlagd sill*, with sour cream and chives, and boiled new potatoes is a must, and it is accompanied by a cold beer and a snaps or two. Strawberries, *jordgubbar*, would likely be dessert, before the obligatory after-dinner coffee. This meal should ideally be eaten outside, as are many Swedish summer meals.

Autumn

Towards the end of August the crayfish season is in full swing with *kräftskivor* (crayfish parties) all over the country. On these occasions people get together, wearing bibs and party hats, to eat *kräftor* boiled with dill, and to drink quite a few glasses of snaps in between the singing of *snapsvisor*, well-known drinking songs.

If you are game you might try the northern autumn speciality, *surströmming*, fermented herring, which tastes somewhat better than its smell suggests. It is eaten with raw onion and *tunnbröd* or *knäckebröd*. Autumn also sees an abundance of funghi, *svamp*, in the woods and the various types of mushrooms collected by eager enthusiasts are a real treat. You must try kantareller – they should be available at markets and well-stocked grocery stores throughout the season.

More berries, such as *lingon* and the northern delicacy *hjort-ron*, appear in autumn, and it's also the season for apples, pears and plums.

Winter

The cold winter requires substantial meals. The traditional Thursday dinner is *ärter med fläsk*, yellow pea soup with pork, and for dessert *pannkakor med lingon*, pancakes with lingonberry jam. December 13 is Lucia, when *lussekatter* (saffron-flavoured sweet buns), *pepparkakor* (ginger snaps) and *glögg* (mulled wine) is served.

At Christmas a special *smörgåsbird* called *julbord* is the tradition. On the *julbord* you will find different sorts of pickled herrings, ham, sausages, *kalvsylta* (brawn), patés, cooked red cabbage, *vörtbröd* (wort-flavoured rye bread), *lutfisk* (dried ling soaked in lye before being boiled), mustard, cheese, *risgrynsgröt* (sweet rice pudding) and more. A special Christmas beer, *julöl*, is served and the children get *julmust*, a sweetish dark brown soft drink which forms a head like beer when poured.

breakfast	**fruh**-kost	frukost
lunch	*luhnfh*	lunch
dinner	**mid**-dah	middag
bakery	baag-eh-**ree**	bageri
coffee shop	kah-**fea**/kon-di-tu-**ree**	kafé/konditori
grocery	spes-eh-**ree**-ahf-**aer**	speceri-affär
delicatessen	dehl-i-kah-**tehs**-ahf-ehr	delikatess-affär
restaurant	rehs-tuh-**rahng**	restaurang

At the Restaurant

There are plenty of restaurants serving the Swedish *husmanskost* (Swedish classic cooking) and the Swedish specialities, but there are a lot of foreign restaurants as well. There is one drawback with Swedish restaurants – they can be a bit expensive. To keep the cost down, don't order any alcoholic drinks, as these tend to be very pricey.

Table for ..., please.
*eht **boord** ferr ..., tahk*   Ett bord för ..., tack.
Can I see the menu please?
*kahn yah for **sea** meh-nüün, tahk*   Kan jag få se menyn, tack.
I'd like the set lunch, please.
*yah skuhl-eh vil-ya haa **luhnfh**-meh-nüün, tahk*   Jag skulle vilja ha lunchmenyn, tack.
What does it include?
*vaad in-eh-**faht**-ahr dea?*   Vad innefattar det?
Is service included in the bill?
*air sehr-**vear**-ings-aav-**yift** in-rairk-nahd i **noot**-ahn?*   Är serveringsavgift inräknad i notan?
Not too spicy please.
*int-eh ferr **krüd-stahrkt**, tahk*   Inte för kryddstarkt, tack.

ashtray	*ahsk-faat*	askfat
the bill	*noot-ahn*	notan
a cup	*ehn kop*	en kopp
dessert	*ehft-ehr-reht/dehs-saer*	efterrätt/dessert
a fork	*ehn gahf-ehl*	en gaffel
fresh	*faeshk*	farsk
a glass	*eht glaas*	ett glas
a knife	*ehn kneev*	en kniv
a plate	*ehn tahl-rik*	en tallrik
spicy	*vairl-krüd-aht*	välkryddat

a spoon	*ehn fhead*	en sked
stale	**uhng-kehn**/*tor*	unken/torr
sweet	*seut*	söt
teaspoon	*tea-fhead*	tesked
toothpick	**tahnd-peat**-*ahr-eh*	tandpetare

Vegetarian Meals

I am vegetarian.

*yah air veh-geh-tahr-ee-**aan***   Jag är vegetarian.

I don't eat meat.

*yah **aet**-ehr int-eh **chert***   Jag äter inte kött.

Breakfast   Frukost

Breakfast tends to be cold in summer and warm in winter.

filmjölk
> Cultured milk, similar to buttermilk, eaten with cereal and a sprinkle of sugar.

knäckebröd
> Crispbread, usually made from rye gruel.

bread	*bröd*
bread roll	*småfranska, frukostbulle*
boiled egg	*kokt ägg*
cereal	*flingor, müsli*
cheese	*ost*
fried egg	*stekt ägg*
jam/marmelade	*sylt/marmelad*
oatmeal	*havregrynsgröt*
scrambled eggs	*omelett*
sugar	*socker*
toast	*rostat bröd*

Sandwiches   Smörgåsar
Swedish sandwiches are always open. If they are very elaborate
you eat them with a knife and fork. In winter you may be served
ovenbaked sandwiches, *varma smörgåsar*, for an evening snack.
The fillings used are called *pålägg*.

Landgång	Gangplank. A long gourmet sandwich with a variety of *pålägg*.
Räksmörgås	Lettuce, sliced hardboiled egg, mayonnaise, lemon and shrimps.
Sillsmörgås	Cold boiled potatoes and pickled herring.

Bread
white French loaf	*franskbröd*
whole grain loaf	*fullkornsbröd*
brown bread roll	*grahamsbulle*
dark sweetened rye bread	*kavring*
crispbread	*knäckebröd*
thin crisp or soft bread made with ground barley	*tunnbröd*
loaf of bread	*limpa*
rye bread	*rågbröd*
wort-flavoured rye bread	*vörtbröd*

Pålägg
butter	*smör*
cheese	*ost*
ham	*skinka*
liver paté	*leverpastej*
pickled herring	*sill*
processed cheese	*mjukost*
sausage meat/salami	*korv*

Soup   Soppa

Ärtsoppa	Yellow pea soup with pork.
Kålsoppa med frikadeller	Cabbage soup with boiled meatballs.
Köttsoppa	Beef broth with meat and vegetables.
Nässelsoppa	Nettle soup served with a hardboiled egg.

broth	*buljong*
chicken soup	*kyckling soppa*
fish soup	*fisksoppa*
mushroom soup	*svampsoppa*
vegetable soup	*grönsakssoppa*

Meat   Kött

Meat tends to be quite expensive in Sweden. So casseroles, *gryta*, are common, as are dishes made with minced meat like *köttbullar*, but perhaps the most famous Swedish meat product is the sausage, *korv*, which comes in all shapes and forms.

Biff á la Lindström	Patties of minced meat mixed with beetroot served with a fried egg.
Blodpudding med lingon	Black pudding with lingonberry jam
Bruna bönor och fläsk	Brown beans in a sweet sauce with bacon
Falukorv	A lean sausage cut in thick slices and fried.
Isterband	Sausage of pork, beef and barley grains.
Kalops	Beef stew with onions and herbs.
Kåldolmar	Stuffed cabbage leaves.
Pytt i panna	Diced meat, boiled potatoes and onion fried and served with beetroot and a fried egg.
Rotmos och fläskkorv	Boiled pork sausage with mashed turnips.

Varm korv	Hot dogs on a breadroll. The special comes with mashed potatoes. Mustard and/or ketchup is a must.
Viltgryta	Game casserole, usually elk or reindeer.

beef	*nötkött*
fillet of beef	*oxfilé*
chicken	*kyckling*
hamburger	*hamburgare, pannbiff*
lamb chops	*lammkotletter*
meatballs	*köttbullar*
minced meat	*köttfärs* (beef), *blandfärs* (beef/pork)
pork	*griskött* (lean), *fläsk* (fat)
pork chops	*fläskkotletter*
roast beef	*oxstek*
roast lamb	*lammstek*
sausage	*korv*
spare ribs	*revbensspjäll*
steak	*biff*
turkey	*kalkon*
veal	*kalvkött*

Seafood

With an enormous coastline and thousands of lakes, seafood is an important part of the Swedish diet and many Swedes enjoy fishing as a hobby. *Kräftor* are caught in creeks and lakes from late August, while many other types of seafood are brought ashore from the North Sea.

Böckling	Smoked herring.
Gravad lax	Cured salmon.
Inlagd sill	Pickled herrings, in a number of varieties.

Lutfisk	Dried ling soaked in lye before being boiled. A dish associated with Christmas.
Sotare	Slightly salted fresh herring grilled over an open fire, hence the name 'chimney sweep'.

baltic herring	*strömming*
caviar	*rysk kaviar*
cod	*torsk*
codroe	*torskrom*
codroe cream	*kaviar*
crab	*krabba*
crayfish	*kräftor*
eel	*ål*
haddock	*kolja*
halibut	*helgeflundra*
herring	*sill*
lobster	*hummer*
mackerel	*makrill*
mussels	*musslor*
oyster	*ostron*
perch	*abborre*
pike	*gädda*
plaice	*rödspätta*
prawns	*havskräftor*
salmon	*lax*
shrimp	*räkor*
sole	*sjötunga*
trout	*forell*
whiting	*vitling*

Potatoes   **Potatis**

Swedes eat potatoes with almost everything, and there is a great number of ways to prepare them for the table.

bakad potatis	Baked potatoes.
färskpotatis	New potatoes, usually boiled with dill.
Janssons frestalse	Potato slices, onion and anchovy baked in the oven with lots of cream.
kokt potatis	Boiled potatoes.
pommes frites	chips, French fries
potatismos	mashed potatoes
potatissallad	potato salad

Vegetables   **Grönsaker**

asparagus	*sparris*
beetroot	*rödbetor*
beans	*bönor, haricot vert*
brussels sprouts	*brysselkål*
cabbage	*vitkål, rödkål*
capsicum	*paprika*
carrot	*morot*
cauliflower	*blomkål*
cucumber	*gurka*
leek	*purjolök*
lettuce	*sallad*
mushrooms	*champinjoner*
onions	*lök*
parsnip	*palsternacka*
peas	*ärter*
spinach	*spenat*
tomato	*tomater*

Staple Foods & Condiments

cooking oil	*matolja*
garlic	*vitlök*
herbs	*örtkryddor*
mustard	*senap* (sweet and fairly mild)
pepper	*peppar*
rice	*ris*
salt	*salt*
sour cream	*gräddfil/creme fraiche*
soy sauce	*soja*
spices	*kryddor*
sugar	*socker*

Fruit & Berries — Frukt och bär

apple	*äpple*
blackberries	*björnbär*
black/red currants	*svarta/röda vinbär*
blueberries	*blåbär*
cherries	*körsbär, bigarråer*
cloudberries	*hjortron*
cranberries	*tranbär*
gooseberries	*krusbär*
grapes	*vindruvor*
lemon	*citron*
lingonberries	*lingon*
orange	*apelsin*
peach	*persika*
pear	*päron*
plum	*plommon*
raspberries	*hallon*
strawberries	*smultron*
wild strawberries	*smultron*

Desserts & Pastries — Efterrätter och Kaffebröd

kanelbulle	Sweet roll with cinnamon and cardamon.
kräm och mjölk	Thickened berry juice with milk.
mazarin	Pastry shell with almond paste filling.
nyponsoppa	Rosehip soup with a dollop of cream.
Prinsesstårta	Layered sponge cake with jam, cream and custard filling covered with green marzipan.
Ris á la Malta	Rice with whipped cream and orange.
Småländsk ostkaka	Baked curd cake with almonds.
småkakor	Small biscuits/cookies.
sockerkaka	Sponge cake, usually flavoured with lemon.
wienerbröd	Danish pastries.

cake	*tårta*
cheesecake	*ostkaka*
custard	*vaniljkräm, maizenakräm*
ginger snaps	*pepparkakor*
ice cream	*glass*
mousse	*fromage*
pancakes	*pannkakor*
whipped cream	*vispgrädde*

Drinks – Nonalcoholic — Alcoholfria Drycker

apple juice	*äppelmust*
coffee	*kaffe*
hot chocolate	*varm choklad*
milk	*mjölk*
orange juice	*apelsinjuice*
soft drink (carbonated)	*läsk*
soft drink (cordial)	*saft*
tea	*te*
water	*vatten*

Drinks – Alcoholic   Alkoholhaltiga Drycker

If a Swede asks you if you would like a drink, they probably have alcohol in mind as the work *drink* denotes an alcoholic drink, usually a cocktail.

brännvin	Spirit distilled from potatoes, may be flavoured with herbs and berries, or plain.
glögg	Mulled wine with raisins and almonds.
snaps	A drink of brännvin, with the words *Skål!*, a small glass is emptied in one go.
punsch	Very sweet liqueur flavoured with arrack.
vinbål	A punch based on wine.

beer	*öl, pilsner*
wine	*starkvin*
liqueur	*likör*
red/white wine	*rödvin, vitt vin*

Shopping

How much is it?

    *hur mük-eht **kost**-ahr dehn?*   Hur mycket kostar den?

bookshop	***book-hahn**-dehl*	bokhandel
camera shop	*foo-tu-ah-**faer***	fotoaffär
general store, shop	*di-va-sheh-**hahn**-dehl, ah-**faer***	diversehandel, affär
laundry	*tveht*	tvätt
market	***mahrk-nahd***	marknad
newsagency	***prehs-büü**-ron/ too-bahks-ah-**faer***	pressbyrån/ tobaksaffär
pharmacy	*ahp-oo-teak*	apotek
stationers	***pahp-ehrs-hahnd**-ehl*	pappershandel
supermarket	***snahb-cheup***	snabbköp

I'd like to buy ...
yah skuhl-eh vil-ya cheu-pah ...

Jag skulle vilja köpa ...

Do you have others?
haar nee nor-grah ahnd-rah?

Har ni några andra?

I don't like it.
yah yil-ahr dehn int-eh

Jag gillar den inte.

May I look at it?
forr yah tit-tah por dehn?

Får jag titta på den?

I'm just looking.
yah tit-ahr baar-ah

Jag tittar bara.

Do you accept credit cards?
taar nee eh-moot kreh-deet-kut?

Tar ni emot kreditkort?

Can I help you?
kahn yah yehl-pah day?

Kan jag hjälpa dig?

Will that be all?
vaar deh ahlt?

Var det allt?

How much/many do you want?
huur mük-eh/mong-ah vil duh haa?

Hur mycket/många vill du ha?

Souvenirs

earrings	*err-heng-ehn*	örhängen
glassware	*glaas*	glas
handicraft	*hehm-sleyd*	hemslöjd
necklace	*hahls-bahnd*	halsband
pottery	*cheh-rah-meek*	keramik
ring	*ring*	ring

Clothing

coat	*rok/kahp-pah*	rock (m)/kappa (f)
jacket	*yahk-kah*	jacka
jumper (sweater)	*trey-ah*	tröja
pants	*büx-oor*	byxor
shirt	*fhur-tah*	skjorta
shoes	*skoor*	skor

It doesn't fit.
    *dehn **pahs**-ahr int-eh*   Den passar inte.

It is too ...	*dehn air ferr ...*	Den är för ...
big	*stoor*	stor
small	*leet-ehn*	liten
short	*kot*	kort
long	*long*	lång

Toiletries

condoms	*kon-dor-mehr*	kondomer
deodorant	*dea-oo-doo-rahnt*	deodorant
hairbrush	*horr-bosh-teh*	hårborste
razor	*raak-hüüiv-ehl*	rakhyvel
sanitary napkins	*daam-bind-ur*	dambindor
shampoo	*horr-fhahm-pu*	hårschampo
shaving cream	*raak-lerd-ehr*	raklödder
soap	*tvorl*	tvål
tampons	*tahm-pong-ehr*	tamponger
tissues	*nairs-duuk-ahr*	näsdukar
toilet paper	*tu-ah-leht-pahp-ehr*	toalettpapper
toothbrush	*tahnd-bosh-teh*	tandborste
toothpaste	*tahnd-krairm*	tandkräm

Stationery & Publications

map	**kaart-ah**	karta
newspaper	**tee-ning**	tidning
newspaper in English	**ehng-ehlsk tee-ning**	engelsk tidning
novels in English	**ehng-ehlsk-ah ru-maan-ehr**	engelska romaner
paper	**pahp-ehr**	papper
pen	**pehn-ah/kuul-spehts-pehn-nah**	penna/ kulspetspenna

Photography

How much is it to process this film?

  huur mük-keh kost-ahr geh aht frahm-kahl-lah dehn haer fil-mehn? Hur mycket kostar det att framkalla den här filmen?

When will it be ready?

  naer air dehn klaar? När är den klar?

I'd like a film for this camera.

  yah skuhl-eh vil-yah haa ehn film til dehn haer kaam-rahn Jag skulle vilja ha en film till den hä kameran.

B&W (film)	**svahrt-veet film**	svart-vit film
camera	**kaam-rah**	kamera
colour (film)	**fary-film**	färgfilm
film	**film**	film
flash	**blixt**	blixt
lens	**ob-yehk-teev**	objektiv
light meter	**yus-mairt-ahr-eh**	ljusmätare

Smoking

A packet of cigarettes, please.

*eht pah-keat sig-ahr-eht-ehr, **tahk***   Ett paket cigaretter, tack.

Are these cigarettes strong/mild?

*air dom **haer** sig-ahr-eht-ehr **stahrk**-ah/**svaag**-ah?*   Är dessa cigaretter starka/svaga?

Do you have a light?

*haar duh **ehld**?*   Har du eld?

cigarette papers	*sigh-ahr-**eht-pahp**-ehr*	cigarettpapper
cigarettes	*sigh-ahr-**eht**-ehr*	cigaretter
filtered	***filt**-ehr*	filter
lighter	***tehnd**-ahr-eh*	tändare
matches	***tehnd**-stik-ur*	tändstickor
pipe	***pee-pah***	pipa
tobacco (pipe)	***peep-tu**-bahk*	piptobak

Sizes & Comparisons

small	***lee**-tehn*	lite
big	***stoor***	stor
heavy	***tuhng***	tung
light	***leht***	lätt
more	***mear***	mer
less	***mind**-reh*	mindre
too much/many	*ferr **mük**-eht/**mong**-ah*	för mycket/många
many	***mong**-ah*	många
enough	***til-rehk**-lit*	tillräckligt
also	*ok-sor*	också

Health

Where is ...?	*vaar air ...?*	Var är ...?
the doctor	**dok**-*torn*	doktorn
the hospital	*fhuuk-huus-eht*	sjukhuset
the chemist	*ah-pu-**teak**-eht*	apoteket
the dentist	*tahnd-**lair**-kah-rehn*	tandläkaren

I am sick.
    yah air fhuuk   Jag är sjuk.
I feel nauseous.
    yah morr il-lah   Jag mår illa.
Could I see a female doctor?
    *kahn yah for **trehf**-fah ehn*   Kan jag få träffa en kvinnlig
    ***kvin-li lair**-kah-reh?*   läkare?
Where does it hurt?
    *vaar gerr deh **unt**?*   Var gör det ont?
I have ...
    yah haar ...   Jag har ...
It hurts here.
    yah haar unt i ...   Jag har ont i ...

Parts of the Body

arm	*ahrm-ehn*	armen
back	*rüg-gehn*	ryggen
chest	*brerst-eht*	bröstet
ear	*er-raht*	örat
eye	*eu-gaht*	ögat
heart	*yart-aht*	hjärtat
leg	*bean-eht*	benet
ribs	*reav-bean-ehn*	revbenen
skin	*huud-ehn*	huden

Ailments

a cold	*ehn ferr-chüül-ning*	en förkylning
constipation	*ferr-stop-ning*	förstoppning
a cough	*hus-tah*	hosta
fever	*feab-ehr*	feber
a headache	*huu-veh-vark*	huvudvärk
indigestion	*maag-beh-svar*	magbesvär
influenza	*in-fluh-ehns-ah*	influensa
low/high blood pressure	*lorgt/herkt blood-trük*	lågt/högt blodtryck
sore throat	*unt i hahl-sehn*	ont i halsen
sprain	*stuuk-ning*	stukning
a stomachache	*unt i maa-gehn*	ont i magen
sunburn	*sool-brehn-ah*	solbränna
a venereal disease	*ehn kerns-fhuuk-dum*	en könssjukdom

Some Useful Words & Phrases

I'm ...	*yah air ...*	Jag är ...
diabetic	*dee-ah-beat-ik-ehr*	diabetiker
epileptic	*ehp-i-lehpt-ik-ehr*	epileptiker
asthmatic	*ahst-maat-ik-ehr*	astmatiker

I'm allergic to antibiotics/
penicillin

    yah air ahl-ehrg-isk moot   Jag är allergisk mot
    ahnt-i-bi-ont-ik-ah/   antibiotika/penicillin
    pehn-i-si-leen

I'm pregnant.

    yah air grah-veed   Jag är gravid.

SWEDISH

I'm on the Pill.
*yah air-tehr **pea-pil**-lehr*   Jag äter p-piller.

I have been vaccinated.
*yah air vahk-see-**near**-ahd*   Jag är vaccinerad.

I have my own syringe.
yaagh haar min eagh-ehn   Jag har min egen spruta.
sprut-ah

I feel better/worse.
*yah morr **beht**-reh/*   Jag mår bättre/sämre.
***sehm**-reh*

accident	*oo-**lük**-ah*	olycka
addiction	***mis**-bruuk*	missbruk
bandage	*ferr-**bahnd***	förband
bite	*beht*	bett
blood pressure	***blood-trük***	blodtryck
blood test	***blood-proov***	blodprov
contraceptive	*preh-vehn-**teev**-mea-dehl*	preventivmedel
injection	***spruu-tah***	spruta
injury	***skaad**-ah*	skada
itch	***klor**-dah*	klåda
oxygen	***süü**-reh*	syre
wound	*sorr*	sår

At the Chemist

I need medication for ...
yah beh-heu-vehr eht   Jag behöver ett medel mot ...
mea-dehl-moot ...

I have a prescription.
*yah haar eht reh-**sehpt*** Jag har ett recept.

At the Dentist

I have a toothache.
*yah haar **tahnd**-vark* — Jag har tandvärk.

I've lost a filling.
*yah haar **tahp**-aht ehn plomb* — Jag har tappat en plomb.

I've broken a tooth.
*yah haar slaa-git **aav** ehn tahnd* — Jag har slagit av en tand.

I don't want it extracted.
*yah vil **int**-eh haa dehn **uut**-draa-gehn* — Jag vill inte ha den utdragen.

Please give me an anaesthetic.
*yah vil haa beh-**deuv**-ning* — Jag vill ha bedövning.

Time & Dates

Swedes often use the 24-hour system for telling the time.

What time is it?
*vaad air **klok**-ahn?* — Vad är klockan?
*huur **mük**-keh air **klok**-kahn?* — Hur mycket är klockan?

It is ...	*dehn air .../hun air ...*	Den är .../Hon är ...
What date is it today?	*vilk-eht **daat**-uum air deht i-**daag**?*	Vilket datum är det idag?
in the morning	*po **mor**-ron-ehn*	på morgonen
in the afternoon	*po **ehft**-ehr-mi-dahn*	på eftermiddagen
in the evening	*po **kvehl**-lehn*	på kvällen

Days of the Week

Monday	*mon-dah*	måndag
Tuesday	*tees-dah*	tisdag
Wednesday	*uns-dah*	onsdag
Thursday	*toosh-dah*	torsdag
Friday	*frea-dah*	fredag
Saturday	*ler-dah*	lördag
Sunday	*sern-dah*	söndag

Months

January	*jahn-uh-**aar**-i*	januari
February	*fehb-ruh-**aar**-i*	februari
March	*mahsh*	mars
April	*ahp-**ril***	april
May	*mai*	maj
June	*juu-ni*	juni
July	*juu-li*	juli
August	*aw-**guhs**-ti*	augusti
September	*sehp-**tehm**-behr*	september
October	*ok-**too**-behr*	oktober
November	*nu-**vehm**-behr*	november
December	*deh-**sehm**-behr*	december

Seasons

summer	*som-ahr*	sommar
autumn	*herst*	höst
winter	*vint-ehr*	vinter
spring	*vorr*	vår

Present

today	*i-daa*	idag
this morning	*i mosh-eh*	i morse

tonight	*i-kvehl*	i kväll
this week	*dehn **haer** veh-kahn*	den här veckan
this year	*i-orr*	i år
now	*nuu*	nu

Past

yesterday	*i-gorr*	igår
day before yesterday	*i-ferr-gorr*	i förrgår
yesterday morning	*i-gorr **mosh**-eh*	igår morse
last night	*i-gorr kvehl*	igår kväll
last week	***ferr**-ah vehk-ahn*	förra veckan
last year	***ferr**-ah orr-eht*	förra året

Future

tomorrow	*i mor-ron*	i morgon
day after tomorrow	*i erv-ehr-mor-ron*	i övermorgon
tomorrow morning	*i mor-ron-**bit**-ti*	i morgon bitti
tomorrow afternoon/evening	*i mor-ron **ehf-tehr-mid**-dah/kvehl*	i morgon eftermiddag/kväll
next week	***nehst**-ah vehk-ah*	nästa vecka
next year	***nehst**-ah orr*	nästa år

During the Day

afternoon	*ehft-ehr-mi-dah*	eftermiddag
dawn, very early morning	*grüü-ning*	gryning
day	*daag*	dag
early	*tee-dit*	tidigt
midnight	*meed-naht*	midnatt

morning	*mor-ron*	morgon
night	*naht*	natt
noon	*mi-daagh*	middag
sunset	*klok-kahn tolv*	klockan tolv
sunrise	*sool-uhp-gong*	soluppgång

Numbers & Amounts

0	*nol*	noll
1	*ehn/eht*	en/ett
2	*tvor*	två
3	*trea*	tre
4	*füü-rah*	fyra
5	*fehm*	fem
6	*sehx*	sex
7	*fhuu*	sju
8	*ot-tah*	åtta
9	*nee-u*	nio
10	*tee-u*	tio
11	*ehlv-ah*	elva
12	*tolv*	tolv
13	*treh-ton*	tretton
14	*fyoo-Ton*	fjorton
15	*fehm-ton*	femton
16	*sehx-ton*	sexton
17	*fhu-ton*	sjutton
18	*aa-Ton*	arton
19	*ni-ton*	nitton
20	*chuu-gu*	tjugo
30	*treh-ti*	trettio
40	*fuhr-ti*	fyrtio
50	*fehm-ti*	femtio

60	*sehx-ti*	sextio
70	*fhuh-ti*	sjuttio
80	*ot-ti*	åttio
90	*ni-ti*	nittio
100	*eht huhnd-rah*	ett hundra
1000	*eht tuu-sehn*	ett tusen
one million	*ehn mil-yoon*	en miljon
1st	*fersh-Tah*	första
2nd	*ahnd-rah*	andra
3rd	*tread-yeh*	tredje
¼	*ehn fyaer-deh-deal/*	en fjärdedel/
	ehn kvaTs	en kvarts
⅓	*ehn trea-dyeh-deal*	en tredjedel
½	*ehn hahlv*	en halv
¾	*trea fyaer-deh-deal-*	tre tjärdedelar/
	ahr/trea kvats	tre kvarts

Some Useful Words

a little (amount)	*leet-eh grahn*	lite grand
double	*duhb-ehl*	dubbel
a dozen	*eht duhs-in*	ett dussin
Enough!	*deh rehk-kehr!*	Det räcker!
just enough/right	*laa-gom*	lagom
once	*ehn gong*	en gång
a pair	*eht paar*	ett par
percent	*pru-sehnt*	procent
too much	*ferr mük-keh*	för mycket
twice	*tvor gong-ehr*	två gånger

Abbreviations

AB	corporation
eKr/fKr	AD/BC
fm/em	am/pm
AB	Corporation
avd/HK	Dept/HQ
EG	EC
fr o m	from and including
Gbg	Göteborg (Gothenburg)
Hr/Fr/Frk	Mr/Mrs/Miss
kl	at (about time)
kr	kronor (Swedish currency)
M	Motorist's National Organisation
moms	VAT (sales tax)
N/S/Ö/V	north/south/east/west
Obs!	note!
SAS	Scandinavian Airline Systems
SJ	Swedish Railways
STF	Swedish Tourist Organisation
Sthlm	Stockholm
T-bana	Metro/Underground
t o m	until and including
v	week

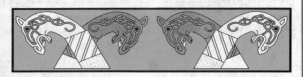

SWEDISH

Index

Finnish 72

Icelandic 141

Swedish 280